The Privilege of Silence

Fifth Amendment Protections against Self-Incrimination

Third Edition

STEVEN M. SALKY

AMERICAN**BAR**ASSOCIATION
Criminal Justice Section

Cover design by ABA Design

Printed in the United States of America.

23 22 21 20 19   5 4 3 2 1

A catalog record for this book is available from the Library of Congress.

Contents

Preface

The genesis of this book was the recognition that the practicing lawyer's library lacked a comprehensive guide to the application of the Fifth Amendment privilege against self-incrimination. This work is designed to fill that void and to become a basic research tool to aid lawyers in thinking about and applying the Fifth Amendment privilege in various contexts and proceedings.

This third edition not only updates the second edition with more recent court decisions but also expands the prior discussion on certain topics in order to elucidate, or in some instances question, a trend or a decision. These topics include the continuing effects of *Chavez v. Martinez* regarding the meaning of the Self-Incrimination Clause, the application of the privilege to the compelled access to encrypted communications, and the continued erosion of the "privilege of silence" that forms the title to this book. Additionally, this third edition highlights decisions by state courts, particularly where they differ from federal court rulings, in order to help readers understand the ambiguity or uncertainty in the law. It also expands the brief history of the Fifth Amendment privilege against compelled self-incrimination and the discussion of its future, especially with regard to brain imaging and other technologies that may extract incriminating information without compelling human expression.

Paul Hynes, who was my co-author for the second edition, was unable to assist with the third edition, but will hopefully return for the fourth. I received significant research help and diligent cite checking from our firm's paralegal and legal research analyst Melissa Lovell and careful editing from our firm's staff attorney Nina Falvello. As in previous writings, I received significant general aid from my assistant Melissa Smith, who often worked on the book after business hours, on her otherwise free time. My law firm deserves acknowledgment for allowing these otherwise busy professionals to help me. My partner David Reiser gave me helpful comments and constructive criticism, as did my friend Andy Good. I have corrected mistakes made in prior editions and tried to improve the presentation. As was the case with the prior editions, errors either in the legal analysis or the editing remain mine, and mine alone, and I encourage readers to bring them to my attention.

About the Author

Steven Salky is a partner at Zuckerman Spaeder LLP, where he represents individuals in a wide variety of white-collar criminal cases, regulatory investigations, and civil litigation. He has extensive experience representing executives of public companies in parallel grand jury and civil litigation as well as congressional proceedings. He also represents professionals, including lawyers, doctors, and accountants, in litigation involving their compliance with applicable professional obligations.

After graduating from Yale Law School in 1981, Mr. Salky clerked for then-Chief Judge Theodore R. Newman Jr. of the District of Columbia Court of Appeals, before beginning a two-year teaching fellowship at the Georgetown University Law Center. As the Stuart Stiller Fellow at Georgetown's Criminal Justice Clinic, he represented indigent criminal defendants and supervised third-year law students in court. He joined Zuckerman Spaeder in 1984.

Mr. Salky has written on various legal subjects. In 2006, he was recognized as "Top Washington Lawyer" for corporate litigation by the *Washington Business Journal*. He has long been interested in the application of the Fifth Amendment privilege against self-incrimination and has spoken on the topic often.

Introduction

The U.S. Constitution provides that "[n]o person . . . shall be compelled in any criminal case to be a witness against himself." U.S. Const. amend. V. While this portion of the Fifth Amendment, most often referred to as the "privilege against self-incrimination," contains only 15 words, its application can be deceptively complex. The clause has generally defied a comprehensive theoretical justification and, instead, has been aptly described as "an unsolved riddle of vast proportions, a Gordian Knot in the middle of our Bill of Rights." *See* Akhil Reed Amar & Renée B. Lettow, *Fifth Amendment First Principles: The Self-Incrimination Clause*, 93 Mich. L. Rev. 857 (1995). Application of the Fifth Amendment right against self-incrimination is highly dependent on the factual setting in which the privilege is asserted, with the values served by the privilege often balanced against the competing interests at stake.

This book is designed primarily to elucidate the contours of the Fifth Amendment privilege against self-incrimination in practice. It intends to guide both the civil litigator, who may confront the privilege infrequently, and the criminal lawyer who seeks to advance a client's interests through creative application of the Fifth Amendment. The book makes only limited attempts to harmonize the often disparate and sometimes contradictory interpretations of the privilege and advances an argument for one interpretation versus a competing interpretation only sparingly. Instead, it attempts to organize and explain the relevant case law so that lawyers may more effectively advise and represent their clients. It is intended to be a starting point for lawyers (and for interested clients) but not the last word on any of the issues addressed.

Many fundamental issues raised by the Self-Incrimination Clause remain unsettled. The separate discussion in Chapter 2 of *McKune v. Lile*, 536 U.S. 24 (2002), for instance, is intended to highlight the degree to which issues relating to the meaning of the word "compelled" remain subject to debate. Chapter 2 also contains a discussion of the implications of *Chavez v. Martinez*, 538 U.S. 760 (2003), where a plurality of the Supreme Court ruled, at least for the purpose of a later civil suit, that the Self-Incrimination Clause is not violated unless and until a person's compelled self-incriminating testimony is actually used against him in a criminal case.

Despite the uncertainty created by *Chavez v. Martinez* as to when the Self-Incrimination Clause is violated, it is well settled that the privilege against self-incrimination may be asserted whenever the speaker reasonably fears that compelled self-incriminating disclosures may later be used against him or her. This third edition therefore continues to focus on the practical aspects of Fifth Amendment assertions in all types of proceedings. Chapter 3 addresses the manner in which courts have treated assertions of the Fifth Amendment in civil cases, in legislative hearings and investigations, and in response to regulatory and administrative agency demands, as well as in interactions with the police (both before and after custody) and during grand jury, criminal trial proceedings, and post-sentencing probation and parole. Although the third edition addresses the exclusionary rule created in *Miranda v. Arizona*, the discussion is intentionally limited and readers are encouraged to seek guidance elsewhere about *Miranda*'s complex and substantial progeny.

The importance of expressly invoking the right to remain silent was highlighted by the Supreme Court decision in *Salinas v. Texas*, 570 U.S. 178 (2013). Thus, the words that must be used to properly invoke the Fifth Amendment privilege and the procedures used by courts to decide the validity of a Fifth Amendment assertion are addressed in Chapters 4 and 5.

Because the legal consequences of asserting the privilege against self-incrimination in non-criminal proceedings are different than when the privilege is asserted in criminal cases, a portion of Chapter 3 is devoted to those issues and contains an expanded discussion of an area of law that remains unsettled: when a proceeding labeled as civil should actually be considered to be criminal for purposes of the right against self-incrimination.

There continues to be a stigma associated with invoking the Fifth Amendment privilege. This stigma is often exaggerated, because the privilege is designed as much to protect the innocent as the guilty. To highlight this point, Chapter 6 is devoted to the topic of stigma.

The case law regarding waiver of the Fifth Amendment, particularly outside the context of custodial interrogation, remains confusing. By discussing a few general principles and then describing how courts approach issues of waiver in various contexts, Chapter 7 attempts to make some sense of this disparate body of law.

It appears settled that the Fifth Amendment protection for documents is limited to the incriminating aspects of the compelled act of producing them. Chapter 8 highlights several of the issues that remain in controversy under the "act of production" privilege, including the foregone conclusion doctrine and the required records exception.

Chapter 9 addresses some of the critical issues associated with immunity, focusing primarily on the federal immunity statute and applicable federal court decisions. As with the second edition, the chapter refers to state cases only when they appear to differ from federal law.

Chapter 10 concerns the issue of brain imaging and the right against self-incrimination. The technology is no longer in its infancy, and the legal issues presented by its potential acceptance in courts are on the horizon. A new Epilogue contains a brief critique of Justice Clarence Thomas's views on the meaning of the Fifth Amendment Self-Incrimination Clause, with the goal of furthering the debate about his "originalist" interpretation of the Self-Incrimination Clause.

CHAPTER 1

The Purpose and Scope of the Fifth Amendment Right Against Compulsory Self-Incrimination

A Very Brief History of the Fifth Amendment

An adequate exploration of the origins of the Fifth Amendment privilege against self-incrimination extends well beyond the purpose of this book. However, as with the application of any constitutional right, it helps to have at least a rudimentary understanding of the history of the language when crafting arguments regarding its application. A student of the historical development of the right against self-incrimination would be well served to spend a few hours reading Leonard W. Levy, *Origins of the Fifth Amendment: The Right Against Self-Incrimination* (1968), which remains an influential work. *See, e.g.*, *McKune v. Lile*, 536 U.S. 24, 56 (2002) (Stevens, J., dissenting). For a different view of the historical development of the privilege, one should also read the essays collected in R.H. Helmholz et al., *The Privilege Against Self-Incrimination: Its Origins and Development* (1997). *See also United States v. Balsys*, 524 U.S. 666, 674 n.5, 687 n.9 (1998).

The Supreme Court traces the roots of our Fifth Amendment right against self-incrimination to the protections the English courts and Parliament granted to religious dissenters who were compelled to take oaths when called before the ecclesiastical courts, as well as the Court of High Commission and the Star Chamber. These bodies used the oath *ex officio* to force heretics from the Church of England to swear before God to answer all questions truthfully, even before the heretics knew the nature of the accusations against them. By use of the oath in conducting their investigations of religious heresy, these bodies left witnesses with the "cruel trilemma" of (1) refusing to take the oath, which constituted contempt and subjected the person to torture; (2) taking the oath and telling the truth about their religious belief, which, if heretical, was punishable by death; or (3) taking the oath and lying, which was also punishable by death. *See Murphy v. Waterfront Comm'n of N.Y. Harbor*, 378 U.S. 52, 55 (1964) (describing the Self-Incrimination Clause as "reflect[ing] many of our fundamental values and most noble aspirations: our unwillingness to subject those suspected of crime to the cruel trilemma of self-accusation, perjury or contempt. . . ."). The ecclesiastical system countenanced methods of interrogating persons designed to lead only to confessions. *See Andresen v. Maryland*, 427 U.S. 463, 470 (1976) (discussing the methods of the ecclesiastical inquisitions and the Star Chamber); *Griffin v. California*, 380 U.S. 609, 620 (1965) (noting that a suspect refusing to testify in front of the Star Chamber suffered "incarceration, banishment, or mutilation").

The English common law courts first sought to prohibit the use of the oath *ex officio* and the attendant inquisitorial methods of interrogating the accused by relying on the Latin maxim *nemo tenetur seipsum prodere* (or *nemo tenetur seipsum accusare*)—"no man is bound to accuse himself." *See, e.g., Brown v. Walker*, 161 U.S. 591, 596–97 (1896) (describing the maxim as a protest against the unjust methods used to extract confessions). Parliament abolished the Court of High Commission and the Star Chamber in 1641, and in 1662 passed a law providing that "no man shall administer to any person whatsoever the oath usually called *ex officio* or any other oath whereby such persons may be charged or compelled to confess to any criminal matter." The English common law courts began to recognize the presumption of innocence by the late 18th century, and judges in criminal cases began affording defendants the right not to incriminate themselves, which eventually established the privilege against self-incrimination as a fundamental rule of evidence.

English common law and the attendant criminal procedures developed there were transplanted to early colonial America. Thus, judges in both England and America adopted limits on the evidentiary use of involuntary pretrial confessions. Additionally, both English common law courts and American courts adopted the *nemo tenetur* principle to preclude the interrogation of suspects under oath. Just as religious dissenters in England protested that interrogation under oath was a forbidden form of torture, religious dissenters in colonial America viewed being placed under oath equally as offensive to their rights as the imposition of bodily harm. Thus in pre-Revolutionary America, justices of the peace, or magistrates, interrogated suspects in advance of bringing charges without placing them under oath. And although any unsworn statements made by the suspect could be introduced at trial, the accused could refuse to respond to such questions and could not be punished for his refusal to speak, as a matter of evidentiary rulings.

After the Revolutionary War, as the colonists sought to ensure that their individual rights in the courts were protected by written constitutions, at least eight of the original states drafted constitutions containing prohibitions against compulsory self-incrimination. Most of these constitutions prohibited compelling either the giving or furnishing of evidence against oneself, without using the word "witness." Section 8 of the Virginia Declaration of Rights, one of the most influential of the early constitutions, proclaimed "[t]hat in all capital or criminal prosecutions, a man hath a right to demand the cause and nature of his accusation . . . ; nor can he be compelled to give evidence against himself. . . ." Similarly, Article XII of the Massachusetts Declaration of Rights, another influential early constitution, provided that "[n]o subject shall . . . be compelled to accuse, or furnish evidence against himself."

Although the Constitutional Convention of 1787 adjourned without establishing a bill of rights, pressure grew for including a guarantee of individual liberties in the federal constitution. After Congress assembled in 1789, James Madison drafted a bill of rights, including a provision that "no person . . . shall be compelled to be a witness against himself." Madison's phrase was initially included in an article concerning both civil and criminal proceedings and apparently drew little attention or debate. An amendment offered in the House of Representatives limited the right to criminal proceedings, and was left unchanged by the Senate in the final Bill of Rights. Unfortunately, references to the right against compulsory self-incrimination are scarce in the congressional proceedings surrounding the ratification of the Bill of Rights. Little explanation exists for the language finally adopted. *See United States v. Balsys*, 524 U.S. 666, 711 (1998) (Breyer, J., dissenting) (observing that the Self-Incrimination Clause "has virtually no legislative history").

In the absence of "legislative history" for the wording adopted for the Self-Incrimination Clause, the Supreme Court has often looked to the common law history of the privilege, on the assumption that the framers adopted the privilege as it existed at the time. *See Ullmann v. United States*, 350 U.S. 422, 506 (1956) ("[T]he privilege against self-incrimination is a specific provision of which it is peculiarly true that 'a page of history is worth a volume of logic.'"). However, just as often, the Court has looked to the general evils that the right was designed to cure for guidance. *See Michigan v. Tucker*, 417 U.S. 433, 439–40 (1974) ("... we must continue to hark back to the historical origins of the privilege, particularly the evils at which it was to strike. The privilege against compulsory self-incrimination was developed by painful opposition to a course of ecclesiastical inquisitions and Star Chamber proceedings.... Certainly anyone who reads accounts of those investigations, which placed a premium on compelling subjects of the investigation to admit guilt from their own lips, cannot help but be sensitive to the Framers' desire to protect citizens against such compulsion."). *See also Couch v. United States*, 409 U.S. 322, 327 (1973) ("Historically, the privilege sprang from an abhorrence of governmental assault against the single individual accused of crime and the temptation on the part of the State to resort to the expedient of compelling incriminating evidence from one's own mouth.").

After the time of ratification, criminal defendants were unable to testify, being deemed incompetent in the eyes of the law by virtue of their biased interest in the outcome. *See generally Ferguson v. Georgia*, 365 U.S. 570, 575–86 (1961) (discussing the evolution of defendant's right to testify). Thus, the courts initially understood the Self-Incrimination Clause to simply affirm the existing common law protections afforded defendants and suspects alike against improper methods used for gaining confessions outside of court. By the end of the 19th century, however, as lawyers became more common in criminal cases, the broad concept of a person's right to remain silent when confronted with compelled examinations by the government became well established, at least in the federal courts. *See Counselman v. Hitchcock*, 142 U.S. 547 (1892) (upholding the right of witnesses to exercise their Fifth Amendment right against self-incrimination before an investigating grand jury absent transactional immunity) and *Brown v. Walker*, 161 U.S. 591 (1896) (upholding the constitutionality of a federal transactional immunity statute that prevented prosecution in exchange for compelling self-incriminating disclosures).

During the McCarthy era of the 1950s, the Fifth Amendment became the basis for invalidating numerous excesses in Congress's attempt to discover and punish Communist Party membership and affiliation. By the 1960s, the Fifth Amendment right against self-incrimination was recognized, in *Malloy v. Hogan*, 378 U.S. 1 (1964), to apply to the states through the Due Process Clause of the Fourteenth Amendment and came to be described as "the essential mainstay of our adversary system." *Miranda v. Arizona*, 384 U.S. 436, 460 (1966).

As we will see throughout this book, the law of the Fifth Amendment right against compelled self-incrimination continues to seesaw between a broad privilege of silence and a narrow exclusion of evidence against criminal defendants at trial, with justices and judges invoking the historical origins and perceived purposes of the right to support their competing interpretations.

Values Served by the Fifth Amendment

In light of the deep historical origins of the Fifth Amendment, the Supreme Court has often stated that the Fifth Amendment should "be accorded liberal construction in favor of the right it was intended to secure." *Hoffman v. United States*, 341 U.S. 479, 486 (1951). The "liberal construction" language was drawn from many of the earliest cases to consider the meaning of the clause. *See, e.g.*, *Bram v. United States*, 168 U.S. 532, 543 (1897) (adhering to rule that the Fifth Amendment should be liberally construed, as "[a] brief consideration of the reasons which gave rise to the adoption of the Fifth Amendment, of the wrongs which it was intended to prevent, and of the safeguards which it was its purpose unalterably to secure, will make it clear that the generic language of the amendment was but a crystallization of the doctrine as to confessions, well settled when the Amendment was adopted."). The "liberal construction" language is often repeated by both federal and state courts, though perhaps less often today than in the 20th century. For instance, in *Ullmann v. United States*, 350 U.S. 422 (1956), Justice Frankfurter, in upholding the federal immunity act that eliminated the witness's right to remain silent, more fully elucidated this proposition by stating:

> This constitutional protection must not be interpreted in a hostile or niggardly spirit. Too many, even those who should be better advised, view this privilege as a shelter for wrongdoers. They too readily assume that those who invoke it are either guilty of crime or commit perjury in claiming the privilege. Such a view does scant honor to the patriots who sponsored the Bill of Rights as a condition to acceptance of the Constitution by the ratifying States. The Founders of the Nation were not naive or disregardful of the interests of justice. . . . They made a judgment, and expressed it in our fundamental law, that it were better for an occasional crime to go unpunished than that the prosecution should be free to build up a criminal case, in whole or in part, with the assistance of enforced disclosures by the accused. The privilege against self-incrimination serves as a protection to the innocent as well as to the guilty, and we have been admonished that it should be given a liberal application.

Id. at 426–27 (citation omitted).

This "liberal construction" contrasts with the manner in which courts construe common law privileges like the attorney-client privilege. The strict construction of common law privileges is justified on the basis that the effect of these privileges is both to impede the full discovery of the truth and to deprive the public of their right to evidence. *See United States v. Bryan*, 339 U.S. 323, 331 (1950) (quoting *Wigmore* regarding the fundamental maxim that the public has the right to every man's evidence, in the context of a witness's failure to comply with a congressional subpoena); *United States v. Nixon*, 418 U.S. 683, 710 (1974) (in refusing to sustain a claim of executive privilege, the Court noted that "exceptions to the demand for every man's evidence are not lightly created nor expansively construed, for they are in derogation of the search for truth"); *Trammel v. United States*, 445 U.S. 40, 50 (1980) (requiring "a public good transcending the normally predominant principle of utilizing all rational means for ascertaining truth" to justify a husband-wife privilege) (quoting *Elkins v. United States*, 364 U.S. 206, 234 (1960)); *Jaffee v. Redmond*, 518 U.S. 1, 9 (1996) (upholding the privilege protecting communications between a psychotherapist and her client despite starting "with the primary assumption that there is a general duty to give what testimony one is capable of giving, and that any exemptions which may exist are distinctly exceptional . . .") (quoting *United States v. Bryan*, 339 U.S. 323, 331 (1950)). Although the Fifth Amendment similarly interferes with the general principle that society is entitled to every man's evidence, it is thought to promote certain fundamental values justifying such interference.

The values thought to justify the privilege against compelled self-incrimination are cataloged in *Murphy v. Waterfront Comm'n of N.Y. Harbor*, 378 U.S. 52, 54–55 (1964), the companion case to *Malloy v. Hogan*, 378 U.S. 1 (1964). There, Justice Goldberg, in deciding "the fundamental constitutional question of whether, absent an immunity provision, one jurisdiction in our federal structure may compel a witness to give testimony which might incriminate him under the laws of another jurisdiction," opened the analysis by describing the values and purposes of the privilege as follows:

> It reflects many of our fundamental values and most noble aspirations: our unwillingness to subject those suspected of crime to the cruel trilemma of self-accusation, perjury or contempt; our preference for an accusatorial rather than an inquisitorial system of criminal justice; our fear that self-incriminating statements will be elicited by inhumane treatment and abuses; our sense of fair play which dictates "a fair state-individual balance by requiring the government to leave the

> individual alone until good cause is shown for disturbing him and by requiring the government in its contest with the individual to shoulder the entire load," our respect for the inviolability of the human personality and of the right of each individual "to a private enclave where he may lead a private life," our distrust of self-deprecatory statements; and our realization that the privilege, while sometimes "a shelter to the guilty," is often "a protection to the innocent."

Murphy, 378 U.S. at 55 (citations omitted). As the Supreme Court subsequently indicated, "[t]his Court has been zealous to safeguard the values which underlie the privilege." *Kastigar v. United States*, 406 U.S. 441, 444–45 (1972).

The Supreme Court's zeal in safeguarding the values underlying the Self-Incrimination Clause is eroding. A more recent Supreme Court has remarked that "the scope of the privilege does not coincide with the complex of values it helps to protect." *Doe v. United States*, 487 U.S. 201, 213 n.11 (1988). *See also Schmerber v. California*, 384 U.S. 757, 762 (1966) ("[T]he privilege has never been given the full scope which the values it helps to protect suggest."). In *United States v. Balsys*, 524 U.S. 666, 691–92 (1998), the Supreme Court criticized *Murphy*'s expansive recitation of the purposes and policies of the Fifth Amendment. The *Balsys* majority specifically rejected *Murphy*'s previous "ambitious conceptualization of personal privacy underlying the Clause," *id.* at 684, and instead opined that its core purpose was simply to "prevent[] government overreaching." *Id.* at 693. In *Balsys*, the Supreme Court found the purposes served by the Fifth Amendment failed to justify extending its scope to fear of *foreign* prosecution, a result overturning substantial prior precedent. *Id.* at 696. *See also Brogan v. United States*, 522 U.S. 398, 404 (1998) (describing the phrase "cruel trilemma" as a *bon mot* used by Justice Goldberg). Indeed, in *Chavez v. Martinez*, 538 U.S. 760, 770 (2003), Justice Thomas, writing for four justices, distinguished between "prophylactic rules designed to safeguard the core constitutional right protected by the Self-Incrimination Clause" and the "core right" simply protecting a person's right not to be compelled to testify against himself at his own criminal trial. In the view of certain justices, the Fifth Amendment should not be accorded a "liberal construction," but must be interpreted strictly or literally in accordance with its text.

As discussed in many of the following sections, courts often balance, either explicitly or implicitly, the right of a party to assert the Fifth Amendment privilege against competing social goals, particularly the government's need to obtain both evidence and criminal convictions. The Supreme Court has explicitly balanced the legitimate interests of the state against the purposes served by the Fifth Amendment—often to the consternation of dissenting justices.

- *McKune v. Lile*, 536 U.S. 24, 37 (2002) (plurality weighed state's "vital interests in rehabilitation goals and procedures within the prison system" in deciding to uphold a state program requiring inmates in sexual abuse treatment to admit prior criminal conduct).
- *Balt. City Dep't of Soc. Servs. v. Bouknight*, 493 U.S. 549, 555–56 (1990) (holding that a mother was required to produce her child at the demand of the Department of Social Services, even though production might incriminate her, because production was part of a non-criminal regulatory regime that served important public policies).
- *New York v. Quarles*, 467 U.S. 649, 686 (1984) (Marshall, J., dissenting) (recognizing a public safety exception to the literal language of the requirements of *Miranda v. Arizona*, despite dissenters' objection that "[t]hough the majority's opinion is cloaked in the beguiling language of utilitarianism, the Court has sanctioned *sub silentio* criminal prosecutions based on compelled self-incriminating statements . . . in direct conflict with the Fifth Amendment. . . .").
- *Braswell v. United States*, 487 U.S. 99, 115 (1988) (the majority held that an agent of a corporation has no self-incrimination privilege when producing official corporate records, and remarked that "recognizing a Fifth Amendment privilege on behalf of the records custodians of collective entities would have a detrimental impact on the Government's efforts to prosecute 'white-collar crime'. . . .").

Of course, an equally compelling argument can be made that the framers had already balanced the interests to be served by the Fifth

Amendment privilege against competing governmental interests and that no further balancing is authorized by the language of the Fifth Amendment.

- *Braswell v. United States*, 487 U.S. 99, 129 (1988) (Kennedy, J., dissenting) ("The majority's abiding concern is that if a corporate officer who is the target of a subpoena is allowed to assert the privilege, it will impede the Government's power to investigate corporations, unions, and partnerships, to uncover and prosecute white-collar crimes, and otherwise to enforce its visitatorial powers. There are at least two answers to this. The first, and most fundamental, is that the text of the Fifth Amendment does not authorize exceptions premised on such rationales.").
- *New Jersey v. Portash*, 440 U.S. 450, 459 (1979) (in holding that the Fifth Amendment prohibits use of a person's immunized *testimony* to impeach the person's credibility when he testifies as a defendant in a criminal trial, the majority remarked that balancing of interests was prohibited by the Fifth Amendment).
- *Kastigar v. United States*, 406 U.S. 441, 467 (1972) (Douglass, J., dissenting) (in arguing that the Constitution did not allow for use and derivative use immunity to compel self-incriminating testimony, Douglass remarked, "[m]y view is that the framers put it beyond the power of Congress to compel anyone to confess his crimes. The Self-Incrimination Clause creates . . . 'the federally protected right of silence,' making it unconstitutional to use a law 'to pry open one's lips and make him a witness against himself.'") (citations omitted).

State courts often construe their state constitutional right against self-incrimination in a manner that provides greater protection to individuals than that provided by the Self-Incrimination Clause of the U.S. Constitution. A few examples include the following:

- *Olevik v. State*, 806 S.E.2d 505 (Ga. 2017) (deciding that the Georgia Constitution protects persons from being forced to perform acts that generate incriminating evidence, not just testimony, and on that basis holding that the state cannot compel a person suspected of driving under the influence of alcohol to blow their deep lung air into a breathalyzer).

- *Commonwealth v. Clarke*, 960 N.E.2d 306, 316–20 (Mass. 2012) (declining to adopt the Supreme Court's decision in *Berghuis v. Thompkins*, 560 U.S. 370 (2010), and holding that Article 12 of the Massachusetts Declaration of Rights allows suspects to invoke the privilege to remain silent after being advised of *Miranda* rights without the same clarity required by federal law).
- *State v. Peterson*, 923 A.2d 585, 593 (Vt. 2007) (refusing to follow *United States v. Patane*, 542 U.S. 630 (2004), as inconsistent with Article 10 of Vermont Constitution); *State v. Knapp*, 700 N.W.2d 899, 913–14 (Wis. 2005) (disagreeing with *United States v. Patane*, 542 U.S. 630 (2004), and holding that the Wisconsin Constitution precludes admission of physical evidence obtained as a direct result of an intentional *Miranda* violation).
- *D'elia v. Pa. Crime Comm'n*, 555 A.2d 864, 870–71 (Pa. 1989) (rejecting *Kastigar v. United States*, 406 U.S. 441 (1972), and holding that statutory use and derivative use immunity was not co-extensive with state constitutional protection against compulsory self-incrimination); *State v. Thrift*, 440 S.E.2d 341, 364–64 (S.C. 1994) (rejecting *Kastigar*, and holding that state constitution requires transactional immunity to preserve a person's rights against compulsory self-incrimination); *State v. Gonzalez*, 853 P.2d 526, 530–32 (Alaska 1993) (same).
- *Opinion of the Justices to the Senate*, 412 Mass. 1201 (Mass. 1992) (rejecting Supreme Court's decision in *South Dakota v. Neville*, 459 U.S. 553 (1983), as inadequate to protect a person's right against self-incrimination under Article XII of the Massachusetts Declaration of Rights and answering a question propounded by the State Senate by deciding that refusal to submit to a breath test is inadmissible under Article XII). *See also State v. Fish*, 893 P.2d 1023 (Or. 1995) (ruling that Oregon Constitution Self-Incrimination Clause protected refusal

to submit to field sobriety test and distinguishing *South Dakota v. Neville* as involving "non-testimonial" blood alcohol test).

- *State v. Reed*, 627 A.2d 630, 637–40 (N.J. 1993) (interpreting New Jersey's right against self-incrimination, founded in common law and statute, to require police officers to inform a suspect that an attorney is present and waiting to talk to him, contrary to Supreme Court's decision in *Moran v. Burbine*, 475 U.S. 412 (1986)).
- *Commonwealth v. Doe*, 544 N.E.2d 860, 861–62 (Mass. 1989) (rejecting *Braswell v. United States*, 487 U.S. 99 (1988), and holding that under the Massachusetts Declaration of Rights, a sole stockholder and sole corporate officer may refuse to produce corporate documents if the act of production would incriminate the custodian personally).
- *Commonwealth v. Turner*, 454 A.2d 537, 540 (Pa. 1982) (taking a more restrictive position than the U.S. Supreme Court in *Fletcher v. Weir*, 455 U.S. 603 (1982), in holding that a defendant cannot be impeached by the use of his silence after arrest, but before receiving *Miranda* warnings).
- *State v. Santiago*, 492 P.2d 657, 662–64 (Haw. 1971) (disagreeing with *Harris v. New York*, 401 U.S. 222 (1971), and holding that under the Hawaii Constitution, a prosecutor may not impeach the defendant with statements made in the absence of *Miranda* warnings).

CHAPTER 2

Elements of the Fifth Amendment

Only compelled self-incriminating testimony is protected by the Fifth Amendment. As expressed by the Supreme Court, "[T]o qualify for the Fifth Amendment privilege, a communication must be testimonial, incriminating, and compelled." *Hiibel v. Sixth Judicial Dist. Court of Nev.*, 542 U.S. 177, 189 (2004). Additionally, the Fifth Amendment privilege belongs only to persons, and not to entities. Further, there is a renewed debate as to whether compelled incriminating testimony must be presented or threatened to be presented in a "criminal case" for the Fifth Amendment to be violated. Each of these issues is discussed in the following sections.

The Meaning of Self-Incrimination

Although the term self-incrimination does not appear in the Fifth Amendment, the words "witness against himself" have consistently been regarded to mean self-incriminating.

Information is self-incriminating if it may subject the speaker, or lead to other information that may subject the speaker, to the possibility of U.S. criminal prosecution or criminal penalties.

- *Kastigar v. United States*, 406 U.S. 441, 445 (1972) (the Fifth Amendment privilege "protects against any disclosures that the witness reasonably believes may be used in a criminal prosecution or could lead to other evidence that might be so used").

- *Hoffman v. United States*, 341 U.S. 479, 486 (1951) ("The privilege afforded not only extends to answers that would in themselves support a criminal conviction under a federal criminal statute, but likewise embraces those which would furnish a link in the chain of evidence needed to prosecute the claimant for a federal crime.").

To constitute incrimination, there must be a realistic possibility of future prosecution or criminal penalties. The Supreme Court has repeatedly stated: "[T]he central standard for the privilege's application has been whether the claimant is confronted by substantial and 'real,' and not merely trifling or imaginary, hazards of incrimination." *Marchetti v. United States*, 390 U.S. 39, 53 (1968). *See also United States v. Apfelbaum*, 445 U.S. 115, 128 (1980) (quoting *Marchetti* with approval); *Zicarelli v. N.J. State Comm'n of Investigation*, 406 U.S. 472, 478 (1972) ("It is well established that the privilege [against self-incrimination] protects against real dangers, not remote and speculative possibilities."); *Brown v. Walker*, 161 U.S. 591, 599–600 (1896) (quoting the English case of *Regina v. Boyes*, 1 Best & S. 311, 321, that distinguished between "danger [that was] . . . real and appreciable, with reference to the ordinary operation of law in the ordinary course of things" and "danger of an imaginary and unsubstantial character, having reference to some extraordinary and barely possible contingency. . . .").

Although the threat of incrimination must be real, the protection afforded by the Fifth Amendment extends to the *possibility* of criminal prosecution, not the probability.

- *Pillsbury Co. v. Conboy*, 459 U.S. 248, 266 n.1 (1983) (Marshall, J., concurring) ("It need not be probable that a criminal prosecution will be brought or that the witness's answer will be introduced in a later prosecution; the witness need only show a realistic possibility that his answer will be used against him.").
- *Resnover v. Pearson*, 965 F.2d 1453, 1462 (7th Cir. 1992) ("We cannot agree that a witness' [*sic*] constitutional privilege against self-incrimination depends upon a judge's prediction of the likelihood of prosecution.").

- *United States v. Sharp*, 920 F.2d 1167, 1171 (4th Cir. 1990) (trial court erred in compelling a witness to testify, despite the witness's assertion of the Fifth Amendment privilege, based solely on the government's representation that it had no present intention of pursuing criminal prosecution).
- *In re Folding Carton Antitrust Litig.*, 609 F.2d 867, 871 (7th Cir. 1979) ("When a witness can demonstrate any possibility of prosecution which is more than fanciful he has demonstrated a reasonable fear of prosecution sufficient to meet constitutional muster.").
- *In re Brogna*, 589 F.2d 24, 27–28 (1st Cir. 1978) (prosecutor's denial of intention to prosecute held insufficient to overrule claim of Fifth Amendment privilege against self-incrimination).
- *United States v. Miranti*, 253 F.2d 135, 139 (2d Cir. 1958) ("We find no justification for limiting the historic protections of the Fifth Amendment by creating an exception . . . which would nullify the privilege whenever it appears that the government would not undertake to prosecute.").
- *Commonwealth v. Leclair*, 17 N.E.3d 415, 420–21 (Mass. 2014) (summary contempt vacated where non-immunized trial witness in criminal trial properly refused to answer questions posed by defense counsel about his prior use of illegal drugs; prosecutor's statement that office had no intention of prosecuting witness for his prior drug use did not matter).
- *Carter v. United States*, 684 A.2d 331, 336–37 (D.C. 1996) (citing cases from the Second, Fourth, Fifth, Seventh, Tenth, and Eleventh Circuits that follow the rule that the inquiry into whether a statement is incriminating should not consider the likelihood of prosecution).

A disclosure that could implicate the witness in any activity addressed by a criminal statute is usually sufficient to justify invocation of the Fifth Amendment privilege against self-incrimination.

- *Counselman v. Hitchcock*, 142 U.S. 547, 576–77 (1892) (describing why two witnesses compelled to give testimony disclosing sources of information, or means by which government could obtain additional evidence that a crime had been committed, would have the effect of connecting the witness to a crime, and thereby constitute self-incriminating disclosures).

- *Blau v. United States*, 340 U.S. 159, 161 (1950) (because the Smith Act forbade knowingly belonging to any organization that advocated overthrow of the government, a grand jury witness could refuse to answer questions regarding whether he was employed by the Communist Party).
- *Albertson v. Subversive Activities Control Bd.*, 382 U.S. 70, 77 (1965) ("[M]ere association with the Communist Party presents sufficient threat of prosecution to support a claim of privilege.") (citations omitted).
- *Oregon v. Martinez-Garcia*, 389 P.3d 405 (Or. Ct. App. 2017) (lower court violated Self-Incrimination Clause of Fifth Amendment when it compelled the defendant, by threatening and imposing contempt, to state his true identity in response to whether he was the person named in multiple criminal charges).
- *But cf. Hiibel v. Sixth Judicial Dist. Ct. of Nev.*, 542 U.S. 177, 190–91 (2004) (although state statute criminalized the refusal to identify oneself when stopped by the police, court found that disclosure of one's name was incriminating only in unusual circumstances and that state statute requiring a person lawfully detained to identify himself did not violate the Fifth Amendment).

Importantly, the privilege extends not only to answers that would themselves constitute admissible evidence in a criminal prosecution but also to any answer that would furnish a "link in a chain" of evidence that could be used to prosecute the person claiming the privilege. In the leading case of *Hoffman v. United States*, 341 U.S. 479, 482 (1951), a witness was subpoenaed to appear before a federal grand jury and asked to state his occupation and whether he knew a certain individual, to which he asserted the Fifth Amendment privilege. The district court overruled his assertion and held him in contempt for refusing to answer on the grounds that the questions posed no risk of a "real and substantial danger of incrimination." The Supreme Court reversed, issuing the often-cited standard: "The privilege afforded not only extends to answers that would in themselves support a conviction under a federal criminal statute, but likewise embraces those which would furnish a link in the chain of evidence needed to prosecute the claimant for a federal crime. . . ." *Id.* at 486. The Court found on the basis of the witness's 21-year police record, presence on a Senate committee's list of known gangsters, being labeled as a gangster by local police, and having served a sentence for narcotics offenses that it was far from "perfectly clear" that the answers to the questions could not possibly incriminate. *Id.* at 488. *See also Molloy v. Hogan*, 378 U.S. 1, 13 (1964) (lower court erred by rejecting a self-incrimination claim by a witness who refused to identify his employer, where ". . . disclosure of his name might furnish a link in a chain of evidence sufficient to connect the [witness] with a more recent crime for which he might still be prosecuted"). The "link in a chain" standard, announced in *Hoffman*, has implications for the waiver of the self-incrimination privilege, a topic addressed in Chapter 7.

Because incrimination includes a "link in a chain of evidence needed to prosecute," even a person who claims innocence may simultaneously assert his or her Fifth Amendment privilege against self-incrimination.

- *Ohio v. Reiner*, 532 U.S. 17, 21–22 (2001) (per curiam) (when the defense theory was that a prosecution witness was responsible for an infant's death, the witness could invoke Fifth Amendment privilege against self-incrimination, despite claims of innocence, because there was reasonable cause to believe that her responses regarding her care of the infant could form a "link in the chain" that could be self-incriminating).
- *In re Proceedings Before a Grand Jury*, 768 N.E.2d 1102, 1107 (Mass. App. Ct. 2002) (reversing a judgment of contempt against a witness who, despite claiming innocence, asserted the Fifth Amendment privilege before a grand jury investigating an arson, where she was one of two individuals in a position to have perpetrated the crime).

The Supreme Court's recognition that the Self-Incrimination Clause protects the innocent and the guilty alike is often misunderstood and is elaborated upon in Chapter 6.

Given the scope and number of federal, state, and local criminal statutes in the United States, including conspiracy statutes, it is relatively easy for a party asserting the right to demonstrate that a question put to him or her may yield an answer that furnishes a link in the chain of incriminating evidence. Indeed, questions concerning not only the witness's potentially criminal conduct but also the whereabouts of records of items that contain potentially incriminating evidence may constitute a link. *Curcio v. United States*, 354 U.S. 118, 121 (1957) (Court found substantial grounds for a fear of possible incrimination where custodian of a union's books and records was asked about the location of those books and records during a grand jury union racketeering investigation). *See also United States v. Hubbell*, 530 U.S. 27, 43 (2000) ("[W]e have no doubt that the constitutional privilege against self-incrimination protects the target of a grand jury investigation from being compelled to answer questions designed to elicit information about the existence of sources of potentially incriminating evidence.").

While courts often place the burden of demonstrating the likelihood of incrimination on the party asserting the Fifth Amendment privilege, some have reasoned that the party opposing the assertion should have the burden of persuasion to demonstrate with clarity that there is no possibility of incrimination for one invoking the privilege. *See, e.g., Kerr v. Hart (In re Christou)*, No. 06–68251-MHM, 2010 WL 4008167, at *5 (Bankr. N.D. Ga. Sept. 24, 2010) ("The 'ultimate burden of persuasion with respect to validity' of a Fifth Amendment claim rests with the opposing party.") (citations omitted); *State v. Manley*, 664 N.W.2d 275, 286 (Minn. 2003) (en banc) ("[T]he trial court should not require the witness to prove the hazard of incrimination, as to do so would require the witness to 'surrender the very protection which the privilege is designed to guarantee.'") (citations omitted); *Commonwealth v. Martin*, 668 N.E.2d 825, 832 (Mass. 1996) ("In attempting to establish his right to the privilege, a witness should not be required to disclose so much that the privilege is effectively destroyed.") (citations omitted).

As the Supreme Court stated in *Hoffman*, "[t]o sustain the privilege, it need only be evident from the implications of the question, in the setting in which it is asked, that a responsive answer to the question or an explanation of why it cannot be answered might be dangerous because injurious disclosure could result." 341 U.S. at 486–87. Indeed, "[c]ompelled testimony that communicates information that may 'lead to incriminating evidence' is privileged even if the information itself is not inculpatory." *Hubbell*, 530 U.S. at 38 (quoting *Doe v. United States*, 487 U.S. 201, 208 n.6 (1988)).

It is rare for courts to overrule assertions of the privilege on the ground that a response is insufficiently incriminating. Only where a criminal prosecution is legally foreclosed or the testimony cannot possibly furnish a link in the chain of incriminating evidence have courts prevented witnesses from invoking the privilege against self-incrimination. For instance, the Fifth Amendment does not protect against testimony that might become incriminating only through the witness's future conduct.

- *United States v. Freed*, 401 U.S. 601, 606–07 (1971) (National Firearms Act registration requirement did not violate defendant's Fifth Amendment right, even though the information the registrant was required to disclose might be used in a prosecution of future firearms offenses defendant might commit).
- *United States v. Harvey*, 869 F.2d 1439, 1448–49 (11th Cir. 1989) (compelled production of information to the Drug Enforcement Administration under a grant of use immunity did not violate the Fifth Amendment with respect to potential future violations of reporting requirements of the tax code).
- *Littlejohn v. United States*, 705 A.2d 1077, 1083 (D.C. 1997) (relying on *Hoffman* to reverse a lower court ruling that allowed a witness to invoke the privilege against self-incrimination based on the witness's fear that his testimony, which placed him on a city block 18 months prior to the commission of a crime he was now charged with, could possibly incriminate him in his pending prosecution for that crime).

The Fifth Amendment does not protect compelled incriminating testimony if the potential for any prosecution has been barred by the applicable statute of limitations or some other complete defense.

- *Hale v. Henkel*, 201 U.S. 43, 67 (1906) ("But if criminality has already been taken away, the [Self-Incrimination Clause of the Fifth] Amendment ceases to apply.").
- *Earp v. Cullen*, 623 F.3d 1065, 1071 (9th Cir. 2010) (noting that the state's argument that a witness had properly invoked her Fifth Amendment privilege was without merit where the applicable statute of limitations had long since expired).
- *United States v. Garrett*, 6 F. App'x 573 (9th Cir. 2001) (rejecting assertion of Fifth Amendment privilege to IRS summons where prosecution for willful failure to file a tax return was time-barred on all tax years relevant to the request for information).
- *United States v. Goodman*, 289 F.2d 256, 262 (4th Cir. 1961), *vacated on other grounds*, 368 U.S. 14 (1961) (determining that defendant had no valid Fifth Amendment privilege because the statute of limitations had already run on any criminal acts committed by him during the time period to which his testimony would relate).
- *Zebbs v. Commonwealth*, 785 S.E.2d 493 (Va. 2016) (finding that where double jeopardy barred any further prosecution, the requirement of a sex offender treatment program that the defendant admit to his crime of conviction could not be incriminating).

Of course, it is often difficult for a party opposing the assertion of the privilege to show with sufficient clarity that any potentially applicable statute of limitations bars the possibility of criminal prosecution. Thus, the majority of cases concerning a statute of limitations "defense" to the assertion of a Fifth Amendment privilege have upheld the right.

- *Convertino v. U.S. Dep't of Justice*, 795 F.3d 587 (6th Cir. 2015) (affirming district court's rulings sustaining a deponent's claim of Fifth Amendment privilege despite assertion that time for prosecuting the deponent would be barred by the applicable statute of limitations, where statute at issue criminalized not only receipt of confidential government documents but also their retention.)

- *In re Flat Glass Antitrust Litig.*, 385 F.3d 350, 371 (3d Cir. 2004) (deponents were found to have provided sufficient proof that several state statutes of limitations had not expired, justifying their assertions of the Fifth Amendment).
- *In re Corrugated Container Antitrust Litig.*, 661 F.2d 1145, 1153 (7th Cir. 1981) (ruling that a witness's assertion of the Fifth Amendment privilege was valid, despite the fact that federal statute of limitations had run on certain federal antitrust charges, because there was still a possibility of prosecution on federal conspiracy charges and state criminal charges).
- *United States v. Nipper*, 210 F. Supp. 2d 1259, 1262 (N.D. Okla. 2002) (court determined that six-year statute of limitations for tax evasion had not expired, justifying assertion of Fifth Amendment privilege).

As a result of the Supreme Court's decision in *Murphy v. Waterfront Commission of New York Harbor*, 378 U.S. 52 (1964), the Fifth Amendment privilege protects witnesses in federal cases against potential incrimination for state crimes, and protects witnesses in state cases against potential incrimination for federal crimes. However, it does not protect a witness whose only justifiable fear is criminal prosecution outside the United States. Rather, in *United States v. Balsys*, 524 U.S. 666, 698–700 (1998), the Supreme Court decided that the Fifth Amendment privilege did not apply to a defendant whose answers could potentially subject him to prosecution in Lithuania and Israel but not in the United States, reasoning that the clause is limited to fear of prosecution by the same government whose powers it limits—the United States federal and state governments. 524 U.S. at 698–700.

Where the risk to the speaker does not involve the possibility of criminal sanctions, but only civil hardships, there is generally no self-incrimination.

- *United States v. Juvenile Male*, 670 F.3d 999, 1011 (9th Cir. 2012) (a probation condition requiring registration as sex offender does not violate the Fifth Amendment's Self-Incrimination Clause because defendant could not fear additional criminal exposure or liability for a crime to which he had already pled guilty).

- *In re Grand Jury Proceedings*, 835 F.2d 375, 376 (1st Cir. 1987) (per curiam) (potential loss of pension benefits not sufficient to invoke Fifth Amendment).
- *Mertsching v. United States*, 704 F.2d 505, 507 (10th Cir. 1983) (per curiam) (right against self-incrimination cannot be invoked to insulate tax preparer from giving testimony because potential penalties assessed for disregarding revenue rules in preparing tax returns are civil in nature).
- *Attor v. Attor*, 894 A.2d 83, 92–93 (N.J. Super. Ct. App. Div. 2006) (ruling that trial court erred in allowing wife to assert her Fifth Amendment privilege where the statute of limitations had run on potential criminal prosecution for false swearing and her fear of deportation, which constituted a civil hardship, was an insufficient basis to invoke the privilege).

Distinguishing between criminal and civil sanctions is often difficult. Relevant cases addressing this issue are discussed in Chapter 3.

Finally, a witness may not claim the privilege against self-incrimination out of fear that he will be prosecuted for perjury for what he is about to truthfully say. However, a witness may claim the privilege if prospective truthful statements will put him at risk for perjury by contradicting his prior testimony.

- *United States v. Allmon*, 594 F.3d 981, 986 (8th Cir. 2010) (noting that while a witness may invoke the privilege where truthful testimony in current proceeding "will reveal perjury that occurred in a *past* proceeding," there could be no claim based on concern that current testimony may lead to perjury charges).
- *United States v. Whittington*, 783 F.2d 1210, 1218 (5th Cir.) (ruling that a witness has no right to "refuse to testify on the basis that the witness may be prosecuted for a lie not yet told"), *reh'g denied*, 786 F.2d 644 (5th Cir. 1986).

- *United States v. Housand*, 550 F.2d 818, 823 (2d Cir. 1977) (holding that a witness may invoke the Fifth Amendment privilege "if he had already lied in the Grand Jury and would now make a truthful contradictory statement").
- *See also Harris v. New York*, 401 U.S. 222, 225 (1971) ("Every criminal defendant is privileged to testify in his own defense or to refuse to do so. But that privilege cannot be construed to include the right to commit perjury.") (citations omitted).

The Meaning of Compulsion

General Propositions

By its terms, the Fifth Amendment protects only communications that are compelled. A subpoena, with its threat of contempt of court for noncompliance, qualifies as compulsion. And the classic example of compulsion is when a court orders the witness to testify under a grant of immunity, accompanied by the threat of contempt for noncompliance. In *New Jersey v. Portash*, 440 U.S. 450 (1979), holding that a person's testimony before a grand jury under a grant of immunity cannot be used to impeach him at trial, the Supreme Court wrote:

> Testimony given in response to a grant of legislative immunity is the essence of coerced testimony. In such cases there is no question whether physical or psychological pressures overrode the defendant's will; the witness is told to talk or face the government's coercive sanctions, notably, a conviction for contempt. The information given in response to a grant of immunity may well be more reliable than information beaten from a helpless defendant, but it is no less compelled. The Fifth and Fourteenth Amendments provide a privilege against *compelled* self-incrimination, not merely against unreliable self-incrimination.

Id. at 459.

The test for compulsion under the Fifth Amendment, in circumstances that do not involve legal process, is not entirely certain. Although subject to criticism, the governing test appears to be "whether, considering the totality of the circumstances, the free will of the witness was overborne."

United States v. Washington, 431 U.S. 181, 188 (1977) (citing *Rogers v. Richmond*, 365 U.S. 534, 544 (1961)). *See also In re Gault*, 387 U.S. 1, 47 (1967) (the state compels production of evidence whenever "whether by force or by psychological domination, [it] overcome[s] the mind and will of the person under investigation and depriv[es] him of the freedom to decide whether to assist the state in securing his conviction").

Certain forms of informal compulsion or pressure are also so severe as to violate the Due Process Clause of the Fifth Amendment (or, in state cases, the Fourteenth Amendment) as well as the Self-Incrimination Clause. The law regarding involuntary confessions is briefly reviewed in Chapter 3. Yet for purposes of the Fifth Amendment's Self-Incrimination Clause, pressures that are not as harsh as those producing involuntary confessions may still render the resulting testimony inadmissible. For instance, requiring public employees either to forfeit their jobs or to incriminate themselves has been determined to constitute impermissible compulsion.

- *Lefkowitz v. Cunningham*, 431 U.S. 801, 802–04 (1977) (political party officer could not be prevented from holding further office for refusing to waive privilege against self-incrimination).
- *Lefkowitz v. Turley*, 414 U.S. 70, 85 (1973) (statutes requiring government contractors to agree that the contract could be cancelled and that they would be disqualified from further state business if they refused to answer questions when called to testify constituted unconstitutional compulsion).
- *Gardner v. Broderick*, 392 U.S. 273, 276–79 (1968) (a police officer may not be compelled by his employer to waive his privilege against self-incrimination under penalty of being fired).
- *Uniformed Sanitation Men Ass'n, Inc. v. Comm'r of Sanitation*, 392 U.S. 280, 284–85 (1968) (employees could not be forced to testify when government was not merely seeking information regarding a possible abuse of public trust, but also seeking information that could be used in a criminal prosecution).
- *Garrity v. New Jersey*, 385 U.S. 493, 496–98 (1967) (police officers' Fifth Amendment rights were violated when answers to questions

obtained by threat of discharge for refusing to answer were used in subsequent criminal prosecution).

The decisions just cited are often referred to as the "penalty cases" and express the Supreme Court's application of its "unconstitutional conditions" doctrine in the context of the Self-Incrimination Clause. These cases analyze the circumstances in which a penalty directly imposed on an assertion of the Fifth Amendment privilege against self-incrimination becomes so great as to deprive the person of the freedom to decide for himself whether to speak. The high-water mark of this line of cases was in *Spevack v. Klein*, 385 U.S. 511 (1967), where the Supreme Court considered the case of a lawyer who had been disbarred for refusing to honor a subpoena duces tecum, on the basis that the production of the records would tend to incriminate him. The New York courts ruled that the Fifth Amendment was not available to Spevak in a bar disciplinary proceeding, as no criminal penalty was threatened in that proceeding. The Supreme Court disagreed. Although the Court recognized that professional disbarment constituted neither a fine nor imprisonment, it considered disbarment to fall within the category of non-criminal sanctions that make the assertion of the Fifth Amendment privilege too costly to survive constitutional scrutiny. According the privilege a liberal construction, the Court found that automatic disbarment for asserting the Fifth Amendment privilege was a "powerful form of compulsion" similar to depriving an individual of employment, and, as such, constituted impermissible compulsion. *Id.* at 516.

Other than depriving a person of government employment or a professional license, however, few recent Supreme Court decisions have found penalties imposed on the out-of-court exercise of the Fifth Amendment privilege to constitute impermissible compulsion. Rather, numerous decisions have upheld the government's right to penalize a refusal to speak without violating a person's Fifth Amendment right against compelled self-incrimination.

- *Selective Serv. Sys. v. Minnesota Pub. Interest Research Grp.*, 468 U.S. 841, 859 (1984) (Military Selective Service Act did not violate

Fifth Amendment right against compulsory self-incrimination by requiring registration for the draft in order to receive financial assistance for higher education).

- *South Dakota v. Neville*, 459 U.S. 553, 564 (1983) (admission at trial of a defendant's refusal to undergo a blood-alcohol test was constitutional because test was not mandatory and, therefore, the defendant's refusal was not compelled).
- *Roberts v. United States*, 445 U.S. 552, 561 (1980) (defendant's refusal to cooperate with officials investigating a conspiracy in which he was a confessed participant was constitutionally appropriate to consider, as one factor, in imposing sentence).

The Supreme Court has been most concerned about penalizing the assertion of a self-incrimination privilege in the criminal courtroom. Thus, in *Griffin v. California*, 380 U.S. 609 (1965), the Court held that the Fifth Amendment forbids a judge or prosecutor to comment on a defendant's decision not to testify. Although a defendant's will is not overborne when he refuses to testify, the cost imposed by allowing an adverse inference to be drawn from the refusal was thought to be too great a penalty, as it "cuts down on the privilege by making its assertion costly." *Id.* at 614. *See also Brooks v. Tennessee*, 406 U.S. 605, 610–11 (1972) (state law requiring a defendant to choose at outset of defense presentation whether or not he would take the stand placed too heavy a burden on defendant's unconditional right not to testify).

Outside of the context of "custodial interrogation," which the Supreme Court recognized in *Miranda v. Arizona* created a presumption of compulsion, and which is separately discussed in Chapter 3, any other forms of governmental pressure to make incriminating admissions have been found lacking the necessary compulsion to violate the Fifth Amendment privilege against self-incrimination. The following examples include cases involving procedures that give defendants a Hobson's choice of forfeiting certain rights in order to preserve their Fifth Amendment protections.

- *Ohio Adult Parole Auth. v. Woodard*, 523 U.S. 272, 287–88 (1998) (no Fifth Amendment–violative level of compulsion where an adverse inference will be drawn from an individual's refusal to answer questions before a clemency board).

- *Minnesota v. Murphy*, 465 U.S. 420, 435 (1984) ("A state may require a probationer to appear and discuss matters that affect his probationary status," as long as the state does not threaten that invocation of the privilege against self-incrimination would lead to revocation of probation.).
- *McGautha v. California*, 402 U.S. 183, 217 (1971) (remarking that "the policies of the privilege against compelled self-incrimination are not offended when a defendant in a capital case yields to the pressure to testify on an issue of punishment at the risk of damaging his case on guilt") *reh'g granted, judgment vacated sub nom. Crampton v. Ohio*, 408 U.S. 941 (1972).
- *Williams v. Florida*, 399 U.S. 78, 82–83 (1970) (Florida's notice of alibi rule does not violate defendant's Fifth Amendment privilege against self-incrimination).
- *United States v. Caira*, 737 F.3d 455, 460–61 (7th Cir. 2013) (deciding there was no impermissible compulsion where an erroneous evidentiary ruling at trial "forc[ed]" the defendant to take the stand and testify in his own defense).
- *United States v. Arrington*, 73 F.3d 144, 149–50 (7th Cir. 1996) (requiring defendant to admit past criminal conduct in order to receive a sentence below statutory minimum does not violate Fifth Amendment privilege against self-incrimination, because no impermissible compulsion).
- *Izazaga v. Superior Court*, 815 P.2d 304, 310–13 (Cal. 1991) (state court order requiring criminal defendant to provide reciprocal discovery did not violate either the Fifth Amendment or California Constitution Article I, § 15 limits on compelled self-incrimination).

In *Salinas v. Texas*, 570 U.S. 178 (2013), the Supreme Court was faced with a case that seemed to require it to determine whether a non-custodial interrogation had involved impermissible compulsion. Although the Court resolved the case on other grounds, as is discussed further in Chapter 3, the case contains an instructive debate on whether the Fifth Amendment prohibited the prosecution's use of an adverse inference, allowed by state law, against a suspect who remained silent in the face of police questioning. Four dissenters concluded that the suspect faced impermissible compulsion, since he was placed in "an impossible predicament"—either answer the police question about a weapon and incriminate himself or remain silent and have that silence used to "suggest a consciousness of guilt." *Id.* at 195 (Breyer, J., dissenting). Two members of the majority—which held that no self-incrimination question was presented because the suspect had not claimed the privilege—disagreed, noting "[a] defendant is not 'compelled . . . to be a witness against himself' simply because an adverse inference may be drawn from his silence." *Id.* at 192 (Thomas, J., concurring in the judgment).

Although the lower courts have divided on the compulsion issue left open by *Salinas*, the decisions more favorable to the accused have held that use of a defendant's pre-arrest silence is prohibited by the right against compelled self-incrimination. *See Commonwealth v. Molina*, 104 A.3d 430 (Pa. 2014) (collecting cases) (ruling on the basis of the Pennsylvania Constitution that the use of pre-arrest silence as substantive evidence of guilt violates a non-testifying defendant's right against compelled self-incrimination). *See also United States v. Okatan*, 728 F.3d 111, 118–120 (2d Cir. 2013) (government's use of evidence in its case-in-chief of a person's invocation of his right to counsel prior to arrest violated rights under Self-Incrimination Clause) and *State v. Horowitz*, 191 So. 3d 429, 438–39, 442–43 (Fla. 2016) (holding that the use of the defendant's pre-arrest, pre-*Miranda* silence as substantive evidence of guilt violates both Florida Constitution and Florida evidence law).

The case of *McKune v. Lile*, 536 U.S. 24 (2002), further demonstrates the struggle within the modern Supreme Court to distinguish permissible from impermissible compulsion. In that case, Lile, who had been convicted and incarcerated for raping a woman at gunpoint, was thereafter ordered to participate in a sexual abuse treatment program (SATP) to minimize the likelihood that he would offend again upon his release. The SATP required that he admit responsibility for his crime, provide a full history of his prior sexual offenses, and undergo a polygraph test to verify his responses. At trial, Lile had testified that the intercourse with the victim was consensual. Thus, if Lile acknowledged responsibility for the rape, or admitted past sexual offenses as required by the SATP, he faced subjecting himself to perjury charges or to other new charges. When he asserted his Fifth Amendment privilege against self-incrimination, he was promptly transferred to maximum security and lost many of his prison privileges.

Four justices concluded that the consequences Lile suffered as a result of his refusal to admit responsibility for past sexual misconduct did not create impermissible compulsion, on the basis that the consequences were not "atypical and significant hardship[s] on [inmates] in relation to the ordinary incidents of prison life." *McKune*, 536 U.S. at 25 (quoting *Sandlin v. Conner*, 515 U.S. 472, 484 (1995)). These four justices, led by Justice Kennedy, distinguished between an ordinary citizen's Fifth Amendment protection and a prisoner's Fifth Amendment protection. They rejected the test for measuring compulsion previously developed in the "so-called penalty cases" of *Garrity v. New Jersey* and its progeny, and applied instead the "atypical and significant hardship" test elucidated in *Sandlin v. Conner*, which the Supreme Court uses for determining due process violations caused by prison requirements. *McKune*, 536 U.S. at 37–40.

In her concurrence, Justice O'Connor declined to analyze the case under *Sandlin*'s due process standard. Instead, she agreed with the four dissenters that the Fifth Amendment standard for evaluating compulsion does not distinguish between prisoners and law-abiding members of the public. Thus, she applied the full-blown Fifth Amendment analysis applied in the "penalty cases." However, under that analysis, she concluded that transfer from a medium to a maximum security prison unit, and the loss of privileges associated with reassignment, did not constitute impermissible compulsion. *Id.* at 48–49.

Four other justices were vehement in their disagreement, both with the plurality's use of the *Sandlin* test and with Justice O'Connor's decision that the sanctions imposed on Lile were not coercive for purposes of the Fifth Amendment. Those justices not only considered the transfer from minimum security to maximum security and the concomitant loss of privileges to be severe, but also protested that the Court, for the first time, "held that a person who has made a valid assertion of the privilege may nevertheless be ordered to incriminate himself and [be] sanctioned for disobeying such an order." *Id.* at 54 (Stevens, J., dissenting).

Subsequently, the lower courts have disagreed over whether various sanctions imposed by other state sex offender programs on the invocation of the privilege against self-incrimination constitute impermissible compulsion. For example, in *Ainsworth v. Stanley*, 317 F.3d 1, 3 (1st Cir. 2002), the First Circuit adopted Justice O'Connor's approach and ruled that New Hampshire's sex offender program did not violate the Fifth Amendment, despite the fact that an inmate's assertion of the Fifth Amendment privilege in response to the admitting questionnaire "almost always results in an inmate being denied parole." Similarly, in *Gwinn v. Awmiller*, 354 F.3d 1211, 1226–27 (10th Cir. 2004), the Tenth Circuit ruled that the reduced likelihood of parole for refusing to participate in a prison treatment program for sexual offenders does not constitute an impermissible penalty of the right against compelled self-incrimination. In *Roman v. DiGuglielmo*, 675 F.3d 204, 214–15 (3d Cir. 2012), the Third Circuit ruled that Pennsylvania's decision to deny an inmate parole unless he admitted his guilt and participated in a sex offender treatment program did not violate the Fifth Amendment, noting that the inmate "has no right or entitlement to parole under Pennsylvania law," and that "[h]is sentence has not been lengthened, nor have the actual conditions of his imprisonment been altered." *Id.* at 214 (citations omitted). In *State v. Pritchett*, 69 P.3d 1278, 1285–87 (Utah 2003), the Utah Supreme Court followed *McKune* and held that a statute requiring sex offenders to admit culpability for the offense for which they were convicted before being considered for probation, did not violate the Fifth Amendment right against self-incrimination. *See also Wirsching v. Colorado*, 360 F.3d 1191, 1202–04 (10th Cir. 2004) (a prisoner's loss of opportunity to earn good time credits and loss of visitation for not making admissions in a sex offender treatment program did not constitute compulsion that violated the Fifth Amendment); *Bleeke v. Lemmon*, 6 N.E.3d 907, 939–40 (Ind. 2014) (a parolee required to participate in a sex offender treatment program requiring admission of past crime or risk of revocation is not a Fifth Amendment violation).

In contrast, the Minnesota Supreme Court, sitting en banc, decided in consolidated cases that an extension of a release date due to loss of good time is the sort of atypical and significant hardship that might compel an inmate to give evidence against himself, thus satisfying the compulsion prong of the Fifth Amendment. *Johnson v. Fabian*, 735 N.W.2d 295, 298, 309 (Minn. 2007). Similarly, in *United States v. Antelope*, 395 F.3d 1128, 1137–38 (9th Cir. 2005), the Ninth Circuit ruled that a longer term of incarceration imposed on a probationer for refusing to disclose his sexual history in the course of court-ordered treatment constituted impermissible compulsion, at least if a real risk of prosecution for past sexual crimes exists. Relying almost entirely on Justice O'Connor's concurrence in *McKune*, the Ninth Circuit determined that the district court's decision to revoke probation and impose an additional period of imprisonment on a person who refused to report his sexual history was unconstitutionally compulsive. *Id.* at 1139. *See also Colorado v. Roberson*, 377 P.3d 1039, 1044 (Colo. 2016) (en banc) (threatening probationer with revocation based on the proper invocation of his Fifth Amendment rights not to answer polygraph questions constituted impermissible compulsion); *State v. Van Komen*, 376 P.3d 738, 744 (Idaho 2016) (where court revoked probation because defendant refused to waive his Fifth Amendment right and answer incriminating questions that could result in new felony charges, the court's action violated his right not to be compelled under the Self-Incrimination Clause); *Capers v. Governor of N.J.*, 525 F. App'x 69, 73 (3d Cir. 2013) (holding that an inmate who lost progressive time credits for refusing to speak about his crimes and to participate in treatment therapy "may be able to sufficiently plead more specific facts to support" a Fifth Amendment claim); *Donhouser v. Goord*, 314 F. Supp. 2d 119, 129 n.8 (N.D.N.Y. 2004), *remanded for clarification by* 181 F. App'x 11 (2d Cir. 2006) ("[A]pplying the vast sea of compulsion principles applied by the various opinions in *McKune* and the federal appellate decisions that followed, [I find that] the loss of good time credits imposed automatically and directly for plaintiff's failure to give up his right to silence and participate in the [sex offender treatment] program, violate every single one of them.").

While *McKune* involved the imposition of sanctions on a prisoner who exercises his Fifth Amendment privilege—a context in which courts have shown considerable deference to the executive branch—the compulsion principles it elucidates cannot be limited to prisoners. A five-member majority of justices in *McKune* agreed that even prisoners enjoy full Fifth Amendment rights. Thus, the divisions among the Justices illustrate the ongoing struggle to define compulsion for purposes of the Fifth Amendment.

Courts appear more sensitive to the degree of coercion thought to violate the Fifth Amendment in the context of parental rights. The following decisions all held, for instance, that the state may not require a parent to choose between exercising the right against self-incrimination and losing parental rights, which are deemed protected liberty interests.

- *In re A.D.L.*, 402 P.3d 1280, 1286 (Nev. 2017) (violation of mother's Fifth Amendment rights to be required to admit to a criminal act in order to be considered in compliance with her case plan).
- *Dep't of Human Svcs. v. K.L.R.*, 230 P.3d 49, 54–55 (Or. Ct. App. 2010) (requiring admission of abuse as a condition of family reunification violates a parent's Fifth Amendment privilege, but terminating parental rights based on parental refusal to participate in therapy does not violate the Fifth Amendment).
- *In re A.W.*, 896 N.E.2d 316, 326 (Ill. 2008) ("[A] trial court may order a service plan that requires a parent to engage in effective counseling or therapy, but may not compel counseling or therapy requiring the parent to admit to committing a crime.") (citation omitted).
- *State v. Brown*, 182 P.3d 1205, 1212 (Kan. 2008) (defendant was placed in a "classic" penalty situation when his parental rights would be terminated if state agency did not receive a full account of his child's injuries).
- *In re J.A.*, 699 A.2d 30, 31 (Vt. 1997) (striking portion of reunification plan that required stepfather to admit he had sexually abused his stepdaughter).
- *In re Amanda W.*, 705 N.E.2d 724, 727 (Ohio 1997) (Fifth Amendment privilege violated when father was forced to admit sexual abuse of daughter as a condition of regaining custody).

- *In re Welfare of J.G.W.*, 433 N.W.2d 885, 886 (Minn. 1989) (en banc) (parent's Fifth Amendment privilege protects against being ordered to admit past abuse as prerequisite to visiting his children).

Private Compulsion vs. Government Compulsion

The Fifth Amendment proscribes only official or governmental compulsion. Purely private compulsion is not prohibited by the Fifth Amendment. The distinction between public and private action can, however, often be blurred. The Supreme Court has ruled that a private party's action may constitute state action, if "there is such a 'close nexus between the State and the challenged action' that the seemingly private behavior 'may be fairly treated as that of the State itself.'" *Brentwood Acad. v. Tenn. Secondary Sch. Athletic Ass'n*, 531 U.S. 288, 295 (2001) (quoting *Jackson v. Metro. Edison Co.*, 419 U.S. 345, 351 (1974)). Facts that "bear on the fairness of such an attribution" include whether the challenged activity "results from the State's exercise of 'coercive power,'" whether "the State provides significant encouragement, either overt or covert," or whether "a private actor operates as a 'willful participant in the joint activity with the State or its agents.'" *Id.* at 296 (citations omitted).

The following Supreme Court decisions have grappled with claims by parties that ostensibly private action constituted de facto state action, in contexts not involving the Self-Incrimination Clause.

- *Edmonson v. Leesville Concrete Co.*, 500 U.S. 614, 621–22 (1991) (Court, in holding that peremptory challenges may not be used to exclude jurors on the basis of race in civil trials, identified three guiding factors to determine whether a particular action or conduct is governmental in character: "the extent to which the actor relies on governmental assistance and benefits; whether the actor is performing a traditional governmental function; and whether the injury caused is aggravated in a unique way by the incidents of governmental authority") (citations omitted).
- *Skinner v. Railway Labor Execs.' Ass'n*, 489 U.S. 602, 633–34 (1989) (while concluding that drug and alcohol tests conducted on railroad engineers by a private railroad company after an accident did

not violate the Fourth Amendment, the Court recognized that the Fourth Amendment applied to private company testing, because tests were required by regulations imposed by the Federal Railway Administration).

- *Lugar v. Edmonson Oil Co.*, 457 U.S. 922, 937 (1982) (a debtor stated a valid claim for relief in a civil rights action against a private creditor, where the creditor had obtained a writ of attachment from a state court judge).
- *Blum v. Yaretsky*, 457 U.S. 991, 1004–05 (1982) (nursing home's decision to transfer patients to a lower level of care did not constitute state action simply because state social service officials were required to approve the decision to discontinue benefits).
- *Jackson v. Metro. Edison Co.*, 419 U.S. 345, 351–52 (1974) (termination of electricity service did not constitute state action simply because state public utility commission approved company's tariff allowing termination of electric service).
- *Griffin v. Maryland*, 378 U.S. 130, 135–36 (1964) (a specially deputized, private security guard was a state actor when he "purported to exercise the authority of a deputy sheriff" and publicly "enforced [the park's] private policy of racial segregation").

Although the Supreme Court has not dealt directly with a case requiring it to decide when private action constitutes de facto government compulsion under the Fifth Amendment, it has come close. In *Estelle v. Smith*, 451 U.S. 454, 467 (1981), the Court ruled that *Miranda* applied during the death penalty phase to a psychiatric competency exam conducted by a court-appointed psychiatrist who was allowed to testify that the respondent would be a danger to society. The Court found that under all the circumstances, the role of the otherwise neutral psychiatrist "changed and became essentially like that of an agent of the State. . . ." The Court has also held that by "intentionally creating a situation likely to induce [a suspect] to make incriminating statements without the assistance of counsel" to a paid informant, "the Government violated [a defendant's] Sixth Amendment right to counsel." *United States v. Henry*, 447 U.S. 264, 274 (1980). Similarly, in *Arizona v. Fulminante*, 499 U.S.

279 (1991), the Court found that a prisoner's confession to an undercover jailhouse informant working as a police agent was involuntary and had been admitted at trial in violation of the defendant's Fourteenth Amendment due process rights. *But cf. Illinois v. Perkins*, 496 U.S. 292, 300 (1990) (*Miranda* does not apply where an undercover police agent, posing as a fellow inmate, questioned an incarcerated suspect).

Lower courts have recognized that private actors may violate the Fifth Amendment Self-Incrimination Clause if their actions are fairly attributed to the direction of the government.

- *United States v. Williamson*, 447 F. App'x 446 (4th Cir. 2011) (deciding that police direction of jailhouse informant, whose questions elicited self-incriminating statements of defendant, could constitute a violation of the Fifth Amendment, and remanding to the district court to determine the degree of police involvement in eliciting the defendant's statements, among other facts).
- *D.L. Cromwell Invs., Inc. v. NASD Reg., Inc.*, 279 F.3d 155, 162–63 (2d Cir. 2002) (upholding district court's decision that an investigator for National Association of Securities Dealers (NASD) was *not* a state actor for purposes of the Fifth Amendment, but suggesting that the evidentiary record could have supported a contrary conclusion, where NASD investigative demands overlapped with FBI demands during parallel investigations).
- *Mathis v. Pac. Gas & Elec. Co.*, 75 F.3d 498, 503–04 (9th Cir. 1996) (dicta remarking that had private entity's internal investigation produced a coerced confession and been conducted in close cooperation with a county task force, a finding of state action for purposes of the Fifth Amendment could be made).
- *United States ex rel. Sanney v. Montanye*, 500 F.2d 411, 415 (2d Cir. 1974) (where an employer administered a polygraph test at the behest of the government, the court held that the state had improperly involved itself in using a "substantial economic threat to coerce a person into furnishing an incriminating statement").
- *Welch v. Commonwealth*, 149 S.W.3d 407, 412 (Ky. 2004) (where defendant admitted uncharged criminal conduct to his counselor

during treatment at court-ordered program for offenders, counselor was considered state actor and statements were suppressed for lack of *Miranda* warnings).

- *State v. Goree*, 950 P.2d 919, 921 (Or. 1997) (defendant's wife was a state actor where she was cooperating with police, was fitted by police with a body wire, and was instructed what to ask the defendant). *But cf. State v. Sanders*, 452 S.W.3d 300, 302–03 (Tenn. 2014) (ruling there was no violation of defendant's right against self-incrimination when he made admissions to a parent of a victim of sexual abuse who was secretly cooperating with law enforcement officials).
- *State v. Bowe*, 881 P.2d 538, 539–41 (Haw. 1994) (recognizing that coercive conduct by a private person may be sufficient to render a defendant's confession involuntary under state's constitutional provision against compelled self-incrimination).

A Second Circuit decision in a highly publicized case involving the Sixth Amendment right to counsel reflects the refusal of courts to ignore state involvement in an ostensibly private action.

- *United States v. Stein*, 541 F.3d 130, 136 (2d Cir. 2008) (government caused KPMG to deny counsel of choice to KPMG employees, in violation of employees' Sixth Amendment rights, when it threatened KPMG with adverse consequences if it advanced legal fees to its indicted employees).

Indeed, although the Second Circuit did not reach the issue, the district court also found that the Department of Justice's pressure on KPMG to require its employees to make statements during the government investigation or be fired resulted in impermissible compulsion requiring suppression of the employees' statements. *United States v. Stein*, 440 F. Supp. 2d 315, 337–38 (S.D.N.Y. 2006).

It is well established that the government may not use, either directly or derivatively, self-incriminating statements made by its employees that are compelled by threat of job termination. *Garrity v. New Jersey*, 385

U.S. 493 (1967). However, when a private corporation conducts an internal investigation and cooperates with the government by turning over to prosecutors the incriminating statements made by its employees under threat of being fired, courts are generally reluctant to find the government involvement sufficient to constitute the necessary state action to suppress the statements (or their fruits) in a subsequent prosecution of the corporate employee. *See Gilman v. Marsh & McLennan & Cos.*, 829 F.3d 69, 76 (2d Cir. 2016) (rejecting a claim by two employees that an internal investigation by their private employer who was cooperating with the government constituted state action). *United States v. Carson*, No. 8:09-cr-00077 (C.D. Cal. May 22, 2012), ECF No. 774 (in holding that private attorneys conducting an internal investigation on behalf of a corporation were not state actors when they interviewed certain employees, the court found insufficient evidence that "the Government 'deliberately precipitated' the supposed coercion employed by [the corporation] in causing the interviews to go forward").

However, in a recent prosecution of a former banker accused of manipulating LIBOR rates, a judge in the Southern District of New York found, after conducting an evidentiary hearing, that a private corporation's actions in conducting an internal investigation should be attributed to the government. The court made extensive factual findings, including that "Deutsche Bank was told by the Government to conduct an investigation . . . , to do so in a particular fashion, to interview particular people including [the defendant], to share its findings with the Government on a regular basis, and to carry out the governmental investigative demands that were generated by its earlier efforts. Deutsche Bank, facing ruin, complied with the Government's directives in every particular." Mem. Decision and Order Den. Def. Gavin Black's Mot. for *Kastigar* Relief, *United States v. Connolly*, No. CR 0370(CM) slip op. at 28 (S.D.N.Y. May 2, 2019). This decision has created a significant degree of uncertainty regarding the typical practices used by the Department of Justice, the Securities and Exchange Commission, the Commodities Future Trading Commission, and other government agencies regarding their usual interactions with corporate counsel conducting internal investigations. Despite finding a *Garrity* violation by Deutsche

Bank, the Court nonetheless denied defendant Black any relief, finding that the government did not make use, directly or derivatively, of the compelled self-incriminating statements obtained during the "internal investigation" from the defendant under threat of termination. *Id.* at 40–43. The subject of when a defendant is entitled to relief for a *Garrity* violation is addressed in Chapter 9.

In an analogous context, the federal courts have considered suppressing evidence obtained by foreign officials, otherwise not subject to Fifth Amendment prohibitions, when law enforcement agents from the United States engage in a joint venture or use foreign officials as their agents. Particularly in the age of international efforts to combat terrorism, cybercrime, and financial corruption, the number of such cases is likely to grow.

- *United States v. Frank*, 599 F.3d 1221, 1228–29 (11th Cir. 2010) (although recognizing the "joint venture doctrine" may justify suppressing statements taken by foreign officials in violation of *Miranda*, court upheld denial of suppression motion where there was no evidence that American officials participated in the foreign interrogation).
- *In re Terrorist Bombings of U.S. Embassies in E. Africa*, 552 F.3d 177, 203 (2d Cir. 2008) (discussing the joint venture doctrine in the context of Fifth Amendment claims).
- *United States v. Covington*, 783 F.2d 1052, 1056–57 (9th Cir. 1986) (case remanded for further proceedings to determine role played by U.S. officials in interrogation of suspect conducted in conjunction with Marshall Islands officials).
- *United States v. Emery*, 591 F.2d 1266, 1267–68 (9th Cir. 1978) (statement suppressed where DEA alerted Mexican police to defendant's activities, coordinated the surveillance at the Mexican airport, and supplied the undercover agent to fly the airplane involved in the drug transaction).
- *United States v. Karake*, 281 F. Supp. 2d 302, 308–09 (D.D.C. 2003) (defendants were entitled to discovery of communications between U.S. and Rwandan government officials to determine whether

Rwandan law enforcement acted as agents of U.S. officials and/or in joint venture).

This "joint venture" doctrine applicable to the cooperation between U.S. law enforcement agents and foreign law enforcement authorities harks back to the Supreme Court's decision to suppress statements obtained by state officials acting as agents for federal law enforcement during the period before *Malloy v. Hogan*, when the Fifth Amendment applied only to federal government officials and not to state officials. *See generally Anderson v. United States*, 318 U.S. 350, 356 (1943) ("There was a working arrangement between the federal officers and the sheriff of Polk County which made possible the abuses revealed by this record. Therefore, the fact that the federal officers themselves were not formally guilty of illegal conduct does not affect the admissibility of the evidence which they secured improperly through collaboration with state officers.") (citations omitted).

A decision by the Second Circuit will have significant implications for the working relationships between United States and foreign prosecutors. In *United States v. Allen*, 864 F.3d 63 (2d Cir. 2017), the court vacated two convictions and dismissed the underlying indictments based on a cooperating witness's exposure to the defendants' statements compelled by a United Kingdom regulatory authority pursuant to a grant of use immunity. The court held that the Fifth Amendment limits the use of a defendant's statements, compelled by a foreign state, in American criminal proceedings regardless of proof of a joint venture with the United States. Because a key cooperating witness had reviewed the compelled statements of the defendants before testifying before the grand jury and at trial in the United States, the defendants successfully argued that both their indictment and conviction were obtained by virtue of violations of their Fifth Amendment rights. The court's ruling, that the Fifth Amendment "applies in American courtrooms even where, as here, the defendant's testimony was compelled by foreign officials *lawfully*," *id.* at 82, will likely be tested in other circuits. The *Allen* case has substantial implications for the use of testimony compelled by immunity, a subject discussed in Chapter 9.

In *United States v. Balsys*, 524 U.S. 666, 698 (1998), the Supreme Court left open the question of whether a defendant who could show certain types of "cooperative conduct" between U.S. and foreign law enforcement authorities could validly exercise his privilege against self-incrimination when the only potential prosecution was in a foreign country. *See also Mattel, Inc. v. MGA Entm't, Inc.*, No. CV 04–9049, 2010 WL 3705782, at *7 (C.D. Cal. Aug. 3, 2010) ("[W]hile *Balsys* may have held that the Fifth Amendment doesn't categorically protect a defendant fearful of foreign prosecution, the scope of its holding didn't include prosecutions in which the United States played such an active role that the prosecution could not be 'fairly characterized as distinctly "foreign."'") (citation omitted). However, this close cooperation exception, if it is an exception, has proven difficult to satisfy. *See, e.g., United States v. All Assets Held at Bank Julius Baer & Co., Ltd.*, 312 F.R.D. 16, 20–21 (D.D.C. 2015).

The Meaning of Testimonial Communication

Although the text of the Self-Incrimination Clause never uses the word "testimony," it is reasonably well settled that to receive Fifth Amendment protection, a compelled self-incriminating communication must be testimonial. The Supreme Court has, however, never defined "testimony." *See, e.g., Crawford v. Washington*, 541 U.S. 36, 68 (2004) (leaving for another day any effort to spell out a comprehensive definition of "testimonial" evidence for purpose of the Sixth Amendment Confrontation Clause). However, it has suggested that "testimony" applies only to spoken words or other actions that explicitly or implicitly make a factual assertion revealing the contents of one's mind. In *Doe v. United States*, 487 U.S. 201, 210 (1988), the Supreme Court held that compelling the defendant in a criminal case to sign a consent form authorizing foreign banks to disclose records of the defendant's accounts did not involve a testimonial communication. The target in the case was ordered to sign a form that "purported to apply to any and all accounts over which Doe had a right of withdrawal. . . ." *Id.* at 204. Because the form did not specify the account to which the authorization applied, the Court reasoned that "neither the form, nor its execution, communicate[d] any factual assertions, implicit or explicit, or convey[ed] any information to the Government." *Id.* at 215. In a telling footnote, the Court commented:

> We do not disagree with the dissent that "[t]he expression of the contents of an individual's mind" is testimonial communication for purposes of the Fifth Amendment. We simply disagree with the dissent's conclusion that the execution of the consent directive at issue here forced petitioner to express the contents of his mind.

Id. at 210 n.9 (citation omitted).

The Supreme Court relied heavily on the *Doe* footnote in deciding *Pennsylvania v. Muniz*, 496 U.S. 582, 582–83 (1990), a case in which it determined that slurred speech and other evidence of lack of muscular coordination revealed by a person arrested for driving under the influence of alcohol were non-testimonial communications. Nevertheless, a plurality of the Court held that one aspect of the field sobriety test administered by police—asking the suspect to recall the date of his sixth birthday—compelled a testimonial communication that expressed "consciousness of the facts and the operations of his mind in expressing it." *Id.* at 594. According to the plurality:

> The content of his truthful answer supported an inference that his mental faculties were impaired, because his assertion (he did not know the date of his sixth birthday) was different from the assertion (he knew the date was [correct date]) that the trier of fact might reasonably have suspected a lucid person to provide. Hence, the incriminating inference of impaired mental faculties stemmed, not just from the fact that Muniz slurred his response, but also from a testimonial aspect of that response.

Id. at 599.

Similarly, in *United States v. Hubbell*, 530 U.S. 27 (2000), the Supreme Court focused on the cognition necessary for a person to produce documents required by a subpoena in determining that the independent counsel had used Hubbell's act of production in violation of an order of immunity. See generally Chapters 8 and 9, concerning the act of production doctrine and immunity, respectively. In that case, the text of the subpoena required Webster Hubbell to produce, inter alia, "[a]ny and all documents reflecting, referring, or relating to any direct or indirect sources of money or other things of value received by or provided to" him. *Hubbell*, 530 U.S. at 46–47. Because of the breadth of such demands, Hubbell was required "to make extensive use of 'the contents of his own mind'" in identifying, assembling, and producing the documents commanded by the subpoena, thereby satisfying the Court that the resulting act of producing the documents was a testimonial communication. *Id.* at 43. According to the Court, "[t]he assembly of these documents was like telling an inquisitor the combination to a wall safe . . . ," a clear testimonial communication. *Id.* at 43.

Taken together, *Doe*, *Muniz*, and *Hubbell* appear to define testimony for the purposes of the Fifth Amendment as any communication (by words or action) expressing the content of a person's mind. *See also Schmerber v. California*, 384 U.S. 757 (1966) (where the majority of the justices recognized that forced physical extractions from the mind are different from forced extraction of blood); *Curcio v. United States*, 354 U.S. 118, 128 (1957) (recognizing that forcing of custodian to testify orally as to the whereabouts of non-produced records is contrary to the Fifth Amendment because it would require him "to disclose the contents of his own mind"). As discussed further in Chapter 10, the definition of testimony will become critical as advances in neuroscience enable law enforcement to extract self-incriminating information directly from one's brain, without the witness ever opening his mouth.

Challenging issues as to what constitutes testimony for purposes of the Self-Incrimination Clause arise when an individual is compelled to decrypt the contents of a computer hard drive, cell phone, or other electronic device with a password and thereby allow the government access to the encrypted files or documents. In *In re Grand Jury Subpoena Duces Tecum Dated March 25, 2011*, 670 F.3d 1335 (11th Cir. 2012), the Eleventh Circuit considered an order holding a defendant in contempt after he had been granted act of production immunity, and still refused, on the basis of his right against self-incrimination, to decrypt and then produce the contents of hard drives seized from him. The circuit court reversed the contempt. It held that the individual's act of decrypting the otherwise inaccessible files on his computer hard drives by use of an alpha-numeric passcode held in his memory was sufficiently testimonial to trigger Fifth Amendment protection. It then ruled that the act of production immunity was insufficient to extinguish the privilege, as it allowed the government derivative use of the decrypted files. In holding that decryption was testimonial, the court—relying on *Fisher v. United States* and *United States v. Hubbell*—reasoned that the decryption required use of the contents of the compelled person's mind, and "would be tantamount to testimony by Doe of his knowledge of the existence and location of potentially incriminating files; of his possession, control, and access to the encrypted portions of the drives; and of his capability to decrypt the files." 670 F.3d at 1346.

Although a few courts have held that a court order can compel a person to tell law enforcement officials the password to his encrypted computer files because the password is not testimonial, the vast majority of courts have correctly decided that compelling the person to provide the password is testimony, as it expresses the contents of the person's mind. Most courts analyzing government efforts to compel individuals to reveal their passwords in order to allow access to the contents of their computers and smartphones focus on the separate issue of whether the "foregone conclusion" doctrine applies. This issue has produced a heated debate that is analyzed at some length in Chapter 8.

The Supreme Court's focus on the disclosure of the content of a person's mind as a defining aspect of "testimony" provides the government with substantial latitude to compel a person to produce otherwise highly self-incriminating evidence consisting of physical matters from a person's body. In the seminal case of *Schmerber v. California*, 384 U.S. 757 (1966), the Supreme Court held that a person could be forced to give blood samples to determine whether he was intoxicated while driving. A 5–4 majority, led by Justice Brennan, held that the privilege against self-incrimination "protects an accused only from being compelled to testify against himself, or otherwise provide the State with evidence of a testimonial or communicative nature, and that the withdrawal of blood and use of the analysis in question . . . did not involve compulsion to these ends." *Id.* at 761.

Following *Schmerber*, courts have upheld, against Fifth Amendment objections, the compelled collection of various types of physical samples:

- Urine samples: *Hess v. Ables*, 714 F.3d 1048, 1053 (8th Cir. 2013) ("[A] urine drug test would not violate her Fifth Amendment right against self-incrimination because urine samples, which are not testimonial evidence, do not trigger Fifth Amendment protections.") (citation omitted); *United States v. Edmo*, 140 F.3d 1289, 1292–93 (9th Cir. 1998) (defendant's Fifth Amendment rights were not violated when police officer required him to give a urine sample); *Walters v. Sec'y of Def.*, 725 F.2d 107, 108–09 (D.C. Cir. 1983) (introduction of compulsory urinalysis evidence into administrative discharge proceeding did not violate Uniform Code of Military Justice Article prohibiting compelled self-incrimination). *See also Nat'l Treasury Emps. Union v. Von Raab*, 489 U.S. 656, 668 (1989) (collection and chemical analysis of drug samples from government employees do not require warrant under Fourth Amendment).
- Hair samples: *United States v. Dougall*, 919 F.2d 932, 935 (5th Cir. 1990) (hair samples are non-testimonial in nature and a requirement to produce them does not violate a person's right against self-incrimination). *See also United States v. Jackson*, 448 F.2d 963, 971 (9th Cir. 1971) (removal of hair samples does not violate a defendant's right to due process).
- DNA samples: *Kaemmerling v. Lappin*, 553 F.3d 669, 685–86 (D.C. Cir. 2008) (compelling prisoner to provide DNA sample for database is not Fifth Amendment violation because blood test evidence is not testimonial); *United States v. Hook*, 471 F.3d 766, 773–74 (7th Cir. 2006) (production of DNA profiles for government database were physical, not testimonial, communications and not protected by Fifth Amendment); *Shaffer v. Saffle*, 148 F.3d 1180, 1181 (10th Cir. 1998) (rejecting Fifth Amendment challenge to collection of DNA samples because such samples are non-testimonial in nature); *Boling v. Romer*, 101 F.3d 1336, 1340 (10th Cir. 1996) (upholding statute

compelling inmates convicted of sex crimes to provide DNA samples before being released on parole). *State v. Heinonen*, 909 N.W. 2d 584, 590–91 (Minn. 2018) (the Fifth Amendment privilege against self-incrimination does not apply when police request and take a DNA sample from a person in custody after arrest, as sample is not a testimonial communication). *See also Maryland v. King*, 569 U.S. 435 (2013) (rejecting Fourth Amendment challenge to police using a cheek swab to obtain a DNA sample from an arrestee in order to match with DNA from unsolved crimes).

Indeed, when a computer or smartphone uses a fingerprint code or a facial or retina recognition passcode instead of an alpha-numeric passcode, the courts have not hesitated to uphold the government's right to compel the person to provide access, on the basis that requiring the person to use a fingerprint or facial features to grant access elicits only physical evidence from a person's body and does not reveal the contents of a person's mind.

- *State v. Diamond*, 905 N.W.2d 870 (Minn.), *cert. denied*, 138 S. Ct. 2003 (2018) (deciding that compelling a person to provide a fingerprint to unlock a cellphone is non-testimonial).
- *Commonwealth v. Baust*, 89 Va. Cir. 267 (2014) ("The fingerprint, like a key, however, does not require the witness to divulge anything through his mental processes.").

On the other hand, a warrant application that sought authority to compel any individual present during the execution of a search warrant to provide fingerprints on an Apple brand device "in order to gain access to the contents of such device" was denied by a magistrate judge in *In re Application for a Search Warrant*, 236 F. Supp. 3d 1066, 1067 (N.D. Ill. 2017). The magistrate judge not only raised various Fourth Amendment concerns with the application but also raised Fifth Amendment concerns about how the warrant would, in effect, compel an individual to "testify[] that he or she has accessed the phone before . . . and that he or she currently has some level of control over or relatively significant connection to the phone and its contents." *Id.* at 1073. Particularly where the warrant sought to compel a number of individuals to press their fingers to the phone and would thereby identify which phone belonged to which person, the fingerprint requirement could be viewed as compelling testimony that "this phone [and its contents] are mine." *See also In the Matter of Search of a Residence in Oakland, California*, No. 4–19–70053, 2019 WL 176937, at *3 (N.D. Cal. Jan. 10, 2019) (denying application for a search warrant seeking to compel any individual present at the time of the search to press a finger or utilize other biometric features to unlock any digital device found on the premises on the basis that "the act of unlocking a phone with a finger or thumb scan far exceeds the 'physical evidence' created when a suspect submits to fingerprinting to merely compare his fingerprints to existing physical evidence (another fingerprint) found at the crime scene. . . .").

Based on the distinction between physical acts and acts revealing the contents of a person's mind, courts have compelled persons to engage in all types of volitional activities that communicate incriminating information, but arguably do not involve cognitive processes. In *United States v. Wade*, 388 U.S. 218, 223 (1967), for instance, the majority remarked that the Fifth Amendment offered no protection "against compulsion to submit to fingerprinting, photography, or measurements, to write or speak for identification, to appear in court, to stand, to assume a stance, to walk, or make a particular gesture" (citation omitted). *See also United States v. Hubbell*, 530 U.S. 27, 35 (2000) (remarking that the Fifth Amendment does not prohibit compelling a suspect "to put on a shirt, to provide a blood sample or handwriting exemplar, or to make a recording of his voice"). Thus, the government may require a person to engage in various courtroom demonstrations or physical acts outside of court that are designed to aid their own conviction, including the following:

- Perform physical actions: *Avery v. Procunier*, 750 F.2d 444, 448 (5th Cir. 1985) (requiring defendant to reenact the crime did not violate his rights against self-incrimination); *State v. Gonzalez*, 895 N.W.2d 580 (Wis. 2014) (to assist jury in identifying the defendant as a participant in a fight, judge could order defendant to display his platinum teeth without violating his right against self-incrimination). *Stave v. Faidley*, 450 P.2d 20, 24 (Kan. 1969) (requiring defendant to perform head-to-toe balance test is non-testimonial and not violative of privilege against self-incrimination).

- Shave a beard or mustache to aid identification: *United States v. Valenzuela*, 722 F.2d 1431, 1433 (9th Cir. 1983) (requiring a defendant to shave is a non-testimonial act and does not implicate Fifth Amendment rights).
- Try on clothing: *Holt v. United States*, 218 U.S. 245, 252–53 (1910) (compelling defendant to try on clothes and demonstrate fit was not Fifth Amendment violation because the act was not testimonial); *State v. Perry*, 230 S.E.2d 141, 145 (N.C. 1976) (instruction requiring defendant to stand before jury and place stocking mask over his face did not violate defendant's constitutional rights against self-incrimination); *State v. Bauman*, 468 P.2d 684, 686 (Wash. 1970) (requiring defendant to put on shirt found at scene of crime and exhibit himself before the jury did not violate his privilege against self-incrimination).
- Provide handwriting examples: *Gilbert v. California*, 388 U.S. 263, 266 (1967) ("[T]he taking of the [handwriting] exemplars did not violate petitioner's Fifth Amendment privilege against self-incrimination. The privilege reaches only compulsion of 'an accused's communications, whatever form they might take, and the compulsion of responses which are also communications, for example, compliance with a subpoena to produce one's papers,' and not compulsion which makes a suspect or accused the source of 'real or physical evidence.'" (quoting *Schmerber v. California*, 384 U.S. 757, 763–64)).
- Dye hair: *United States v. Brown*, 920 F.2d 1212, 1215 (5th Cir. 1991) (likening requiring a defendant to dye his hair to other non-testimonial evidence and finding that the action did not violate defendant's Fifth Amendment rights), *overruled on other grounds sub nom. United States v. Candia*, 454 F.3d 468, 471 (5th Cir. 2006).
- Demonstrate speech in order to reveal physical characteristics of voice: *Pennsylvania v. Muniz*, 496 U.S. 582, 592 (1990) (compelling

drunk driving defendant to respond to routine booking questions and thereby demonstrate slurred speech and lack of coordination on videotape was not testimonial); *United States v. Dionisio*, 410 U.S. 1, 6–7 (1973) (compelling defendant to read a transcript of an electronically recorded conversation for the purpose of identifying a physical characteristic was not testimonial in nature); *United States v. Wade*, 388 U.S. 218, 222–23 (1967) (compelling defendant to appear in a lineup and to speak within hearing distance of witness and to exhibit physical characteristics for purpose of identification was not within the scope of the privilege).

If the government can compel courtroom demonstrations without violating the defendant's Fifth Amendment privilege, it stands to reason that a defendant can engage in similar demonstrations without waiving his Fifth Amendment right not to testify, a subject briefly addressed in Chapter 7.

Because the compelled extraction of physical evidence is most often deemed non-testimonial, the refusal to allow the extraction of physical samples may itself be used as evidence of a person's guilt.

- *Pennsylvania v. Muniz*, 496 U.S. 582, 604–05 (1990) (holding that the introduction into evidence of both a person's incriminating statements in response to routine booking questions and a refusal to take a Breathalyzer test did not violate the Fifth Amendment privilege against self-incrimination).
- *Deering v. Brown*, 839 F.2d 539, 543–44 (9th Cir. 1988) (defendant's refusal to submit to Breathalyzer was admissible, even though refusal was punishable by three-day prison sentence).
- *Rowley v. Commonwealth*, 629 S.E.2d 188, 190 (Va. Cir. Ct. 2006) (because administration of breathalyzer test is not compelled testimony, the imposition of criminal penalties for refusing to submit to the test does not violate the Self-Incrimination Clause).
- *Am. Fork City v. Cosgrove*, 701 P.2d 1069, 1075 (Utah 1985) (citing prior cases, and holding that defendant's rights under the Utah Constitution's self-incrimination clause were not violated when,

after arrest, defendant was required to submit to a Breathalyzer test under threat of losing his driver's license).

- *But cf. Olevik v. State*, 806 S.E.2d 505 (Ga. 2017) (Georgia Constitution protects against compelled Breathalyzer tests and the admission of evidence of a refusal to take the test).

Indeed, all 50 states have enacted implied consent statutes, most of which allow the admission into evidence of a person's refusal to undergo a Breathalyzer test, the constitutionality of which was impliedly upheld in *South Dakota v. Neville*, 459 U.S. 553, 566 (1983). *See also Missouri v. McNeely*, 569 U.S. 141, 156 (2013) (holding that the Fourth Amendment prevents the taking of a warrantless blood sample); and *Birchfield v. North Dakota*, 136 S. Ct. 2160, 2163 (2016) (holding that the search incident to arrest doctrine permits law enforcement to conduct warrantless breath tests but not warrantless blood tests on suspected drunk drivers).

A testimonial communication in violation of the Fifth Amendment may be found where the government's efforts to compel a person to provide physical evidence, or to engage in otherwise potentially self-incriminating conduct, would reveal the contents of the person's mind. For instance, in *In re Layden*, 446 F. Supp. 53, 55–56 (N.D. Ill. 1978), the government sought an order to compel a grand jury witness to furnish handwriting exemplars in what the court described as a "convoluted" manner to be compared with handwriting samples previously determined to have been disguised. Despite the Supreme Court's earlier approval of the compulsory production of a defendant's normal handwriting, the district judge refused to extend that decision to require the defendant to provide exemplars in an unnatural writing style, reasoning that such handwriting would reveal the contents of the mind.

Other courts have agreed with this reasoning:

- *United States v. Campbell*, 732 F.2d 1017, 1021–22 (1st Cir. 1984) (suppressing handwriting exemplars obtained by dictation, which provided the government not only samples of defendant's penmanship but also evidence of spelling and constituted "a testimonial message in addition to a physical display").

- *United States v. Kallstrom*, 446 F. Supp. 2d 772, 773 (E.D. Mich. 2006) (government's proposed manner of obtaining handwriting exemplars—through dictation that allows the examiner to pose spelling questions to the subject—contravenes Fifth Amendment privilege against self-incrimination).
- *United States v. Matos*, 990 F. Supp. 141, 143–44 (E.D.N.Y. 1998) (where a defendant misspelled a dictated word in the same manner that the word was misspelled in the bank robbery note, the court found the exemplar to be testimonial in nature and a roundabout way of compelling the defendant to respond to a spelling test).
- *State v. Fish*, 893 P.2d 1023 (Or. 1995) (distinguishing *South Dakota v. Neville* and ruling that Oregon Constitution protected refusal to submit to field sobriety test from use against the defendant on the basis that administration of the test required testimonial acts).
- *Commonwealth v. Conkey*, 714 N.E.2d 343, 346–48 (Mass. 1999) (admission of fact that defendant initially agreed to return to police station to provide fingerprints, but then did not do so, was used to show consciousness of guilt and was therefore testimonial and erroneously admitted at trial).
- *See also United States v. Greer*, 631 F.3d 608, 610 (2d Cir. 2011) (although deciding that there was no Fifth Amendment violation because the tattoo was not the product of government compulsion, the court decided that government reliance on the content of the defendant's tattoo to link him to another person made the tattoo "testimonial").
- *United States v. Ledbetter*, 188 F. Supp. 3d 674, 682–84 (S.D. Ohio 2016) (Marbley, J.) (ruling that where government relied on gang affiliated tattoos to help establish the existence of the conspiracy, the display of hidden tattoos was testimonial and the government could not compel the defendants to allow inspection of those tattoos or require them to be displayed in court).
- *People v. Slavin*, 807 N.E.2d 259 (N.Y. 2004) (both majority and dissenting justices agreed that white supremacist tattoos were testimonial, but majority ruled that photographic evidence of tattoos admitted at trial did not violate Fifth Amendment because defendant created the tattoos on his own).

- *Serratore v. People*, 497 P.2d 1018, 1021–22 (Colo. 1972), *limited sub nom. People v. Ramirez*, 609 P.2d 616, 621 (Colo. 1980) (prosecution's attempt to have the defendant touch a line at a certain height in order to communicate to jury the his ability to perform a physical act is no different than calling him to the witness stand to testify, and was therefore inadmissible).

Absence of a Fifth Amendment Privilege for Collective Entities

While a natural person may assert a Fifth Amendment right not to testify or produce documents, it has long been held that the Fifth Amendment privilege does not apply to corporations.

- *Hale v. Henkel*, 201 U.S. 43, 74–75 (1906) (after affirming the right of an individual to resist a grand jury subpoena duces tecum for his private papers that might incriminate him, the Court stated, "Upon the other hand, the corporation is a creature of the state. . . . It would be a strange anomaly to hold that a state, having chartered a corporation to make use of certain franchises, could not in the exercise of its sovereignty . . . demand the production of the corporate books and papers. . . .").
- *Wilson v. United States*, 221 U.S. 361, 384–85 (1911) (relying on *Hale v. Henkel* in upholding contempt of corporation president for refusal to produce corporate documents).
- *Wheeler v. United States*, 226 U.S. 478, 489–90 (1913) (relying on *Hale v. Henkel* in affirming order of district court that held former officers of dissolved corporation in contempt for refusing to produce corporate records in their possession in response to grand jury subpoena).

The Supreme Court has extended the inapplicability of the Fifth Amendment to other types of artificial entities. As first explained by the Court in *United States v. White*, 322 U.S. 694, 701 (1944), the Fifth Amendment privilege does not apply to any group or association that "has a character so impersonal in the scope of its membership and activities that it cannot be said to embody or represent the purely private interests of its constituents, but rather to embody their common or group interest only." *See also Rogers v. United States*, 340 U.S. 367, 371–72 (1951) (Communist Party may not claim the Fifth Amendment privilege). Thereafter, in *Bellis v. United States*, 417 U.S. 85, 92–93 (1974), the Court decided that a three-person law partnership has no Fifth Amendment privilege. Again, the Court focused on whether the organization had an established identity independent of its individual members and decided that, if it does, then neither it nor its agents may resist a grand jury subpoena for its records on the basis of the Fifth Amendment. *Id.* at 95. In accordance with these decisions and *Braswell v. United States*, which is discussed later in the chapter, the lower courts have held that even grantor trusts are collective entities and that their creator cannot invoke the Fifth Amendment privilege to avoid producing the trust's records, deeming the creator of the trust to be holding the documents in a representative capacity. *See Bank of America v. Roberts*, Case No. 4:12CV609AGF, 2014 WL 1259779, at *8 (E.D. Mo. Mar. 26, 2014).

The Supreme Court's decisions in *Citizens United v. Federal Election Commission*, 558 U.S. 310 (2010), and *Burwell v. Hobby Lobby Stores, Inc.*, 573 U.S. 682 (2014) have generated discussion about whether corporations should be able to invoke constitutional rights—including the Fifth Amendment right against self-incrimination—previously thought to be limited to natural persons. In *Citizens United*, the Court held that political spending was a form of protected speech under the First Amendment, and the government may not prohibit corporations or unions from seeking to persuade voters by spending money on political advertising. In *Hobby Lobby*, the Court ruled that closely held corporations could not be compelled to provide certain types of contraception in their health plans over their owner's religious objections. Commentators have questioned why a corporation has First Amendment speech and religious rights, but not Fifth Amendment rights. Similarly, commentators question the denial of the right against compelled self-incrimination for collective entities, given that collective entities can be convicted of crimes and subjected to punishment like natural persons. The inability of a collective entity to assert a self-incrimination privilege arguably relieves the government of its constitutional obligation to "shoulder the entire load" in any criminal prosecution of a collective entity. Given the current makeup of the Supreme Court, however, the long-standing difference between the right of a natural person to invoke a Fifth Amendment right against compelled self-incrimination and the absence of such a right by an artificial entity is unlikely to change.

Of course, a "collective entity" can respond to a demand for information only through its agents. The question arises, then, whether the agent is able to assert a Fifth Amendment privilege when responding to a demand for the collective entity's records. The Supreme Court answered that question in the negative in *Braswell v. United States*, 487 U.S. 99, 102–03 (1988). A sole shareholder, and the only corporate officer with authority over the business affairs of two corporations he had formed, resisted complying with a grand jury subpoena duces tecum seeking the production of corporate records. He argued that he was the corporation's alter ego and the act of production would incriminate him personally. *Id.* at 109–10. A closely divided Court ruled that because a corporation had no Fifth Amendment privilege, the individual acting on the corporation's behalf in producing its documents could not claim the benefit of the privilege. The Court relied on what the dissenting justices called "the fiction" that the custodian acts only as a representative of the entity, and not personally, in producing the entity's documents. The Court said:

> The custodian of corporate or entity records holds those documents in a representative rather than a personal capacity. Artificial entities such as corporations may act only through their agents, and a custodian's assumption of his representative capacity leads to certain obligations, including the duty to produce corporate records on proper demand by the Government. Under those circumstances, the custodian's act of production is not deemed a personal act, but rather an act of the corporation. Any claim of Fifth Amendment privilege asserted by the agent would be tantamount to a claim of privilege by the corporation—which of course possesses no such privilege.

Id. (citation omitted).

A person who conducts his or her business affairs alone and does not use the collective entity form may still refuse to produce documents on the basis of the Fifth Amendment if the act of producing the records would incriminate the person personally. Chapter 8 discusses the act of production doctrine.

- *United States v. Doe*, 465 U.S. 605, 612–17 (1984) (recognizing that an individual sole proprietor could resist the production of business records to a grand jury on the basis of the Fifth Amendment).
- *In re Kave*, 760 F.2d 343, 358 (1st Cir. 1985) (confirming sole practitioner attorney's Fifth Amendment privilege not to produce documents before a special master).
- *United States v. Fox*, 721 F.2d 32, 36 (2d Cir. 1983) (holding that a sole proprietor stands on different constitutional footing than a representative of a corporation or other collective entity because a sole proprietorship has no legal existence apart from its owner).
- *Slone-Stiver v. Broock (In re Tower Metal Alloy Co.)*, 200 B.R. 598, 610 (Bankr. S.D. Ohio 1996) (allowing husband and wife to invoke their Fifth Amendment privilege for records created under an entity name, where court determined entity was not a collective entity for purposes of invoking the privilege).
- *In re Grand Jury Subpoena Duces Tecum Dated Nov. 13, 1984*, 616 F. Supp. 1159, 1162 (E.D.N.Y. 1985) (treating partner in two-person consulting firm as sole proprietor where compelled production of partnership ledgers, cash receipts, and records of disbursements would be incriminatory).

Numerous questions remain unresolved in the wake of *Braswell*. First, does *Braswell* apply to former employees of a collective entity? Two circuits have held that former employees who possess corporate documents obtained prior to the termination of employment are still regarded as the corporation's agents when subpoenaed for production of those documents. In the following cases, the former employee was held not to have a Fifth Amendment privilege to assert with respect to the self-incriminating aspects of the production of corporate records.

- *In re Grand Jury Subpoena Dated Nov. 12, 1991*, 957 F.2d 807, 810–12 (11th Cir. 1992) (per curiam) (holding that *Braswell* applies to former corporate employees of a defunct bank).
- *In re Sealed Case (Gov't Records)*, 950 F.2d 736, 740 (D.C. Cir. 1991) (holding that *Braswell* applies to former government officials and government documents).
- *Halloran v. Williams (In re Keller Fin. Servs. of Fla., Inc.)*, 259 B.R. 391, 406 (Bankr. M.D. Fla. 2000) (holding that *Braswell* applies to former corporate director).

Two other circuits have reasoned that once the employee has terminated his relationship with the corporation (or any other collective entity), he can no longer be considered its agent and is no longer acting as a corporate representative of records that he or she is compelled to produce. In these circuits, a former employee has a personal Fifth Amendment privilege to assert if the act of producing the documents belonging to the collective entity will incriminate him.

- *In re Three Grand Jury Subpoenas Duces Tecum Dated Jan. 29, 1999*, 191 F.3d 173, 181 (2d Cir. 1999) ("The rule in *Braswell* was predicated on the rationale that corporate custodians hold and produce documents only in a representative capacity and that when a corporate custodian produces subpoenaed corporate records, at bottom, the corporation produces the documents subpoenaed. It follows . . . that once the agency relationship terminates, the former employee is no longer an agent of the corporation and is not a custodian of the corporate records.") (citation omitted).
- *Mora v. United States (In re Grand Jury Proceedings)*, 71 F.3d 723, 724 (9th Cir. 1995) ("[T]he collective entity rule does not apply to a former employee of a collective entity who is no longer acting on behalf of the collective entity.").

In the case of *Park v. Cangen Corp.*, 7 A.3d 520 (Md. 2010), the highest court of Maryland considered these decisions in a replevin action by a corporation against its former president seeking corporate documents and other information he allegedly stole after his termination. Despite accepting the former president's argument that the act of production was both testimonial and incriminating, the majority held "that a former employee of a corporation cannot assert the privilege against compelled incrimination to the act of producing corporate documents in his possession," at least not insofar as applied to corporate documents he allegedly stole. *Id.* at 533. The ruling appears to be based in part on the majority's satisfaction that a prosecutor could not make evidentiary use of the former president's court-ordered production of documents in a subsequent prosecution against him.

Second, does *Braswell* apply to a single-member limited liability corporation (LLC), a corporate form used by sole entrepreneurs for conducting business? In a footnote at the end of the majority opinion, *Braswell* explicitly left open "the question whether the agency rationale supports compelling a custodian to produce corporate records when the custodian is able to establish, by showing for example that he is the sole employee and officer of the corporation, that the jury would inevitably conclude that he produced the records." *Braswell*, 487 U.S. at 118 n.11. The answer provided by the lower courts as of this writing appears to be unanimous that a limited liability corporation's sole member does not enjoy Fifth Amendment privilege protection against producing the corporation's documents.

- *In re Twelve Grand Jury Subpoenas*, 908 F.3d 525, 527 (9th Cir. 2018) ("[W]e join all of our sister circuits to have considered the issue in holding that the Fifth Amendment provides no protection to a collective entity's records custodian—and that the size of the collective entity and the extent to which the jury would assume that the individual seeking to assert the privilege produced the documents are not relevant.").
- *In re Grand Jury Empaneled on May 9, 2014*, 786 F.3d 255, 263 (3d Cir. 2015) ("Appellants have advanced no persuasive rationale as to why the reasoning of *Bellis* and *Braswell* does not apply to one-person corporations like that operated by Doe.").
- *United States v. Roe*, 421 F. App'x 881, 884–85 (10th Cir. 2011) (controlling members of a limited liability corporation had no right

to refuse to produce its business records in response to IRS summonses seeking to determine the corporation's taxable income, despite the fact that the LLC was a pass-through entity and its members would be taxed on its income).

- *In re Grand Jury Subpoena Issued June 18, 2009*, 593 F.3d 155, 158–59 (2d Cir. 2010) (per curiam) ("a one-person corporation cannot avail itself of the Fifth Amendment privilege" and district court did not abuse its discretion in holding LLC in contempt for refusing to produce its records in accordance with a grand jury subpoena).
- *United States v. Lu*, 248 F. App'x 806, 808 (9th Cir. 2007) (affirming denial of motion to quash a grand jury subpoena directed to owner of single-member LLC).
- *Amato v. United States*, 450 F.3d 46, 53 (1st Cir. 2006) (refusing to allow sole officer and sole shareholder of a corporation to invoke Fifth Amendment privilege in response to subpoena directed to him for corporation's records).
- *See also In the Matter of Civil Investigative Demands to Cellmark Biopharma LLC & Lexium Int'l, LLC Dated May 24, 2016*, File No. 162–3133, 2016 WL 4128222, at *3 (July 25, 2016) (FTC denied LLC's motion to quash because civil investigative demands were directed to LLCs and sought only LLC documents, and opined that a corporation must appoint agent other than a sole shareholder who was asserting the privilege to produce the corporation's documents).

Braswell created an exclusionary rule for the corporate custodian required to produce the documents of a collective entity. According to the *Braswell* majority, during trial the government may not make evidentiary use of the fact that a particular individual produced the documents in question:

> Because the custodian acts as a representative, the act is deemed one of the corporation and not the individual. Therefore, the Government concedes, as it must, that it may make no evidentiary use of the "individual act" against the individual. For example, in a criminal prosecution against the custodian, the Government may not introduce into

> evidence before the jury the fact that the subpoena was served upon and the corporation's documents were delivered by one particular individual, the custodian. . . . The Government may offer testimony—for example, from the process server who delivered the subpoena and from the individual who received the records—establishing that the corporation produced the records subpoenaed. The jury may draw from the corporation's act of production the conclusion that the records in question are authentic corporate records, which the corporation possessed, and which it produced in response to the subpoena. And if the defendant held a prominent position within the corporation that produced the records, the jury may, just as it would had someone else produced the documents, reasonably infer that he had possession of the documents or knowledge of their contents. Because the jury is not told that the defendant produced the records, any nexus between the defendant and the documents results solely from the corporation's act of production and other evidence in the case.

Braswell, 487 U.S. at 118.

Although this exclusionary rule is sometimes described as granting the individual custodian "immunity," it does not prevent the government from making derivative use of the fact that the individual produced the documents. Thus, *Braswell* does not constitute use and derivative use immunity extinguishing the Fifth Amendment right against self-incrimination. *See, e.g., In re Three Grand Jury Subpoenas Duces Tecum Dated Jan. 29, 1999*, 191 F.3d at 182. Nonetheless, by limiting the evidentiary use that can be made of the fact that a person is compelled by the government to produce collective entity documents, this judicially created exclusionary rule is of value to the custodian.

- *United States v. McLaughlin*, 126 F.3d 130, 134 (3d Cir. 1997) (*Braswell* means that the government may not use the testimonial act of non-production against the defendant. "The government's repeated reference [at trial] to [defendant's] incomplete act of production as evidence of his culpability flies in the face of *Braswell*. . . .").

- *In re Grand Jury Witnesses*, 92 F.3d 710, 713 (8th Cir. 1996) (following *Braswell*, when government issued identical subpoenas to multiple corporate employees seeking to determine who had possession of a particular record, government may not tell the grand jury which corporate custodian produced particular document).

The protection that the *Braswell* exclusionary rule provide to a corporate custodian called as a witness at trial to qualify the documents produced as business records, under the "business records" exception to the hearsay rule, is somewhat unclear. Well-reasoned decisions have ruled that although the custodian can be required to testify that the documents produced were responsive to the subpoena, and that the documents are authentic within the meaning of the applicable rules of evidence, the government may not compel testimony that qualifies the documents as business records.

- *In re Grand Jury Subpoena (John Doe, Inc.)*, 991 F. Supp. 2d 968, 980 (E.D. Mich. 2014) (concluding that although custodian could be compelled to certify that the responsive documents produced are corporate records and within the possession, custody and control of the corporation, she may assert her Fifth Amendment privilege to refuse to answer any other questions about the documents).
- *In re Grand Jury Proceedings (ABC Corp.)*, 473 F. Supp. 2d 201, 209–10 (D. Mass. 2007) (concluding that testimony sufficient to qualify documents as business records cannot be compelled from a corporate custodian who asserts a valid Fifth Amendment privilege; unlike testimony authenticating the documents, testimony that lays a business records foundation is not implicit in the production of the documents).
- *In re Grand Jury Empaneled on Apr. 6, 1993*, 869 F. Supp. 298, 306 (D.N.J. 1994) (concluding that testimony to qualify documents produced to grand jury as business records "will often entail independent incrimination separate and apart from the act of production itself and required authentication testimony").

- *In re Grand Jury 83–8 (MIA) Subpoena Duces Tecum*, 611 F. Supp. 16, 23 (S.D. Fla. 1985) (government could use authentication implicit in corporate representatives' act of production in subsequent proceedings brought against corporation but could not compel witnesses to authenticate corporate documents in subsequent proceedings against witnesses personally).

These decisions would appear in line with the Supreme Court's decision in *Curcio v. United States*, 354 U.S. 118 (1957), which stated that although the custodian may be compelled to produce a corporation's (or, in that case, a labor union's) records, he cannot be compelled, absent a grant of immunity, to condemn himself by his own oral testimony about other matters.

Not all courts agree:

- *In re Custodian of Records of Variety Distrib., Inc.*, 927 F.2d 244, 251 (6th Cir. 1991) ("Because a custodian of corporate records has no necessary relation to the *contents* of the documents which he has produced, we do not believe that statements that he is familiar with the company's recordkeeping practices and knows that the company regularly keeps such records in the course of a regularly conducted business activity is sufficiently incriminating in and of itself.").

Court decisions make reasonably clear that a custodian required to produce the records of a collective entity cannot be required to testify, over a Fifth Amendment objection, to the location of documents not in the custodian's possession and thereby unable to be produced.

- *Curcio v. United States*, 354 U.S. at 118–19 ("The issue in this case is whether the custodian of a union's books and records may, on the ground of his Fifth Amendment privilege against self-incrimination, refuse to answer questions asked by a federal grand jury as to the whereabouts of such books and records which he has not produced pursuant to subpoena. . . . [W]e hold that the privilege against self-incrimination attaches to such questions.").

- *Armstrong v. Guccione*, 470 F.3d 89, 100 (2d Cir. 2006) ("Although [witness] has no Fifth Amendment right to refuse to produce the property, he does retain the right to refuse to testify as to the whereabouts of the missing corporate property.") (citations omitted).
- *In re Grand Jury Subpoena Dated Apr. 9, 1996*, 87 F.3d 1198, 1204 (11th Cir. 1996) (reversing order of contempt for sole corporate officer and director who refused to testify about the location of corporate records sought by a grand jury subpoena).

Similarly, a corporate custodian cannot be personally compelled to produce an accounting for the company he controls over his Fifth Amendment objection. Because such an accounting is deemed "testimony," a custodian can only be ordered to secure an accounting by or on behalf of the corporation, which does not have a right not to testify. *See SEC v. Dunlap*, 253 F.3d 768, 770–778 n.15 (4th Cir. 2001); *U.S. Commodity Futures Trading Comm'n v. Garcia*, No. 2:15-cv, 2015 U.S. Dist. LEXIS 69957 (M.D. Fla. May 29, 2015).

However, a witness should raise his or her Fifth Amendment privilege to any questions posed about the whereabouts of documents the witness is not producing at the time the questions are initially posed. Waiting until a hearing for contempt may be too late.

- *United States v. Rylander*, 460 U.S. 752, 756–57 (1983) (The Court stated, "a contempt proceeding does not open to reconsideration the legal or factual basis of the order alleged to have been disobeyed" and held that, where a claim of lack of possession was first raised at the contempt hearing, the witness had the burden of proving a present inability to comply with a demand for the production of records, even where this requires the witness's potentially incriminating testimony.) (citation omitted).
- *United States v. Ali*, 874 F.3d 825, 829–30 (4th Cir. 2017) (affirming district court order holding respondent in contempt for failing to

produce documents pursuant to IRS summons, and finding *Rylander* controlling).

- *But cf. United States v. St. John*, No. 8:11-mc-00099-JDW-MAP, 2013 WL 411402, at *4 (M.D. Fla. Feb. 1, 2013) (finding *Rylander* inapposite where respondent consistently invoked his Fifth Amendment privilege in meetings with IRS revenue officer and was, therefore, entitled to rely on it during contempt proceedings).

The Meaning of "Any Criminal Case"

The Fifth Amendment protects only a person compelled to be a "witness against himself" in "any criminal case." A compelled statement used against a defendant at trial or as a source leading to other evidence used at trial meets this criteria, but whether it also protects compelled testimony used in proceedings before a criminal trial is under debate.

In *Chavez v. Martinez*, *supra*, the Supreme Court considered whether a suspect who had been shot and paralyzed by the police could bring a civil suit under 42 U.S.C. § 1983 for the violation of his constitutional rights against both compelled self-incrimination and due process resulting from his coercive interrogation in the hospital, or whether the police officer was immune from damages. As to Mr. Martinez's Self-Incrimination Clause claim, the Court was splintered. Justices Scalia, O'Connor, and Chief Justice Rehnquist, led by Justice Thomas, were satisfied that because Mr. Martinez was never charged with a crime and his answers were never used against him in any criminal prosecution, the police officer had not deprived him of his Fifth Amendment rights against compelled self-incrimination. Justices Ginsberg, Kennedy, and Stevens, each of whom wrote separately, disagreed with Justice Thomas for different reasons. Justice Souter, joined by Justice Breyer, agreed that Mr. Martinez's Fifth Amendment claim did not satisfy the stringent requirements for bringing a claim for civil damages under section 1983, but steered clear of agreeing with Justice Thomas that there could never be a violation of the Fifth Amendment Self-Incrimination Clause unless and until a compelled incriminating statement was used against the defendant in a trial or other adversarial proceeding.

Mr. Martinez took the position that the meaning of "any criminal case" in the text of the Self-Incrimination Clause "should encompass the entire criminal investigatory process, including police interrogations." 538 U.S. at 766. Justice Thomas claimed instead that "a 'criminal case' at the very least requires the initiation of legal proceedings," *id.* at 760, and suggested in other respects that the right against compelled self-incrimination could only be violated if a suspect's statements had been presented at his trial. *Id.* However, because the case did not require it, even Justice Thomas's plurality opinion made no decision about the "precise moment when a 'criminal case' commences" for the purpose of the right against compelled self-incrimination. *Id.* at 767. Instead, the majority of the Court determined that Mr. Martinez's claim that the police interrogation violated his due process rights might survive, and remanded the case to the Ninth Circuit on that claim alone.

In *City of Hays v. Vogt*, 138 S. Ct. 1683 (2018), the Supreme Court appeared poised to resolve the unanswered question in *Chavez* about when a "criminal case" commences. Although the case has a complicated set of facts that eventually led the Court, after oral argument, to dismiss the prior grant of certiorari as improvident, the question presented to the Court was whether in a section 1983 civil suit for damages, allegations that a person was compelled to make incriminating statements that were later used against him in a criminal preliminary hearing, but not at trial, stated a violation of the Fifth Amendment right against self-incrimination. According to the Tenth Circuit, whose opinion holds after the Supreme Court dismissed certiorari, the Fifth Amendment definition of "any criminal case" includes a probable cause hearing. *Vogt v. City of Hays,* 844 F.3d 1235, 1239 (10th Cir. 2017).

In their briefs and at oral argument, neither the City of Hayes nor the United States, as *amicus curiae*, challenged the Tenth Circuit's conclusion that the probable cause hearing was part of the criminal case for purposes of the Fifth Amendment. Instead, they argued that the use of compelled statements at that stage did not make Vogt "a witness against himself," claiming that could only occur at proceedings where guilt and punishment were determined. Because the Supreme Court dismissed the case, this question remains unanswered.

As the city of Hays pointed out in its certiorari petition, after the *Chavez* decision, a split exists in the lower courts about whether a constitutional violation of the Self-Incrimination Clause arises from various uses of allegedly improperly compelled incriminating statements in advance of a criminal trial, at least for the purposes of a damages action under section 1983. Four circuits and at least one state supreme court have held that the Fifth Amendment right against self-incrimination is a constitutional right that can only be violated if the compelled statements are used at a criminal trial.

- *Renda v. King*, 347 F.3d 550, 558–59 (3d Cir. 2003) (affirming lower court's denial of a section 1983 claim alleging Fifth Amendment violations, where the coerced incriminating statements were used to file charges but never used at trial, reasoning "it is the use of coerced statements during a criminal trial, and not in obtaining an indictment, that violates the Constitution") (citation omitted).
- *Burrell v. Virginia*, 395 F.3d 508, 513–14 (4th Cir. 2005) (holding that the defendant's section 1983 claim failed because he did not allege any trial action that violated his Fifth Amendment rights).
- *Murray v. Earle*, 405 F.3d 278, 285 (5th Cir. 2005) ("The Fifth Amendment privilege against self-incrimination is a fundamental trial right which can be violated only at trial. . . .").
- *Winslow v. Smith*, 696 F.3d 716, 731 (8th Cir. 2012) (deciding that plaintiffs self-incrimination claims failed "because Plaintiffs did not proceed to a criminal trial").
- *State v. Mems*, 708 N.W.2d 526, 534 (Minn. 2006) ("Even assuming appellant's police statement was obtained in violation of *Miranda*, there was no Fifth Amendment violation where his statement was not admitted at trial.").

At least four other circuits have determined that a coerced statement does not have to be introduced at trial to violate a person's Fifth Amendment rights. Several courts agree with Justice Ginsburg in *Chavez*, who said she "would hold that the Self-Incrimination Clause applies at the time and place police use severe compulsion to extract a statement from a suspect." 538 U.S. at 799 (Ginsberg, J., concurring in part and dissenting in part).

- *Vogt v. City of Hays,* 844 F.3d 1235, 1246 & n.7 (10th Cir. 2017) (admission of compelled statement and its fruits at probable cause hearing preceding indictment was actionable under section 1983).
- *Aleman v. Village of Hanover Park*, 662 F.3d 897, 905–06 (7th Cir. 2011) (despite fact that criminal charges were dropped, the violation of respondent's *Miranda* rights was actionable in a suit under section 1983 because prosecutors used custodial statement to obtain an indictment).
- *Stoot v. City of Everett*, 582 F.3d 910, 922–25 (9th Cir. 2009) (a compelled statement had been used in "a criminal case" when relied upon in affidavit filed in support of charging document).
- *Higazy v. Templeton*, 505 F.3d 161, 174–75 (2d Cir. 2007) (section 1983 relief was available when a coerced confession was used in bail determination).
- *Sornberger v. City of Knoxville*, 434 F.3d 1006, 1022–23 (7th Cir. 2006) (a section 1983 claim was established by use at a variety of pretrial proceedings).
- *See also Moody v. Michigan Gaming Control Bd.*, 790 F.3d 669 (6th Cir. 2015) (harness racing drivers, who are state licensees and protected under *Garrity*, could pursue section 1983 claim against Board for violating their self-incrimination rights by suspending their racing licenses after they invoked their right to refuse to answer Board questions relating to illegal race fixing).

Chavez, a case for civil damages, did not force the Court to face the meaning of the Self-Incrimination Clause in the usual context of its application to evidence sought to be used in the prosecution of an individual. Although the splintered decision of the Supreme Court is best analyzed as a decision limited to its section 1983 context, much of the language in both the plurality opinion and the dissents foreshadowed the use of the competing interpretations of the clause outside the context of a civil damages action and in actual prosecutions. The resolution of the debate in *Chavez* over what constitutes "any criminal case" for purposes of the Fifth Amendment Self-Incrimination Clause and when a person becomes a "witness against himself" is highly consequential for more reasons than whether a civil claim for damages may be pursued. Given that the vast majority of criminal prosecutions are resolved by bargained guilty pleas, a decision that the Self-Incrimination Clause only applies at trial would neuter the right for the vast majority of criminal cases. Indeed, such a ruling would seem to jeopardize many of the Court's seminal Self-Incrimination Clause decisions, whose reasoning establishes that the "criminal case" under the Fifth Amendment commences at least at the stage of a grand jury, and perhaps sooner; and that a person becomes "a witness against himself" whenever the government compels a self-incriminating admission, regardless of whether it is ever used in a court proceeding.

Counselman v. Hitchcock, 142 U.S. 547 (1892) is the first and perhaps most important decision, prior to *Chavez*, on the meaning of the words "any criminal case." Counselman, who was involved as a receiver and shipper of grain, was called before a grand jury investigating violations of a criminal statute regarding the rates that could be charged for transporting grain. On the basis of his right against self-incrimination, he refused to answer a variety of questions, and was held in contempt and jailed for doing so. His writ of habeas corpus was denied on the basis that a provision of the criminal statute in question immunized any statements or evidence obtained from Mr. Counselman from use in future criminal proceedings.

A unanimous Supreme Court reversed and granted Mr. Counselman's writ of habeas corpus. Although the decision is best remembered for ruling that the statutory use immunity granted to Mr. Counselman was not co-extensive with the constitutional right against compelled self-incrimination and that only transactional immunity would be constitutionally sufficient, the key to the Court's decision was its refutation of the appellee's contention "that a witness is not entitled to plead the privilege of silence, except in a criminal case against himself. . . ." 142 U.S. at 562. To that proposition, the Supreme Court said: "but such is not the language of the constitution." *Id.* (emphasis added). The Court then went on to explain why "[t]he case before the grand jury was therefore a criminal case." *Id.* According to the Court, "[i]t is impossible that the meaning of the [Self Incrimination Clause] can only be that a person shall not be compelled to be a witness against himself in a criminal prosecution against himself. It would doubtless cover such cases; but it is not limited to them. The object was to insure that a person should not be compelled, when acting as a witness in any investigation, to give testimony which might tend to show that he himself had committed a crime." *Id.* Indeed, the appellee argued "that the investigation before the grand jury was not a criminal case . . . and that a case could arise only when an indictment should be returned," to which the Court responded that the Fifth Amendment, distinct from the Sixth Amendment, applied in advance of a court proceeding, including in grand jury proceedings. *Id.* at 563.

The Supreme Court's more recent decision in *United States v. Hubbell*, 530 U.S. 27 (2000), also seems to establish that a criminal case includes a grand jury proceeding. In *Hubbell*, the Court ruled that the grand jury indictment must be dismissed where *Hubbell* was compelled to give incriminating testimony, by producing documents to a grand jury under an immunity order. Although the case is primarily remembered for elucidating when the act of producing documents is deemed "testimonial" under the Self-Incrimination Clause, the second issue addressed by the Court was whether the government was prevented from using Hubbell's testimonial act of production to prepare criminal charges against him. Justice Stevens, writing for the majority, made clear that what mattered for purposes of the Fifth Amendment was whether the constitutionally protected act of producing documents was used to help indict Hubbell, regardless of whether it was used at trial. In the introduction, the majority opinion says ". . . the phrase 'in any criminal case'. . . might have been read to limit its coverage to compelled testimony that is used against the defendant in the trial itself. It has, however, long been settled that its protection encompasses compelled statements that lead to the discovery of incriminating evidence even though the statements themselves are not incriminating and not introduced into evidence." 530 U.S. at 37. The majority opinion addressed the fact that the Independent Counsel intended not to introduce Hubbell's act of production at his criminal trial, pointing out that this concession "leaves open the separate question of whether it has already made 'derivative use' of the testimonial aspect of that act in obtaining the indictment against respondent. . . ." *Id.* at 41. After analyzing the evidence presented to the grand jury that had been compelled by the grant of immunity extinguishing Hubbell's right against self-incrimination, the Court determined that the Fifth Amendment privileged act of production had been so used. The opinion concluded that the compelled testimony had been used in a "criminal case" by virtue of aiding the return of Hubbell's indictment. *Id.* at 43–44.

As for when a person becomes "a witness against himself," the Supreme Court has long held that the Fifth Amendment protects a person from being compelled to make an incriminating statement that can be subsequently used in a criminal case, without regard to whether it is in fact used. This is the teaching of *Hoffman v. United States*, 341 U.S. 479 (1951); *Malloy v. Hogan*, 378 U.S. 1 (1964); and numerous other cases defining the term "self-incriminating," as reviewed earlier in this chapter. *Chavez* did not purport to overrule this long-standing interpretation of the Self-Incrimination Clause. Indeed, a year before *Chavez* was decided, all nine justices agreed in *McKune v. Lile*, 536 U.S. 24 (2002), that if the change in an inmate's prison conditions were deemed compulsory, the inmate's answer to questions posed in his sex abuse treatment program would have violated his Fifth Amendment rights because of their potential use in a future criminal prosecution. Justice Thomas's plurality opinion in *Chavez* never mentions *McKune v. Lile*. Thus, a compelling argument can be made that *Chavez* applies only in section 1983 civil damage actions and has no application to the interpretation of the Self-Incrimination Clause in any other context.

CHAPTER 3

Proceedings in Which the Fifth Amendment May Be Asserted and the Consequences of Remaining Silent

The Supreme Court has remarked on numerous occasions that the Fifth Amendment "can be asserted in any proceeding, civil or criminal, administrative or judicial, investigatory or adjudicatory," in which the witness reasonably believes the information sought, or discoverable as a result of his testimony, could be used in a subsequent criminal proceeding.

- *McCarthy v. Arndstein*, 266 U.S. 34, 40 (1924) ("The [Fifth Amendment] privilege is not ordinarily dependent upon the nature of the proceeding in which the testimony is sought or is to be used. It applies alike to civil and criminal proceedings, wherever the answer might tend to subject to criminal responsibility him who gives it. The privilege protects a mere witness as fully as it does one who is also a party defendant. It protects, likewise, the owner of goods which may be forfeited in a penal proceeding.") (citation omitted).
- *Kastigar v. United States*, 406 U.S. 441, 444–45 (1972) ("[The Fifth Amendment] can be asserted in any proceeding, civil or criminal, administrative or judicial, investigatory or adjudicatory; and it protects against any disclosures which the witness reasonably believes

could be used in a criminal prosecution or could lead to other evidence that might be so used.") (citations omitted).

- *Lefkowitz v. Turley*, 414 U.S. 70, 77 (1973) ("The [Fifth] Amendment not only protects the individual against being involuntarily called as a witness against himself in a criminal prosecution but also privileges him not to answer official questions put to him in any other proceeding, civil or criminal, formal or informal, where the answers might incriminate him in future criminal proceedings.") (citation omitted).
- *Minnesota v. Murphy*, 465 U.S. 420, 426 (1984) ("The Fifth Amendment, in relevant part, provides that no person 'shall be compelled in any criminal case to be a witness against himself.' It has long been held that this prohibition not only permits a person to refuse to testify against himself at a criminal trial in which he is a defendant, but also 'privileges him not to answer official questions put to him in any other proceeding, civil or criminal, formal or informal, where the answers might incriminate him in future criminal proceedings.'") (quoting *Lefkowitz*, 414 U.S. at 77).
- *United States v. Balsys*, 524 U.S. 666, 672 (1998) ("[The Self-Incrimination Clause] 'can be asserted in any proceeding, civil or criminal, administrative or judicial, investigatory or adjudicatory,' in which the witness reasonably believes that the information sought, or discoverable as a result of his testimony, could be used in a subsequent state or federal criminal proceeding.") (quoting *Kastigar*, 406 U.S. at 444–45).

Furthermore, numerous U.S. Supreme Court decisions have recognized that a person asserting the self-incrimination privilege does not have to wait until a criminal prosecution has been initiated to resolve the dispute over the assertion. These cases recognize that the Fifth Amendment protects not only the use of compelled self-incriminating statements in a criminal case but also a distinct and independent right not to be compelled, most often by the threat of contempt, to make self-incriminatory statements in other proceedings that could be used in a future criminal case.

- *Pillsbury Co. v. Conboy*, 459 U.S. 248, 256–57 (1983) (Grant of immunity at the earlier criminal trial did not require a witness to testify at his later civil deposition, even when the questions asked at the deposition closely tracked the testimony the witness had previously given in the criminal case under the grant of immunity. Instead, the Court recognized that the witness retained a Fifth Amendment privilege to refuse to answer questions posed at his civil deposition.).
- *Garner v. United States*, 424 U.S. 648, 653 (1976) ("[T]he privilege protects against the use of compelled statements as well as guarantees the right to remain silent absent immunity.").
- *Murphy v. Waterfront Comm'n of N.Y. Harbor*, 378 U.S. 52, 57 n.6 (1964) ("The constitutional privilege against self-incrimination has two primary interrelated facets: [t]he Government may not use compulsion to elicit self-incriminating statements . . . and the Government may not permit the use in a criminal trial of self-incriminating statements elicited by compulsion.") (citations omitted).

Although there are circumstances where the privilege against self-incrimination is self-executing, a person's failure to invoke their Fifth Amendment privilege can be fatal to their claim.

- *Salinas v. Texas*, 570 U.S. 178, 183 (2013) ("To prevent the privilege from shielding information not properly within its scope, we have long held that a witness who 'deserves the protection of the privilege . . . must claim it' at the time he relies on it.").
- *Minnesota v. Murphy*, 465 U.S. 420, 427 (1983) (an individual seeking to avail himself of the protections of the privilege against self-incrimination must actually "claim it" (quoting *U.S. v. Monia*, 317 U.S. 424, 427 (1943))).

This chapter therefore considers when assertion of the self-incrimination privilege is required and the consequences of invoking the privilege and/or remaining silent. Chapter 5 addresses how the privilege should be invoked.

Assertions of the Fifth Amendment Right Against Self-Incrimination in Criminal Proceedings and the Consequences of Invoking and/or Remaining Silent

During Custodial Police Interrogation

As mentioned in Chapter 2, several recent Supreme Court decisions have suggested that the core right against compelled self-incrimination protected by the Fifth Amendment does not apply until a person is tried (or at least charged) in a court of law.

- *United States v. Patane*, 542 U.S. 630, 641 (2004) (plurality opinion) ("Potential violations [of the Self-Incrimination Clause] occur, if at all, only upon the admission of [compelled incriminatory] statements into evidence at trial.").
- *Chavez v. Martinez*, 538 U.S. 760, 766 (2003) (plurality rejected defendant's argument that a "criminal case" encompasses the entire investigatory process, stating that "[i]n our view, a 'criminal case' at the very least requires the initiation of legal proceedings.") (citation omitted).
- *United States v. Verdugo-Urquidez*, 494 U.S. 259, 264 (1990) (stating in dicta that "[t]he privilege against self-incrimination guaranteed by the Fifth Amendment is a fundamental trial right of criminal defendants. Although conduct by law enforcement officials prior to trial may ultimately impair that right, a constitutional violation occurs only at trial.") (citations omitted).

Nonetheless, to protect an individual's Fifth Amendment right against compelled self-incrimination in a criminal case, a 5–4 majority of the U.S. Supreme Court in *Miranda v. Arizona*, 384 U.S. 436 (1966), established a safeguard requiring law enforcement officials to give certain warnings to persons in police custody before questioning them. *Miranda* requires law enforcement officials to inform a suspect being held in custody that he has a right to remain silent, that his statements may be used against him at trial, and that during questioning he has the right to an attorney, including a court-appointed attorney if he cannot afford one. *Id.* at 478–79. Absent proof that police gave such warnings and a suspect validly waived the rights, incriminating statements obtained during custodial interrogation are inadmissible at trial. *Id.* at 479.

Since 1966, the Supreme Court has decided almost 90 cases construing the *Miranda* decision, the vast majority of which are beyond the scope of this book. However, the following discussion seeks to cover the critical contours of the *Miranda* rule.

The *Miranda* Court was faced with four cases in which law enforcement officials questioned defendants "in a room in which [each] was cut off from the outside world." *Id.* at 445. Although the Court cited to numerous instances of police brutality toward witnesses undergoing interrogation while in custody at the police station, the Court was just as concerned with psychological police tactics designed to secure self-incriminating statements. The Court "perceive[d] an intimate connection between the privilege against self-incrimination and police custodial questioning," announcing itself "satisfied that all the principles embodied in the privilege apply to informal compulsion exerted by law-enforcement officers during in-custody questioning." *Id.* at 458, 461. The Court reasoned

> that without proper safeguards, the process of in-custody interrogation of persons suspected or accused of crime contains inherently compelling pressures which work to undermine the individual's will to resist and to compel him to speak where he would not otherwise do so freely. In order to combat these pressures and to permit a full opportunity to exercise the privilege against self-incrimination, the accused must be adequately and effectively apprised of his rights and the exercise of those rights must be fully honored.

Id. at 467.

The Supreme Court crafted an exclusionary rule to effectuate its recognition of an accused's right to remain silent during custodial interrogation. It stated the rule as follows:

> After such warnings have been given, . . . the individual may knowingly and intelligently waive these rights and agree to answer questions or

> make a statement. But unless and until such warnings and waiver are demonstrated by the prosecution at trial, no evidence obtained as a result of interrogation can be used against him.

Id. at 479.

The *Miranda* majority appeared to hold that the Fifth Amendment privilege against self-incrimination was fully applicable during custodial interrogation. However the decision, including its exclusionary rule for statements produced by custodial interrogation without having been advised of one's rights, has subsequently been described as merely setting forth prophylactic procedures and not a constitutional rule. It has been subject to numerous exceptions, and not expanded beyond its limited holding.

- *Moran v. Burbine*, 475 U.S. 412, 425 (1986) (refusing to expand *Miranda* to require police to inform a suspect that an attorney retained by his sister was seeking to contact him).
- *Michigan v. Tucker*, 417 U.S. 433, 435–37 (1974) (limiting the remedy for a *Miranda* violation to the exclusion of testimonial evidence obtained from the suspect and allowing third parties identified in the excluded testimony to testify at trial).
- *New York v. Quarles*, 467 U.S. 649, 655–56 (1984) (*Miranda* was subject to a "public safety" exception, allowing testimonial evidence obtained directly from a suspect interrogated while in custody to be admitted at trial, reasoning that when a threat to public safety necessitated immediate questioning, failure to give *Miranda* warnings was excused). *See also Arizona v. Londo*, 158 P.3d 201 (Ariz. 2006) (finding admissible under the so-called rescue doctrine a statement made during non-*Mirandized* custodial interrogation, and reviewing other state cases holding the same).

The decision in *Moran v. Burbine* has not held sway with a number of state courts, many of which have suppressed statements obtained by custodial interrogation after the police failed to inform the suspect that a lawyer was seeking to contact him. *See, e.g., State v. Stoddard*, 537

A.2d 446 (Conn. 1988); *Bryan v. State*, 571 A.2d 170 (Del. 1990); *State v. Reed*, 627 A.2d 630 (N.J. 1993); *West v. Commonwealth*, 887 S.W.2d 338 (Ky. 1994); *People v. McCauley*, 645 N.E.2d 923 (Ill. 1994); *State v. Roache*, 803 A.2d 572 (N.H. 2002); and *State v. McAdams*, 193 So. 3d 824, 832 (Fla. 2016) (due process under Florida Constitution requires that police notify the suspect—whether or not he is in custody—of the fact that his attorney is present and available to provide legal advice).

The Supreme Court seemed to breathe new life into *Miranda*'s Fifth Amendment justification when it ruled in *Dickerson v. United States*, 530 U.S. 428, 444 (2000), that "*Miranda* announced a constitutional rule" that could not be overruled by Congress. In *Dickerson*, the petitioner was indicted on federal charges, and, before trial, moved to suppress a statement he had made at an FBI field office on the ground that he had not received *Miranda* warnings before being interrogated. The district court granted his motion to suppress, but the Fourth Circuit granted the government's interlocutory appeal and reversed. The Fourth Circuit agreed with the district court that Dickerson had not received *Miranda* warnings, but found that 18 U.S.C. § 3501, which allowed un-*Mirandized* statements to be admitted into evidence if made voluntarily, governed the case.

The Supreme Court reversed. While it recognized that section 3501 was intended to legislatively overrule *Miranda*, the Court concluded that Congress had no authority to supersede *Miranda*. Although the Court admitted that language in some of its prior decisions indicated that *Miranda* was merely "prophylactic" (*New York v. Quarles*) and the warnings were "not themselves rights protected by the Constitution" (*Michigan v. Tucker*), it struck down 18 U.S.C. § 3501 as a violation of the Fifth Amendment. *Dickerson*, 530 U.S. at 444.

Enthusiasm for *Miranda*'s constitutional basis was short-lived. In *United States v. Patane*, 542 U.S. 630, 637 (2004), a divided Supreme Court decided that the failure to give a suspect *Miranda* warnings does not require suppression of the physical fruits of the suspect's voluntary statements. The plurality, once again led by Justice Thomas, characterized the *Miranda* rule as prophylactic, employed to protect against violations of the Self-Incrimination Clause. The plurality reasoned that because *Miranda*'s prophylactic rule extended beyond the specific prohibition contained in the Fifth Amendment, the further exclusion of non-testimonial evidence gained from *Miranda*'s violation could not be justified by the values served by the Fifth Amendment. Thus, "[t]here is simply no need to extend (and therefore no justification for extending) the prophylactic rule of *Miranda* to this context." *Id.* at 643.

Regardless of how *Miranda v. Arizona* is characterized, it applies only if the suspect is subjected to custodial interrogation. In *Miranda*, the Supreme Court defined custodial interrogation as "questioning initiated by law enforcement officers after a person has been taken into custody or otherwise deprived of his freedom of action in any significant way." 384 U.S. at 444. For a number of reasons, this book does not address what constitutes "interrogation" for purposes of *Miranda*, but instead briefly focuses attention on the meaning of "custody." *See, e.g., United States v. Moore*, 104 F.3d 377, 385 (D.C. Cir. 1997) (arguing that "custody and not interrogation [i]s the trigger for the attachment of the Fifth Amendment"). *See also United States v. Mandujano*, 425 U.S. 564, 579 (1976) (plurality rejected argument that putative defendant called before a grand jury was entitled to *Miranda* warnings, which they described as "aimed at the evils seen by the Court as endemic to police interrogation of a person in custody").

"Custody" is an objective determination, depending neither on the subjective views of the person being interrogated nor on the expectations of the police.

- *Howes v. Fields*, 565 U.S. 499, 508–09 (2012) ("... custody is a term of art that specifies circumstances that are thought generally to present a serious danger of coercion").
- *Thompson v. Keohane*, 516 U.S. 99, 112 (1995) ("Two discrete inquiries are essential to the [custodial] determination: first, what were the circumstances surrounding the interrogation; and second, given those circumstances, would a reasonable person have felt he or she was not at liberty to terminate the interrogation and leave. Once the scene is set and the players' lines and actions are reconstructed, the court must apply an objective test to resolve 'the ultimate inquiry': [was] there a 'formal arrest or restraint on freedom

of movement' of the degree associated with a formal arrest.") (citations omitted).

- *Stansbury v. California*, 511 U.S. 318, 323 (1994) (per curiam) ("[T]he initial determination of custody depends on the objective circumstances of the interrogation, not on the subjective views harbored by either the interrogating officers or the person being questioned.").
- *Pennsylvania v. Bruder*, 488 U.S. 9, 11 (1988) (per curiam) (no custody during routine traffic stop during which officer administered sobriety test).
- *Berkemer v. McCarty*, 468 U.S. 420, 440 (1984) (after holding *Miranda* was not applicable to roadside questioning of motorist stopped for traffic violation, the Court remarked that the controlling question is whether a reasonable person would believe he was in police custody to the degree associated with an arrest).
- *Oregon v. Mathiason*, 429 U.S. 492, 493–95 (1977) (per curiam) (*Miranda* warnings not required when parolee voluntarily submitted to questioning at the police station).

See also

- *J.D.B. v. North Carolina*, 564 U.S. 261, 280–81 (2011) (holding that a child's age may properly be taken into consideration in determining whether a juvenile was in custody for purposes of *Miranda*).
- *Yarborough v. Alvarado*, 541 U.S. 652, 665–66 (2004) (juvenile was not in custody when he was brought to the police station for questioning by his parents, who remained in the lobby while he was questioned for two hours about a murder).

"Custody" is not limited to interrogations at the police station. Rather, *Miranda* warnings have been required in a variety of settings where the suspect has been deprived of his freedom of action and would reasonably consider himself in custody. Because there are literally thousands of cases addressing an incredible variety of settings and circumstances in order to determine whether a person is in custody for *Miranda* purposes, only a few situations are mentioned here.

- *Maryland v. Shatzer*, 559 U.S. 98, 113 n.8 (2010) (Court assumed that "[w]hen a prisoner is removed from the general prison population and taken to separate location for questioning," he was in custody for *Miranda* purposes, despite holding that waiver of *Miranda* rights was valid and that prior invocation of counsel was no longer effective).
- *Estelle v. Smith*, 451 U.S. 454, 468–69 (1981) (*Miranda* applicable to a court-ordered psychiatric examination by court-appointed psychiatrist who later testifies for the state).
- *Orozco v. Texas*, 394 U.S. 324, 327 (1969) (late-night questioning by four police officers of a suspect in his boarding-house bedroom amounted to custodial interrogation).
- *Mathis v. United States*, 391 U.S. 1, 2–3 (1968) (IRS agent's questioning of inmate serving a sentence on unrelated matters required *Miranda* warnings).
- *United States v. Cowan*, 674 F.3d 947, 957–58 (8th Cir. 2012) (suspect was in custody when handcuffed, patted down, questioned, and not told he was free to leave).
- *United States v. Cavazos*, 668 F.3d 190, 194 (5th Cir. 2012) (suspect was in custody at home when he was handcuffed, guarded by armed agents at all times, and not told he was free to leave).
- *United States v. Rogers*, 659 F.3d 74, 77–78 (1st Cir. 2011) (suspect was in custody, even at home, because military superior ordered him to go home and three police officers conducting a search there did not indicate he was free to leave).
- *United States v. Martinez*, 462 F.3d 903, 909–10 (8th Cir. 2006) (holding that a suspect who was frisked, handcuffed, and questioned, but not arrested, was in custody for *Miranda* purposes).
- *United States v. Hemphill*, No. 1:10-CR-053, 2010 WL 3366137, at *4 (S.D. Ohio Aug. 20, 2010) (parolee was in custody when he was handcuffed and led around his home by his parole officer with four police officers present).
- *B.A. v. Indiana*, 100 N.E.3d 225, 233–34 (Ind. 2018) (student taken to principal's office and questioned by "resource officers" about bomb threat was deemed to be in custody and should have been given *Miranda* warnings).

- *State v. Hammonds*, 804 S.E.2d 438, 444 (N.C. 2017) (where defendant's freedom was already restricted by civil commitment order and officers told suspect he could leave only after he spoke to them about a robbery, suspect was in custody for *Miranda* purposes).
- *But cf. Burlew v. Hedgpeth*, 448 F. App'x 663, 664–65 (9th Cir. 2011) (reviewing cases from numerous circuits addressing whether a defendant in a police car before arrest was in custody, and deciding that state court finding that suspect was not in custody when placed in the back of the squad car was not so unreasonable as to support habeas relief).

Neither probationers nor prison inmates are necessarily in custody for *Miranda* purposes, however.

- *Howes v. Fields*, 565 U.S. 499, 515–17 (2012) (a prisoner questioned in prison conference room by armed sheriff's deputies for five to seven hours was not in custody when he was told several times he could end the questioning and return to his cell).
- *Minnesota v. Murphy*, 465 U.S. 420, 430 (1984) (probationer required to meet with his probation officer to answer questions was not in custody for purposes of *Miranda* because doing so does not involve a significant restraint on freedom).
- *Schreane v. Ebbert*, 864 F.3d 446, 453 (6th Cir. 2017) (no *Miranda* custody where incarcerated defendant was questioned in jail service center and thereafter returned to county jail).
- *United States v. Stoterau*, 524 F.3d 988, 1004 (9th Cir. 2008) (*Miranda* warnings not required before polygraph exam administered to probationers).
- *People v. Elliot*, 833 N.W.2d 284, 307 (Mich. 2013) (a parolee meeting in jail library with his parole officer after being incarcerated for parole violation was not in custody for purposes of *Miranda*).

If a person in custody remains completely silent in response to questioning after receiving *Miranda* warnings, it is reasonably well established that such silence cannot be used against the person in a criminal trial for any purpose.

- *Salinas v. Texas*, 570 U.S. 178, 188–89 n.3 (2013) (both plurality and dissent agreed that if Salinas had been in custody and had been given *Miranda* warnings, he would not have been required to invoke his right to remain silent to have claimed the protection of the Fifth Amendment).
- *Wainwright v. Greenfield*, 474 U.S. 284, 295 (1986) (substantive use of silence after receiving *Miranda* warnings violates due process).
- *Doyle v. Ohio*, 426 U.S. 610, 617–20 (1976) (due process violated by assuring suspect that his silence will not be used against him and then using his silence to impeach an explanation subsequently offered at trial).
- *United States v. Shannon*, 766 F.3d 346, 355–56 (3d Cir. 2014) (prosecutor violated defendant's due process rights when he asked the defendant on cross-examination whether he had ever told anyone about his exculpatory version of the facts, where defendant had remained silent after receiving *Miranda* warnings).
- *Hurd v. Terhune*, 619 F.3d 1080, 1087 (9th Cir. 2010) (reversing conviction where prosecutor made multiple references to suspect's post-*Miranda* silence at trial. "*Miranda* does not apply only to specific subjects or crimes. It applies to every question investigators pose.").
- *United States v. Rodriguez*, 260 F.3d 416, 421–22 (5th Cir. 2001) (prosecutor's closing, which urged jury to infer guilt from defendant's decision to remain silent after arrest and *Miranda* warnings, violated Fifth Amendment).
- *Thomas v. Indiana*, 910 F.2d 1413, 1416–17 (7th Cir. 1990) (defendant's silence after *Miranda* warnings could not be used as substantive evidence of sanity).

Some courts also prohibit prosecutors from commenting on or asking juries to draw adverse inferences from a person's selective silence after receiving *Miranda* warnings.

- *Moreno v. Borg*, 921 F.2d 280, at *4 (9th Cir. 1990) (mem.) (defendant's invocation of right to remain silent mid-interrogation could not be used as substantive evidence of guilt, even though he initially waived his *Miranda* rights).

- *State v. Rogers*, 512 N.E.2d 581, 585 (Ohio 1987) (ordering new trial when defendant's silence after receiving *Miranda* warnings was used for substantive purposes).

Indeed, the defendant's silence in the face of statements made by an alleged co-conspirator during custodial interrogation of both suspects was held, by at least one court, inadmissible against the defendant at trial.

- *United States v. Lafferty*, 503 F.3d 293, 305–07 (3d Cir. 2007) (trial court committed reversible error by admitting defendant's silence and defendant's failure to deny statements made by her alleged co-conspirator during joint custodial police interrogation of both suspects).

Despite *Miranda*'s clear protection of the right to remain silent during custodial interrogation, an improper comment at trial about a suspect's silence in response to *Miranda* warnings does not invariably result in a reversal of a conviction.

- *United States v. Lopez*, 500 F.3d 840, 843–45 (9th Cir. 2007) (eliciting testimony regarding defendant's pre- and post-*Miranda* silence violated defendant's Fifth Amendment rights, but was harmless error).
- *United States v. Whitehead*, 200 F.3d 634, 639–40 (9th Cir. 2000) (prosecutor's comments that stressed defendant's guilt because of defendant's custodial silence violated Fifth Amendment, but was harmless error).
- *State v. Hernandez*, 159 P.3d 950, 966–67 (Kan. 2007) (prosecutor's comment that defendant had not given his version of events until trial violated defendant's constitutional rights, but was harmless error).
- *Jones v. State*, 748 So. 2d 1012, 1021–22 (Fla. 1999) (police officer's comment on defendant's silence was error, though harmless).

- *But cf. Coleman v. State*, 75 A.3d 916, 923 (Md. 2013) (petitioner's ineffective assistance of counsel entitled him to a new trial when counsel repeatedly failed to object to state's evidence that he had remained silent in the face of police questioning after he was arrested and given *Miranda* warnings).

Miranda's exclusionary rule does not require that statements obtained in violation of its requirements be excluded from use in any proceeding or for all purposes. Rather, such statements may be admissible in proceedings other than a criminal trial.

- *I.N.S. v. Lopez-Mendoza*, 468 U.S. 1032, 1039 (1984) (federal appellate courts have held that "the absence of *Miranda* warnings does not render an otherwise voluntary statement . . . inadmissible in a deportation case") (citations omitted).
- *United States v. Nichols*, 438 F.3d 437, 444 (4th Cir. 2006) (statements obtained in violation of *Miranda* can be used against defendant at sentencing, unless "actually coerced or otherwise involuntary").
- *United States v. Patterson*, 812 F.2d 1188, 1192–93 (9th Cir. 1987) (statement taken in violation of *Miranda* could be used in an affidavit to establish probable cause for the issuance of a search warrant).
- *Commonwealth v. Kates*, 305 A.2d 701, 711 (Pa. 1973) (statements taken in violation of *Miranda* are admissible during a probation revocation proceeding).

But see

- *State v. Smith*, 542 P.2d 1115, 1116–18 (Ariz. 1975) (en banc) (statements made by suspect in custody in response to police interrogation, without the benefit of *Miranda* warnings, were inadmissible in a probation revocation proceeding).

Importantly, statements secured in violation of *Miranda* are admissible for purposes of impeachment in a criminal trial.

- *Kansas v. Ventris*, 556 U.S. 586, 593 (2009) (prosecutor can offer statements elicited in violation of *Miranda* to impeach the testifying defendant's credibility).
- *Harris v. New York*, 401 U.S. 222, 224–26 (1971) (statements made in violation of *Miranda* may be used to impeach testimony that bears on the crime charged).

Some state courts disagree on the basis of their state constitutions. *See, e.g.*, *Alaska v. Batts*, 195 P.3d 144, 153–55 (Alaska Ct. App. 2008) (holding Alaska Rule of Evidence 412, allowing the state to impeach a defendant's trial testimony with prior statements taken in violation of *Miranda*, to be unconstitutional under Alaska Constitution, when violation of *Miranda* was either intentional or egregious).

It is also clear that post-arrest, pre-warning silence may be used to impeach a defendant's trial testimony under the U.S. Constitution. States are free to fashion different rules.

- *Fletcher v. Weir*, 455 U.S. 603, 606–07 (1982) (per curiam) (impeachment use of post-arrest, pre-*Miranda* silence does not violate due process, and states are allowed to determine the admission of such silence for impeachment under their rules of evidence).
- *Jenkins v. Anderson*, 447 U.S. 231, 237–39 (1980) (permitting prosecutor's reference to the defendant's pre-arrest silence to impeach defendant's testimony that he acted in self-defense).

Again, some state courts have fashioned different rules on the basis of their state constitutional self-incrimination clause.

- *State v. Hoggins*, 718 So. 2d 761, 772 (Fla. 1998) (holding that Florida Constitution prevents impeachment of testifying defendant with silence he maintained at the time of arrest but prior to receipt of *Miranda* warnings).

However, courts are split on whether a defendant's pre-*Miranda* custodial silence can be used to prove guilt.

- *Wainwright v. Greenfield*, 474 U.S. 284, 291 (1986) (not addressing whether admitting a defendant's pre-*Miranda* custodial silence to prove guilt violates the privilege against self-incrimination).

Contrast

- *United States v. Velarde-Gomez*, 269 F.3d 1023, 1029 (9th Cir. 2001) (holding that use of post-arrest pre-*Miranda* silence violated the defendant's self-incrimination rights, reasoning that allowing it would put suspect into an impossible "Catch 22").

with

- *United States v. Frazier*, 394 F.3d 612, 619–20 (8th Cir. 2005) (allowing use of post-arrest pre-*Miranda* silence as substantive evidence of guilt on basis that government arrest did not induce silence).

Even if police comply with all the requirements of *Miranda*, an involuntary statement given in a custodial setting is still inadmissible in a criminal case under both the Self-Incrimination Clause and the Due Process Clause of the Fifth or Fourteenth Amendment.

- *Miranda v. Arizona*, 384 U.S. 436, 464 n.33 (1966) ("It is now axiomatic that the defendant's constitutional rights have been violated if his conviction is based, in whole or in part, on an involuntary confession, regardless of its truth or falsity.") (citations omitted).
- *Bram v. United States*, 168 U.S. 532, 542–43 (1897) ("But a confession, in order to be admissible, must be free and voluntary; that is, must not be extracted by any sort of threats or violence, nor obtained by any direct or implied promises, however slight, nor by the exertion of any improper influence.").
- *Tankleff v. Senkowski*, 135 F.3d 235, 242 (2d Cir. 1998) (a defendant's claims that a confession was involuntary and that it was obtained in violation of *Miranda* were held by the court to be "interrelated, but analytically distinct").

Indeed, in *Corley v. United States*, 556 U.S. 303 (2009), the Supreme Court ruled that even voluntary confessions may be thrown out if suspects are not presented in court in a timely manner.

The Supreme Court has formulated the test for voluntariness in the context of confessions in various ways. In *Arizona v. Fulminante*, 499 U.S. 279, 288 (1991), the Court directed lower courts to consider whether a defendant's will was "overborne in such a way as to render his confession the product of coercion." In *Culombe v. Connecticut*, 367 U.S. 568, 602 (1961), the plurality said that to be admissible, the statement must be "the product of an essentially free and unconstrained choice by its maker," a formulation later approved in *Schneckloth v. Bustamonte*, 412 U.S. 218, 225 (1973). Some form of police coercion is necessary to render a statement involuntary. *Colorado v. Connelly*, 479 U.S. 157, 164–67 (1986) (finding no due process violation where allegedly involuntary statement was not accompanied by police coercion). Involuntariness may be shown not only by physical coercion, *Brown v. Mississippi*, 297 U.S. 278, 286–87 (1936) (whipping and hanging suspect from a tree), but by a variety of more subtle types of psychological coercion. *Mincey v. Arizona*, 437 U.S. 385, 397–402 (1978) (hospital interview of seriously wounded suspect after police ignored requests to see attorney). However, the Supreme Court has approved the use of deception during interrogation. *See Frazier v. Cupp*, 394 U.S. 731, 739 (1969) (police are allowed to falsely claim that a suspect's cousin confessed); *Oregon v. Mathiason*, 429 U.S. 492, 495–96 (1977) (police allowed to falsely claim that a suspect's fingerprints had been found at the crime scene).

In federal courts, when a defendant moves to suppress statements in a criminal case on the ground that they were made involuntarily, the government has the burden to prove voluntariness by at least a preponderance of the evidence. *Lego v. Twomey*, 404 U.S. 477, 489 (1972). However, the Supreme Court noted that the states were free, pursuant to their own constitutions, to adopt a higher standard. *Id.* And various states have, either by case law or state statute, required the prosecution to prove voluntariness beyond a reasonable doubt. *See, e.g., Commonwealth v. Taveres*, 430 N.E.2d 1198, 1206 (Mass. 1982) (deciding that Article 12 of the Massachusetts Constitution requires the state to prove the voluntariness of a defendant's confession beyond a reasonable doubt for it to be admissible in a jury trial); *State v. Collins*, 297 A.2d 620, 627 (Me. 1972) (deciding that safeguarding "the right of an individual, entirely apart from his guilt or innocence, not to be compelled to condemn himself by his own utterances" demands the State prove voluntariness beyond a reasonable doubt).

The admission of an involuntary confession at trial is subject to a constitutional harmless error analysis. *Arizona v. Fulminante*, 499 U.S. 279 (1991) (five justices agreed that error of admitting an involuntary confession into evidence was subject to the harmless error test of *Chapman v. California*, although a different five-justice majority held that the error was not harmless in the present case) (citation omitted).

The circumstances in which courts have found statements to have been involuntary and therefore inadmissible in a prosecution against the defendant as a violation of either Self-Incrimination Clause or due process are extremely varied. The following cases—from both federal and state courts—serve merely as examples.

- *Fulminante*, 499 U.S. at 286–88 (inmate's confession was coerced when he was interrogated by an undercover informant, who presented himself as an organized crime figure and offered to protect the inmate from "rough treatment" at the hands of his fellow inmates).
- *Greenwald v. Wisconsin*, 390 U.S. 519, 521 (1968) (statements were involuntary where defendant was questioned for four hours during a 13-hour detention, requested counsel, and was given neither food nor medication for high blood pressure).
- *Gallegos v. Colorado*, 370 U.S. 49, 54–55 (1962) (written statement of 14-year-old obtained after five days of being held incommunicado was involuntary).
- *Ashcraft v. Tennessee*, 322 U.S. 143, 153 (1944) (arrest statements were involuntary where suspect was subjected to 36 hours without sleep or rest as well as over 30 hours of continuous interrogation).
- *United States v. Swint*, 15 F.3d 286, 290 (3d Cir. 1994) (statements were involuntary when defendant came to the courthouse to give

an informal, off-the-record interview, his attorney was not present, he was not given *Miranda* warnings, and the officers present were carrying clearly visible weapons).

- *United States v. Rogers*, 906 F.2d 189, 192 (5th Cir. 1990) (statements given in an interview conducted by federal agents under the auspices of the sheriff's department, which had previously promised defendant that he would not be prosecuted for a related crime, were involuntary).
- *People v. Thomas*, 8 N.E.3d 308, 316 (N.Y. 2014) (when officers repeatedly offered false assurances that they believed child's injuries were accidental and that defendant would not be arrested, and falsely told defendant that his child was alive and he should disclose what he did to save child's life, combined with a lengthy interrogation during defendant's hospitalization, rendered statements inadmissible as involuntary).
- *State v. Morton*, 186 P.3d 785, 799 (Kan. 2008) (when investigator affirmatively misrepresented the true nature of the interview to the defendant, the defendant's self-incriminatory statements were involuntary).
- *State v. Hoppe*, 661 N.W.2d 407, 418 (Wis. 2003) (suppressing statements elicited by a five-hour interrogation while the defendant was in the hospital suffering from chronic, end-stage alcohol dependence and alcohol-related dementia).

Although the U.S. Supreme Court in *Colorado v. Connelly*, 479 U.S. 157, 163 (1986) decided that absent "the crucial element of police overreaching . . . there is simply no basis for concluding that any state actor has deprived a criminal defendant of due process," several states have held that police wrongdoing is not a necessary element of determining that a confession is involuntarily and inadmissible under the state constitution's Due Process Clause.

- *State v. Kula*, 616 N.W.2d 313, 325 (Neb. 2000) (rejecting state's contention that court need not determine whether a confession was voluntary if it was made to a private person).

- *Commonwealth v. Cooper*, 899 S.W.2d 75, 79 (Ky. 1995) (pressure of private investigators was not deemed sufficient in this case to justify suppression of confession, but court recognized common law rule that such pressure by private persons could justify suppression).
- *State v. Bowe*, 881 P.2d 538 (Haw. 1994) (distinguishing *Connelly* and deciding that a private person's coercive conduct could make confession involuntary under state Due Process Clause).

The recent decision of the en banc Seventh Circuit in *Dassey v. Dittmann*, 877 F.3d 297 (7th Cir. 2017), demonstrates just how difficult the determination of when a confession is involuntary and inadmissible can be. In that case, after the state court found the confession of an intellectually impaired juvenile voluntary, a federal district court and a divided panel of the Seventh Circuit disagreed and found the state court decision "unreasonable." The en banc circuit court reversed the panel decision under the deferential standard applicable to federal habeas corpus cases, but only by a 4–3 margin. *Id.* at 301. Unfortunately, the Supreme Court denied certiorari, precluding clarification of the standard for judging when a confession is voluntary. *See generally* Brief for Professors of Criminal Law, Criminal Procedure and Constitutional Law as Amici Curiae Supporting Petitioner, *Dassey v. Dittmann*, No. 17–1172 (U.S. Mar. 26, 2018).

The admissibility of confessions taken by U.S. investigators from non-Americans abroad or taken by foreign police from Americans abroad are topics that have become more than a matter of academic interest during the "war on terror." Although the subject deserves a lengthy discussion, the book only cites some of the cases a lawyer should consider when wading into this doctrinally difficult area.

- *United States v. Straker*, 800 F.3d 570, 613–15 (D.C. Cir. 2015) (per curiam) (assuming, without deciding, that *Miranda* applies to statements obtained by U.S. authorities from suspects held in foreign custody abroad).
- *In re Terrorist Bombings of U.S. Embassies in E. Africa*, 552 F.3d 177, 198–202 (2d Cir. 2008) (concluding that the Fifth Amendment

governs the admissibility in domestic courts of statements made to U.S. law enforcement agents by foreign nationals held in foreign custody, and proceeding on the assumption that *Miranda* generally applies to interrogations conducted by U.S. law enforcement agents abroad).

- *United States v. Abu Ali*, 528 F.3d 210, 227–28 (4th Cir. 2008) (a U.S. citizen's voluntary statements to foreign law enforcement officials without *Miranda* warnings are "generally admissible" if the foreign officials are not "(1) engaged in a joint venture with, or (2) acting as agents of, United States law enforcement officers") (citations omitted).
- *United States v. Yousef*, 327 F.3d 56, 145–46 (2d Cir. 2003) (in holding that an alien's statements to foreign law enforcement officials without *Miranda* warnings were admissible, the court explained that "statements taken by foreign police in the absence of *Miranda* warnings are admissible if voluntary" unless (1) "United States law enforcement agents actively participate in questioning conducted by foreign authorities" (known as the "joint venture doctrine") or (2) the circumstances under which the statements were obtained "shock the judicial conscience") (citations omitted).
- *United States v. Martindale*, 790 F.2d 1129, 1131–32 (4th Cir. 1986) (holding that a former State Department officer's statements to British law enforcement officials were "admissible absent proof of duress or of a willful attempt of American authorities to evade the strictures of *Miranda* or *Massiah* by employing the foreign authorities") (citation omitted).
- *United States v. Chavarria*, 443 F.2d 904, 905 (9th Cir. 1971) (in holding that a U.S. citizen's confession to Mexican police was admissible, the court explained: "When the interrogation is by the authorities of a foreign jurisdiction, the exclusionary rule has little or no effect upon the conduct of foreign police. Therefore, so long as the trustworthiness of the confession satisfies legal standards, the fact that the defendant was not given *Miranda* warnings before questioning by foreign police will not, by itself, render his confession inadmissible.") (citations omitted).

- *United States v. Bin Laden*, 132 F. Supp. 2d 168, 181 (S.D.N.Y. 2001) (extending the Fifth Amendment privilege and *Miranda* to foreign suspects interrogated abroad by American law enforcement personnel).

It is noteworthy that, in several cases involving statements taken by U.S. investigators from non-Americans abroad, the government conceded that the Fifth Amendment right against self-incrimination applied. *United States v. Straker*, 800 F.3d 570 (D.C. Cir. 2015); *In re Terrorist Bombings of U.S. Embassies in E. Africa*, 552 F.3d 177 (2d Cir. 2008); *United States v. Clarke*, 611 F. Supp. 2d 12, 29 (D.D.C. 2009); *United States v. Straker*, 596 F. Supp. 2d 80, 90–91 (D.D.C. 2009).

In an analogous context, it is worth noting that although the Fifth Amendment does not apply to Indian tribal court proceedings, the Indian Civil Rights Act of 1968 provides that "no Indian tribe in exercising powers of self-government shall . . . compel any person in any criminal case to be a witness against himself." 25 U.S.C. § 1302(a)(4). Based on this provision, at least one state court has explained that defendants testifying in tribal proceedings "enjoy a federally imposed privilege against self-incrimination that is substantially coextensive with the fifth amendment privilege," such that an Indian tribe "could not compel [a defendant's] testimony without a grant of use and derivative use immunity sufficient to meet the dictates of the fifth amendment." *Tracy v. Superior Court of Maricopa County*, 810 P.2d 1030, 1048 (Ariz. 1991) (citation omitted). In general, tribal police must give *Miranda*-like warnings during a custodial interrogation, and statements taken by tribal police in violation of *Miranda* are not admissible in a tribal, federal, or state prosecution.

- *Fort Peck Tribes v. Bighorn*, 1 Am. Tribal Law 121, 123 (Fort Peck Ct. App. 1997) ("[T]ribal police officers must upon arrest, and taking a person into custody, give that person notice of his Tribal Rights, which includes his right to protection against self-incrimination.").
- *Lower Elwha Klallam Indian Tribe v. Bolstrom*, 19 Ind. L. Rep. 6026, 6027 (L. Elwha Ct. App. 1991) (the proper remedy for the

tribal police's failure to give *Miranda*-like warnings is exclusion of the defendants' statements).

- *United States v. Medearis*, 775 F. Supp. 2d 1110, 1117 (D.S.D. 2011) (suppressing custodial statements that the defendant made to tribal police without receiving any *Miranda*-like warnings).

During Non-Custodial Police Interrogation

Self-incriminating statements made to law enforcement agents outside of custodial interrogation are presumed not to have resulted from coercion, thereby generally making such statements admissible against the defendant. In such circumstances, the defendant's decision to speak is generally deemed voluntary as well.

- *Beckwith v. United States*, 425 U.S. 341, 346–48 (1976) (upholding denial of motion to suppress statements made during interview by IRS agents at defendant's home).
- *United States v. Czichray*, 378 F.3d 822, 830 (8th Cir. 2004) (reversing order suppressing confession when defendant was interrogated in his home and, thus, not in custody).
- *United States v. Coleman*, 208 F.3d 786, 790–91 (9th Cir. 2000) (self-incriminating statements made by defendant in his apartment, five days after he was first arrested and released, were admissible against him at trial).
- *United States v. Erekson*, 70 F.3d 1153, 1157 (10th Cir. 1995) (self-incriminating statements made during voluntary appearance at IRS agent's office were admissible at trial).
- *State v. Evans*, 495 N.W.2d 760, 762–64 (Iowa 1993) (sustaining conviction when statements admitted against defendant at trial were obtained by police questioning that took place in defendant's home).

Whether a person's invocation of his right to remain silent in non-custodial settings can be used as substantive evidence of guilt remains unanswered by the Supreme Court. In *Salinas v. Texas*, 570 U.S. 178, 183 (2013), the Supreme Court granted certiorari "to resolve a division of authority in the lower courts over whether the prosecution may use a defendant's assertion of the privilege against self-incrimination during a non-custodial police interview as part of its case in chief." But the Court found it unnecessary to resolve the split, ruling instead that Salinas had failed to unequivocally invoke the privilege, thereby allowing his silence to be used against him for that reason. Although a few courts have upheld the use at trial of defendant's invocation of the privilege if the questioning occurred in a non-custodial setting, most courts said no before *Salinas* and most courts continue to say no, which is consistent with *Griffin v. California*, a case discussed later in this section, guaranteeing a defendant's silence at trial cannot be used against him.

For instance, in *United States v. Okatan*, 728 F.3d 111, 120 (2d Cir. 2013), the Second Circuit not only answered the question left open in *Salinas* but confirmed the principle that a person's request for counsel is an effective invocation of the right against self-incrimination. In *Okatan*, a border patrol agent stopped the defendant's vehicle near the border and asked him questions about why he had engaged in certain activities, at which point Okatan said he wanted a lawyer and was arrested. At trial on charges of attempting to bring an alien into the country illegally, the government was permitted to offer evidence of Okatan's request for counsel in response to the border agent's question and was permitted to argue to the jury that his asking for a lawyer was evidence of his guilt.

The Second Circuit reversed the conviction, holding that even if Okatan was not in custody, a request for counsel in response to law enforcement questioning was an invocation of the Fifth Amendment privilege. The Court also held that use at trial of a pre-arrest invocation of the privilege was prohibited, analogizing to the prohibition of government comments on a defendant's failure to testify at trial. The Court ruled that the logic of *Griffin v. California* made any comment on the invocation of the privilege—"no matter the context in which the invocation is made"—too costly to withstand constitutional scrutiny. *Id*. at 120.

While *Salinas* would appear to allow the use of pre-arrest silence at trial where a person fails to clearly invoke his Fifth Amendment privilege, not all courts agree.

- *State v. Horwitz*, 191 So. 3d 429, 442 (Fla. 2016) (holding that use of defendant's pre-arrest silence violated Florida Constitution self-incrimination clause even in the absence of an invocation of the right).
- *Commonwealth v. Molina*, 104 A.3d 430, 432 (Pa. 2014) (holding that the state cannot "use a non-testifying defendant's pre-arrest silence" to support its claim of defendant's guilt, and reversing the conviction upon determining that the error was not harmless) (collecting cases).
- *State v. Lovejoy*, 89 A.3d 1066, 1073–75 (Me. 2014) (the prosecution violated both federal and state constitutions by eliciting testimony that defendant did not return phone calls from police).

During Grand Jury Proceedings

For the federal government to initiate a serious criminal case, the Constitution requires the approval of a grand jury. U.S. Const. amend. V ("No person shall be held to answer for a capital, or otherwise infamous crime, unless on a presentment or indictment of a Grand Jury . . . ."). Most state constitutions have similar provisions. The grand jury is empowered to issue subpoenas—either *ad testificandum*, calling for a witness to testify, or *duces tecum*, requiring the witness to produce documents or other tangible items. (The Fifth Amendment "act of production" privilege applicable to the compelled production of documents is addressed in Chapter 8.) The Supreme Court has repeatedly affirmed a person's right to invoke the Fifth Amendment privilege against self-incrimination in response to subpoenas issued by grand juries, at least as to subpoenas directed to them personally.

- *United States v. Mandujano*, 425 U.S. 564, 575 (1976) (describing the process for adjudicating a grand jury witness's assertion of the privilege against self-incrimination).
- *United States v. Calandra*, 414 U.S. 338, 346 (1974) (stating that a grand jury may not force a witness to testify in violation of his Fifth Amendment rights).

- *Counselman v. Hitchcock*, 142 U.S. 547, 562–63 (1892) (finding that Fifth Amendment right against self-incrimination is a broader right than the right to counsel under the Sixth Amendment, and, thus, may be exercised in a larger number of settings).

Procedures for Invoking the Fifth Amendment in the Grand Jury

Although the self-incrimination privilege has long been held to prohibit the prosecution from forcing a defendant to appear as a witness at his own trial, to claim the Fifth Amendment privilege in response to a grand jury subpoena a witness must either appear before the grand jury and assert the privilege after each question calling for a potentially incriminating answer or move to quash the subpoena on the ground that responses to any question would be protected by the Fifth Amendment privilege. Simply refusing to honor a grand jury subpoena on the basis of the Fifth Amendment privilege is unwarranted and may be grounds for contempt.

- *United States v. Mandujano*, 425 U.S. 564, 572 (1976) (plurality) ("The Fifth Amendment does not confer an absolute right to decline to respond in a grand jury inquiry. . . .").
- *In re Grand Jury Subpoenas Dated Dec. 7 & 8, Issued to Bob Stover, Chief of Albuquerque Police Dept.* 40 F.3d 1096, 1104 (10th Cir. 1994) (police officer's fear that grand jury may consider compelled internal affairs statement and return an indictment against him does not provide sufficient basis for blanket assertion of Fifth Amendment before grand jury).
- *A v. Dist. Ct. of Second Jud. Dist.*, 550 P.2d 315, 322–23 (Colo. 1976) ("A witness before a grand jury cannot assert his Fifth Amendment right against self-incrimination by a [b]lanket refusal to answer all questions put to him. When asked a specific question or series of questions, the answers to which he believes will tend to incriminate him, he may refuse to answer.") (citations omitted).

However, at least in federal grand jury investigations, witnesses who announce their intention to assert their Fifth Amendment rights in response to any question calling for a potentially incriminating answer (i.e., in a blanket fashion) may often be excused from having to appear.

- *See* U.S. Dep't of Justice, Justice Manual § 9–11.154 (2018) (authorizing prosecutors to decide to withdraw a subpoena where the witness has indicated in advance that he intends to assert the privilege, but warning against doing so too readily).

Although three judges of one federal court opined that a person whom the prosecutor knows will assert a Fifth Amendment privilege could not be subpoenaed to appear under the circumstances of that case, *Jones v. United States*, 342 F.2d 863, 867–70 (D.C. Cir. 1964) (en banc), and some states have provided the same protection by statute, Nev. Rev. Stat. § 172.197; Neb. Rev. Stat. § 29–1411, the great weight of authority is to the contrary.

- *United States v. Wong*, 431 U.S. 174, 179 n.8 (1977) ("[T]here is no constitutional prohibition against summoning potential defendants to testify before a grand jury.") (citations omitted).
- *United States v. Dionisio*, 410 U.S. 1, 10 n.8 (1973) ("The obligation to appear is no different for a person who may himself be the subject of the grand jury inquiry.") (citations omitted).

Department of Justice internal guidelines recommend against compelling a target of a grand jury investigation to appear before the grand jury to assert his Fifth Amendment privilege, unless in exceptional cases.

- U.S. Dep't of Justice, Justice Manual § 9–11.150 (2018) (advising prosecutors to consider, among other factors, "whether the questions the prosecutor and the grand jurors intend to ask or the other information sought would be protected by a valid claim of privilege" in determining whether to subpoena a target).

Such internal guidelines or policies are not, however, enforceable against the Department of Justice.

- *United States v. Myers*, 123 F.3d 350, 358 (6th Cir. 1997) (despite being "troubled by the government's violations of the DOJ Manual," court refused to use its supervisory powers to suppress grand jury testimony when the government failed to comply with relevant DOJ manual provisions requiring warnings to grand jury targets and subjects).

See generally

- *United States v. Caceres*, 440 U.S. 741, 755–56 (1979) (while recognizing that federal agencies should follow their own procedures and guidelines when individual rights are affected, failure of IRS to follow rules regarding recording of conversation provided no basis to suppress evidence obtained).

Although the Supreme Court has not definitively resolved the question whether *Miranda*-type warnings must be given to a target of the grand jury investigation, the Court has hinted that warnings regarding the witness's rights under the Fifth Amendment are not required.

- *Minnesota v. Murphy*, 465 U.S. 420, 431 (1984) (in the course of ruling that *Miranda*-type warnings need not be given to a probationer being questioned by a probation officer, the Court noted that it has "never held that [warnings] must be given to grand jury witnesses") (citation omitted).
- *United States v. Mandujano*, 425 U.S. 564, 579–80 (1976) (while finding it unnecessary to consider whether any warnings were required, the plurality remarked that "grand jury questioning[] take[s] place in a setting wholly different from custodial police interrogation").

The lower federal courts have generally recognized that even though it is the policy of the Department of Justice to append an "Advice of Rights" form to all grand jury subpoenas served on targets or subjects, U.S. Dep't of Justice, Justice Manual § 9–11.151 (2018), advice regarding

Fifth Amendment rights is not constitutionally required to be given to grand jury witnesses.

- *United States v. Williston*, 862 F.3d 1023, 1032–33 (10th Cir. 2017) (rejecting claim that district court erred by not suppressing at trial the defendant's grand jury testimony that was given without his receiving *Miranda* warnings, when defendant was in custody on unrelated charges at the time).
- *United States v. Quam*, 367 F.3d 1006, 1008 (8th Cir. 2004) (declining to fashion a rule that would require warnings regarding the right against self-incrimination to be given to witnesses testifying before a grand jury).
- *United States v. Gomez*, 237 F.3d 238, 242 (3d Cir. 2000) (where grand jury covered only topics witness could have reasonably believed would be covered in questioning and witness had adequate opportunity to consult an attorney before the grand jury, prosecutor did not have a constitutionally mandated obligation to inform the witness that he could remain silent and that anything he said could be used against him).
- *United States v. Goodwin*, 57 F.3d 815, 818 (9th Cir. 1995) (failure to provide the DOJ "Advice of Rights" form containing Fifth Amendment warnings did not, without more, establish a deprivation of defendant's rights).
- *United States v. Russell*, 916 F. Supp. 2d 305, 310 (E.D.N.Y. 2013) (listing numerous cases in which courts have concluded that *Miranda*-like warnings are not required for targets or subjects subpoenaed to testify before grand juries).

Similarly, the Fifth Amendment does not require the suppression of grand jury testimony elicited without previously advising the witness that he is the target of the grand jury investigation.

- *United States v. Washington*, 431 U.S. 181, 188 (1977) ("After being sworn, respondent was explicitly advised that he had a right to remain silent and that any statements he did make could be used to convict him of crime. It is inconceivable that such a warning would fail to alert him to his right to refuse to answer any question which might incriminate him. This advice also eliminated any possible compulsion to self-incrimination which might otherwise exist.").

However, a number of states have required either that grand jury witnesses be advised of their rights against compulsory self-incrimination or that targets be advised of their status.

- Ariz. R. Crim. P. 12.5 ("A person under investigation by the grand jury may be compelled to appear before the grand jury, or may be permitted to appear upon the person's written request. The person must be advised of the right to remain silent and the right to have counsel present to advise the person while giving testimony."); *State v. Doolittle*, 746 P.2d 924, 929 (Ariz. 1987) (affirming suppression of evidence obtained in violation of defendant's right to be informed of privilege against self-incrimination).
- Ind. Code Ann. § 35–34–2-5(b) ("If the subpoena is issued to a target, the subpoena shall also contain a statement informing the target that: (1) he is a subject of the grand jury investigation; (2) he has the right to consult with an attorney and to be assisted by an attorney under section 13 of this chapter; and (3) if he cannot afford an attorney, the court inpaneling [*sic*] the grand jury will appoint one for him, upon request."); *State ex rel. Pollard v. Criminal Court of Marion Cty., Div. One*, 329 N.E.2d 573, 589 (Ind. 1975) (targets of the grand jury investigation may refuse to testify, and need not exercise the privilege against self-incrimination on a question-by-question basis as required of other witnesses).
- *Commonwealth v. Woods*, 1 N.E.3d 762, 720–21 (Mass. 2014) ("[W]here, at the time a person appears to testify before a grand jury, the prosecutor has reason to believe that the witness is either a 'target' or is likely to become one, the witness must be advised, before testifying, that (1) he or she may refuse to answer any question if a truthful answer would tend to incriminate the witness, and

(2) anything that he or she does say may be used against the witness in a subsequent legal proceeding.").

- *State v. Cook*, 464 N.E.2d 577, 581 (Ohio 1983) (holding that a grand jury witness who was potentially the focus of the investigation should have been warned of her Fifth Amendment privilege).
- *People ex rel. Gallagher v. District Court*, 601 P.2d 1380, 1383 (Colo. 1979) (oral advisement of rights before the grand jury did not comply with statute requiring that a suspect be advised of rights before a grand jury appearance).
- *State v. De Cola*, 164 A.2d 729, 732 (N.J. 1960) ("[A] person whose criminal liability is the object of a grand jury inquiry must be informed of his privilege to withhold evidence tending to his own incrimination.").

And in several states, witnesses compelled to testify before a state grand jury are entitled to transactional immunity merely for testifying.

- Tenn. R. Crim. P. 6(j)6: "Immunity of Certain Witnesses from Prosecution. No witness shall be indicted for any offense in relation to which the district attorney general has compelled the witness to testify before the grand jury."
- N.Y. Crim. Proc. § 190.40.1: "Every witness in a grand jury proceeding must give any evidence legally requested of him regardless of any protest or belief on his part that it may tend to incriminate him." N.Y. Crim. Proc. § 190.40.2: "A witness who gives evidence in a grand jury proceeding receives immunity unless" certain circumstances apply. *See People v. Chin*, 490 N.E.2d 505, 513 n.4 (N.Y. 1986) (the statutory immunity that a grand jury witness receives is transactional rather than use immunity).

When a witness appears before the grand jury and exercises his privilege against self-incrimination, the invocation should not be used to impeach a defendant who chooses to testify at trial. *See also Grunewald v. United States*, 353 U.S. 391 (1957) (Court emphasized that because the grand jury witness, later indicted, was not represented by counsel during questioning, could not summon any witnesses, and had no opportunity to cross-examine those who might testify against him, his silence was probative of very little).

Absence of a Fifth Amendment Privilege in Response to Grand Jury Subpoena for Documents That Incriminate Others

The Fifth Amendment provides no basis for a person to object to a grand jury subpoena requiring the production of documents in the possession of a third party. In *Couch v. United States*, 409 U.S. 322 (1973), a person transferred her financial records, including bank statements, canceled checks, and deposit slips, to her accountant. The IRS, which was investigating the person for tax fraud, served the accountant with an administrative summons. The taxpayer asserted her Fifth Amendment privilege to enjoin enforcement of the summons. The Supreme Court rejected the taxpayer's arguments, reasoning that the Fifth Amendment protects only against personal compulsion, and that the enforcement of the summons to compel the production of documents in the possession of her accountant did not compel the taxpayer to do anything. *Id.* at 329. Accordingly, courts have routinely overruled Fifth Amendment objections posed by parties to subpoenas for their records in the possession of third parties.

- *SEC v. Jerry T. O'Brien, Inc.*, 467 U.S. 735, 742 (1984) (no Fifth Amendment violation when subpoena was issued to third party and target was not compelled to produce any materials).
- *Johnson v. United States*, 228 U.S. 457, 458 (1913) (Fifth Amendment privilege did not apply to books and records that had been transferred involuntarily by a bankrupt party to a trustee in bankruptcy).
- *United States v. Mickens*, 926 F.2d 1323, 1331 (2d Cir. 1991) (no Fifth Amendment violation with respect to customers when bank was required to report large cash transactions, because customers were not under compulsion).
- *In re Grand Jury Subpoena (Maltby)*, 800 F.2d 981, 984 (9th Cir. 1986) (former police chief cannot assert Fifth Amendment right to

prevent production of incriminating records in possession of his successor).

- *Ryerson v. I.R.S.*, 371 F. Supp. 2d 1130, 1134 (D. Ariz. 2005) (taxpayer's motion to quash third-party subpoenas directed to Wells Fargo and Arizona Public Service Co. denied, as "[p]laintiff ha[d] no [Fifth Amendment] protectable interest in these 'third party' records").
- *United States v. One Hundred Four Thousand Seven Hundred Sixty-Eight Dollars*, No. 97 CV 5257 (RJD), 1999 WL 684152, at *2–3 (E.D.N.Y. July 12, 1999) (although requiring claimant in forfeiture proceeding to produce her prior tax returns was protected by her Fifth Amendment privilege, she could be compelled to execute an authorization form allowing the IRS to release copies of her tax returns).

It is also clear that a person may not shield documents from a grand jury subpoena by giving the documents to her lawyer. Although the lawyer may cite attorney-client privilege to resist producing documents given by the client for the purpose of obtaining legal advice, the fact that the client could assert a Fifth Amendment privilege over the documents does not give the lawyer a right to resist production on the basis of the client's Fifth Amendment privilege.

- *Fisher v. United States*, 425 U.S. 391, 405 (1976) (explaining that the Fifth Amendment does not protect documents that a person has given to his attorney because once the attorney possesses the documents and the government demands them, the threat of compulsion is removed from the witness).
- *In re Sealed Case*, 162 F.3d 670, 673–75 (1998) (D.C. Cir. 1998) (attorney for Monica Lewinsky was compelled to produce to grand jury documents and tangible objects given to him by his client).

The Supreme Court in *Couch* recognized a possible exception to the rule regarding the absence of a Fifth Amendment right in the production of records in the possession of a third party, stating: "[s]ituations may well arise where constructive possession is so clear or the relinquishment of possession is so temporary and insignificant as to leave the personal compulsions upon the accused substantially intact." 409 U.S. at 333. Chapter 8 reviews cases applying the exception.

Absence of Protection Against Grand Jury Considering Evidence Previously Obtained in Violation of the Fifth Amendment

Indictments returned by a grand jury that considers evidence previously obtained in violation of the privilege against self-incrimination are nevertheless normally valid.

- *United States v. Williams*, 504 U.S. 36, 49 (1992) (noting that "our cases suggest that an indictment obtained through the use of evidence previously obtained in violation of the privilege against self-incrimination is nevertheless valid") (citations omitted).
- *United States v. Calandra*, 414 U.S. 338, 346 (1974) (in dicta indicating that evidence obtained in violation of Fifth Amendment right against self-incrimination may be presented to grand jury).
- *United States v. Blue*, 384 U.S. 251, 255 n.3 (1966) (defendant is not entitled to challenge an indictment on the ground that the grand jury heard evidence obtained in violation of the Fifth Amendment privilege against self-incrimination; sole remedy is suppression of the testimony at trial).
- *State v. Case*, 928 P.2d 1239, 1242 (Alaska 1996) (reinstating indictment that lower court had dismissed on grounds that grand jury considered evidence obtained in violation of the defendant's Fifth Amendment right against self-incrimination).
- *See also United States v. Mechanik*, 475 U.S. 66, 70 (1986) (a petit jury's guilty verdict renders harmless any error that may flow from a violation of the federal rules governing its activities).

Indictments returned by a grand jury that considers testimony of the defendant that had been compelled by a grant of immunity—which protects against use of such testimony in "any criminal case"—are, however, generally invalid. Only if the government can establish that the evidence relied upon by the grand jury was derived from independent, legitimate sources may an indictment survive the use of such "tainted" testimony.

- *United States v. Hubbell*, 530 U.S. 27, 45 (2000) (affirming decision dismissing an indictment obtained in part through evidence derived from act of producing documents compelled by order of immunity pursuant to 18 U.S.C. § 6003).
- *United States v. Allen*, 864 F.3d 63, 101 (2d Cir. 2017) (where the prosecution witness reviewed the prior testimony of the defendant compelled by foreign authority's grant of limited immunity and the government could not satisfy their burden under *Kastigar* to prove that the witness's review did not "shape, alter, or affect the evidence" used to indict, such impermissible use was not harmless beyond a reasonable doubt and required indictment to be dismissed).
- *United States v. Palumbo*, 897 F.2d 245, 248–49 (7th Cir. 1990) (citing cases from Eighth, Ninth, and Eleventh Circuits reversing convictions where indictments were obtained on the basis, at least in part, of testimony given by the defendant under a grant of immunity).
- *State v. Conrad*, 552 N.E.2d 214, 216 (Ohio 1990) (dismissing indictment obtained by use of defendant's prior immunized testimony).
- *But cf. United States v. Rivieccio*, 919 F.2d 812, 816 (2d Cir. 1990) (affirming conviction after use of immunized testimony at trial).
- *In re Misc. 4281*, 149 A.3d 1253, 1267 (Md. Ct. Spec. App. 2016) (holding that Fifth Amendment does not prohibit a grand jury from compelling the production of a public agency's report containing employees' self-incriminating statements coerced by *Garrity* immunity).

The apparent discrepancy between the consequences for a grand jury indictment based on the violation of a person's Fifth Amendment right against self-incrimination and a grand jury indictment based on the violation of an order of immunity is hard to square, since use and derivative use immunity is deemed co-extensive with the Fifth Amendment. Chapter 9 discusses this in greater depth. Indeed, if a grand jury proceeding is part of "any criminal case" under the Fifth Amendment and an immunity order similarly prevents the use of testimony compelled by it in "a criminal case," as is provided by 18 U.S.C. § 6002, there should be no difference. This conundrum, though beyond the scope of this book, deserves treatment elsewhere.

During Pretrial Proceedings

In *Simmons v. United States*, 390 U.S. 377, 394 (1968), the Supreme Court held that "when a defendant testifies in support of a motion to suppress evidence on Fourth Amendment grounds, his testimony may not thereafter be admitted against him at trial on the issue of guilt unless he makes no objection." In that case, the defendant moved to suppress a suitcase containing incriminating materials that had been seized, he alleged, in violation of the Fourth Amendment. To establish his standing to contest the search and seizure, the defendant testified at the pretrial suppression hearing that he was the suitcase's owner. At trial, the defendant's pretrial hearing testimony was used against him. While acknowledging that the pretrial hearing testimony was not compelled, the Supreme Court was concerned that the defendant was required to surrender his Fifth Amendment right against self-incrimination in order to assert an arguably valid Fourth Amendment claim. Thus, the Court fashioned the exclusionary rule prohibiting the use of such testimony in the government's case in chief at trial.

The *Simmons* exclusionary rule has been extended to testimony given at certain other pretrial hearings where the protection of other constitutional rights is at stake. Despite the fact that the Supreme Court expressly declined to decide whether "The Simmons principle" could be extended to Sixth Amendment claims for the appointment of counsel, *United States v. Kahan*, 415 U.S. 239, 243 (1974), *Simmons* has been extended to statements made by a defendant to protect his right to counsel, to avoid double jeopardy, and to proceed to trial.

- *United States v. Aguirre*, 605 F.3d 351, 358–59 (6th Cir. 2010) (Fifth Amendment privilege violated by use at trial of financial affidavit prepared by defendant to obtain court-appointed counsel, though it did not amount to plain error).

- *United States v. Garcia*, 721 F.2d 721, 723 (11th Cir. 1983) (defendant may testify at a pretrial double jeopardy hearing and disclose self-incriminating information "without fear that the evidence will be used against him at the ensuing trial") (citation omitted).
- *United States v. Inmon*, 568 F.2d 326, 333 (3d Cir. 1977) (defendant could not be required, as the cost of litigating a valid Fifth Amendment double jeopardy claim, to waive the Fifth Amendment privilege against self-incrimination in a later trial).
- *United States v. Branker*, 418 F.2d 378, 380 (2d Cir. 1969) (defendant's testimony in a hearing on an application to proceed *in forma pauperis* could not be used as evidence against him at trial).
- *Hayes v. State*, 581 So. 2d 121, 126 (Fla. 1991) (defendant may testify at a suppression hearing and not waive his Fifth Amendment privilege; collecting cases detailing a wide variety of situations in which *Simmons* applies).

See also

- *United States v. Weston*, 36 F. Supp. 2d 7, 13 (D.D.C. 1999) ("[T]he scope of the competency hearing shall be limited to determining whether the defendant is . . . mentally incompetent. . . . If any information is obtained beyond this limited scope that would be relevant to the defendant's guilt and/or future death penalty phase, that information would be exclud[able]. . . .") (citations omitted).
- *United States v. Salemme*, 985 F. Supp. 197, 200 (D. Mass. 1997) (for purposes of deciding whether defendant was eligible for court-appointed counsel, court first agreed to accept ex parte submission from the parties and, if a further adversary proceeding was necessary, to then provide defendant with immunity for his statements).
- *Cooper v. State*, 422 P.3d 722, 727–28 (Nev. 2018) (en banc) (invoking its supervisory power, the court fashioned an exclusionary rule that prevents government from using probationer's testimony given at a probation revocation hearing held before the disposition of criminal charges arising out of the alleged violation of the conditions of probation).

- *People v. Pokovich*, 141 P.3d 267, 276–77 (Cal. 2006) (deciding that a testifying defendant may not be impeached at trial with statements made during a court-ordered examination to determine defendant's mental competency to stand trial).
- *People v. Jablonski*, 126 P.3d 938, 957 (Cal. 2006) ("[B]ecause a defendant may not invoke his right against compelled self-incrimination in a competency examination, neither the statements of [the defendant] to the psychiatrists appointed under section 1369 nor the fruits of such statements may be used in trial of the issue of [the defendant's] guilt. . . .") (citation omitted).
- *People v. Arcega*, 651 P.2d 338, 346–48 (Cal. 1982) (establishing a rule under California law that statements made to psychiatrists or psychologists appointed for purposes of a competency hearing or the fruits of their examination may not be admitted at the guilt or sanity phase of trial).

Although the Supreme Court has not specifically ruled on the issue, the prevailing case law favors allowing the testifying defendant to be impeached by his prior pretrial testimony, including prior testimony given to vindicate Fourth Amendment rights.

- *United States v. Salvucci*, 448 U.S. 83, 93–94 (1980) (reserving question of whether *Simmons* "use immunity" extends beyond the government's case in chief to the cross-examination of the defendant in the event he chooses to testify at trial).
- *Walder v. United States*, 347 U.S. 62, 65 (1954) (allowing prosecution to impeach a defendant's trial testimony that he had never possessed narcotics with evidence of his possession, which had been previously suppressed because it had been obtained in violation of the Fourth Amendment).
- *United States v. Jaswal*, 47 F.3d 539, 543 (2d Cir. 1995) (no error for government to use testimony from suppression hearing to impeach defendant's testimony at trial).
- *United States v. Beltran-Gutierrez*, 19 F.3d 1287, 1291 (9th Cir. 1994) ("[Defendant] elected to testify in his own defense at his trial.

The Fifth Amendment protected him from the use of his suppression hearing testimony in the Government's case in chief to prove his guilt. It did not protect him from impeachment for testifying falsely.").

- *United States v. Quesada-Rosadal*, 685 F.2d 1281, 1283 (11th Cir. 1982) ("[T]he use of prior inconsistent statements given at a suppression hearing can be used to impeach a defendant's trial testimony, whether given during direct or cross-examination.") (citation omitted).
- *United States v. Vaughn*, No. 05–00482 OWW, 2008 WL 4104241, at *7–8 (E.D. Cal. Sept. 3, 2008) (holding that the defendant cannot complain that his choice to testify at suppression hearing was used to impeach his inconsistent testimony at trial).
- *Bobb v. United States*, 758 A.2d 958, 964 (D.C. 2000) (no plain error for government to use pretrial hearing testimony to impeach defendant's credibility as trial witness).
- *State v. Schultz*, 448 N.W.2d 424, 427–32 (Wis. 1989) (not per se impermissible to require a defendant to choose between asserting his right to suppress statements and asserting his right to remain silent, by allowing statements at suppression hearing to be used to impeach his testimony at trial).

The Supreme Court has upheld at least one rule requiring the making of potentially incriminating statements before trial. In *Williams v. Florida*, 399 U.S. 78, 85 (1970), the Court, while recognizing that the Florida notice of alibi disclosure called for a "testimony" by the defendant, decided there was no prohibited compulsion where the required notice simply accelerated the disclosure that would be required at trial. The Court distinguished *Brooks v. Tennessee*, 406 U.S. 605, 610–11 (1972), which held that an unconstitutional burden was placed on defendant's right not to testify by a state rule requiring his testimony prior to other defense witnesses. However, not all state courts have agreed with the "mere acceleration" rationale of *Williams* and there are undoubtedly situations where statutorily required pretrial disclosures violate the Fifth Amendment. For instance in *Binegar v. Eighth Judicial Dist. Court*,

915 P.2d 889 (Nev. 1996) (per curiam), the Nevada Supreme Court held that a statutory reciprocal discovery provision violated the defendant's privilege against self-incrimination insofar as it required defense disclosure of (1) the reports of scientific experts who were not expected to testify at trial, and (2) the names, addresses, and recorded statements of prospective witnesses not expected to testify at trial.

During Trial Fifth Amendment Rights of the Defendant

In accordance with the plain meaning of its words, the Fifth Amendment guarantees the criminal defendant an unqualified right to choose whether or not to testify at his or her trial. When a defendant chooses not to testify, the Fifth Amendment generally prohibits the prosecutor, the trial judge, or counsel for a co-defendant from making adverse comments about the defendant's decision. In *Griffin v. California*, 380 U.S. 609, 613–14 (1965), the Supreme Court held that any inference of guilt to be drawn from the defendant's exercise of the Fifth Amendment at trial was tantamount to improper compulsion.

Although Justice Thomas and the late Justice Scalia criticized the *Griffin* adverse inference rule, the Supreme Court seems unlikely to overrule it any time soon. In 1999, the *Griffin* rule was described as "an essential feature of [our] legal tradition" in *Mitchell v. United States*, 526 U.S. 314, 316, 330 (1999), where the Court extended *Griffin*'s prohibition of an adverse inference from silence to the sentencing decision. As the Court later explained, *Griffin* held that "[t]he defendant's right to hold the prosecution to proving its case without his assistance is not to be impaired by the jury's counting the defendant's silence against him." *Portuondo v. Agard*, 529 U.S. 61, 67 (2000). And in *Salinas v. Texas*, 570 U.S. 178, 192 (2013), only the dissenters in *Mitchell*, Justices Thomas and Scalia, took the opportunity to criticize *Griffin* as inconsistent with the text of the Self-Incrimination Clause ("*Griffin* is impossible to square with the text of the Fifth Amendment . . . A defendant is not 'compelled . . . to be a witness against himself' simply because a jury has been told that it may draw an adverse inference from his silence.") (Thomas, J., concurring) (citations omitted). The dissenters in *Salinas*—Justices Breyer, Sotomayor, Ginsburg, and

Kagan—endorsed the *Griffin* decision in arguing that the prosecutor should not have been allowed to comment at trial on the defendant's silence in response to non-custodial police questioning. *Id.* at 193. The three justices constituting the plurality in *Salinas*—Justices Alito and Kennedy and Chief Justice Roberts—took no position on the wisdom of *Griffin*.

There are hundreds of cases addressing prosecutors' comments at trial that violate the defendant's Fifth Amendment right to remain silent. A few examples include the following:

- *Griffin v. California*, 380 U.S. 609, 611 (1965) (prosecutor's comment that defendant "has not seen fit to take the stand and deny or explain" violated the Fifth Amendment).
- *United States v. Hills*, 618 F.3d 619, 640 (7th Cir. 2010) (prosecutor's comments in closing arguments that "you don't really need to worry about that Fifth Amendment protection unless you're worried that you're [d]oing something illegal" and that the defendants were "using the Fifth Amendment not as a shield to protect themselves from incrimination, but as a sword to prevent the IRS from getting the information that they are entitled to," violated non-testifying defendant's Fifth Amendment rights).
- *Ben-Yisrayl v. Davis*, 431 F.3d 1043, 1049–51 (7th Cir. 2005) (prosecutor's comment, "[l]et the Defendant tell you," violated defendant's Fifth Amendment rights because jury could reasonably interpret it as suggestion that the jury should infer guilt from defendant's silence).
- *United States v. Rodriguez*, 215 F.3d 110, 122 (1st Cir. 2000) (improper to suggest that the defendant could have contradicted a government witness).
- *United States v. Hardy*, 37 F.3d 753, 757 (1st Cir. 1994) (prosecutor's comment that non-testifying defendants were "still running and hiding today" violated Fifth Amendment).

A comment on a non-testifying defendant's demeanor during trial (or during custodial interrogation) may also constitute a violation of a defendant's Fifth Amendment right not to testify.

- *United States v. Green*, 541 F.3d 176, 187 (3d Cir. 2008) (conviction reversed where prosecutor elicited testimony that defendant "widened his eyes, lowered his head and sighed" when shown videotape of narcotics transaction during custodial interrogation in which *Miranda* warnings were not given), *vacated on other grounds* 556 F.3d 151 (3d Cir. 2009).
- *United States v. Rivera*, 944 F.2d 1563, 1568–69 (11th Cir. 1991) (error for prosecutor to comment on defendant's "deadpan" demeanor).
- *United States v. Schuler*, 813 F.2d 978, 981 (9th Cir. 1987) ("[P]rosecutorial comment on a defendant's non-testimonial behavior may impinge on that defendant's fifth amendment right not to testify.").

The prohibition on commenting on the invocation of the right against self-incrimination at a criminal trial is not absolute. In *United States v. Robinson*, 485 U.S. 25 (1988), the Supreme Court considered a mail fraud case involving false insurance claims. The defense attorney suggested during closing argument that the government was not being fair because it had not allowed him to tell his client's side of the story. In rebuttal, the prosecutor argued that the defendant had an adequate opportunity to explain his position when he gave a statement to the authorities, when he spoke to an insurance company investigator, and that he "could have taken the stand and explained it to you, anything he wanted to." *Id.* at 40 n.3. The Court distinguished *Griffin* and upheld the conviction, in effect recognizing a "fair response" exception to the *Griffin* rule.

Most courts have followed *Robinson*'s lead, and only a few examples are described here.

- *Graham v. Dormire*, 212 F.3d 437, 439–40 (8th Cir. 2000) (prosecutor's comment that the jury could determine when the defendant needed to testify was a "fair response" to defense counsel's statement that defendant did not need to testify).
- *De La Riva v. Garcia*, 121 F.3d 715, at *1 (9th Cir. 1997) (mem.) (trial court reasonably interpreted defense attorney's comments to

suggest that defendant could not testify on his own behalf, thereby allowing prosecutor to make "fair response" that defendant could testify on his own behalf).

- *Commonwealth v. Trivigno*, 750 A.2d 243, 248–49 (Pa. 2000) (defense counsel's statement to jury that they could infer defendant's innocence from defendant's not guilty plea authorized prosecutor to inform jury of actual legal effect of a not guilty plea).
- *People v. Austin*, 28 Cal. Rptr. 2d 885, 895 (Cal. Ct. App. 1994) ("It must be remembered [that] the defendant's right to remain silent is a shield. It cannot be used as a sword to cut off the prosecution's 'fair response' to the evidence or argument of the defendant.") (citation omitted).
- *State v. Brecht*, 421 N.W.2d 96, 102–03 (Wis. 1988) (state was allowed to elicit police officer's testimony about defendant's pre-*Miranda* silence on redirect after defense counsel elicited facts about defendant's pre-arrest conduct on cross-examination of police officer).

Additionally, a prosecutor's adverse comments in violation of *Griffin* may constitute harmless error. Thus, in *Chapman v. California*, 386 U.S. 18 (1967), the Supreme Court decided that the *Griffin* rule did not involve rights so basic to a fair trial that their violation can never be harmless. Rather, if the prosecutor can prove beyond a reasonable doubt that the jury would have returned a guilty verdict in any event, the conviction can be upheld. *Id.* at 24. While imposing a high bar, numerous cases have upheld a defendant's conviction despite a violation of the *Griffin* rule. A few representative cases include the following:

- *United States v. Hasting*, 461 U.S. 499, 512 (1983) (prosecutor's comments regarding uncontradicted testimony constituted harmless error in the face of overwhelming evidence of guilt).
- *United States v. McMillan*, 600 F.3d 434, 452 (5th Cir. 2010) (prosecutor's comment "not one of these defendants is stepping up" was harmless error, where court instructed jury to disregard and prosecutor explained to jury that he misspoke).

- *United States v. Rodriguez-Velez*, 597 F.3d 32, 45 (1st Cir. 2010) (where court issued instruction to disregard prosecutor's comments and evidence of guilt was overwhelming, *Griffin* error was harmless).
- *United States v. Forrest*, 402 F.3d 678, 686 (6th Cir. 2005) (prosecutor's comments regarding defendant's failure to provide testimony to support his defense argument were harmless, where evidence of guilt was strong and comments were not extensive).
- *United States v. Barbour*, 393 F.3d 82, 90–91 (1st Cir. 2004) (prosecutor's comments that might reasonably be interpreted as a reference to defendant's failure to testify, such as "[the conspirators] are the only people who laid it out for you" and "this [tape recorder] allowed you to listen to th[e] defendant," did not likely affect the outcome of the trial and were mitigated by jury instructions).
- *People v. Brasure*, 175 P.3d 632, 647 (Cal. 2008) (court's immediate and unequivocal direction to jury not to consider prosecutor's improper comment, combined with overwhelming evidence of guilt, rendered *Griffin* error harmless).

Extensive adverse comments, combined with evidence that could have supported acquittal, will support a finding of reversible constitutional error.

- *Anderson v. Nelson*, 390 U.S. 523, 525–27 (1968) (prosecutorial comments such as "I give him credit for not getting up on the stand and trying to tell you a lie," combined with questionable evidence of guilt, led to reversal of conviction under *Chapman*).
- *United States v. Rodriguez*, 260 F.3d 416, 421–23 (5th Cir. 2001) (prosecutor's argument that jury should infer guilt from defendant's silence after his arrest required reversal, when comments were linked directly to prosecutor's argument regarding the implausibility of the defense theory of the case).
- *People v. Guzman*, 80 Cal. App. 4th 1282, 1288–90 (Cal. Ct. App. 2000) (*Griffin* error required reversal because prosecutor's comments on defendant's failure to testify were "relentless" and evidence of guilt was not overwhelming).

Comments by counsel for a co-defendant on a defendant's decision not to testify can also be improper, but they are often found to constitute harmless error.

Compare

- *De Luna v. United States*, 308 F.2d 140, 154–55 (5th Cir. 1962) (repetitious comments by defense counsel for co-defendant on defendant's failure to testify were too prejudicial to be cured by a no-inference jury instruction and thereby required new, separate trials for both defendants).

with

- *United States v. Spencer*, 592 F.3d 866, 881 (8th Cir. 2010) (comment by counsel for co-defendant that he would not "hide behind the Fifth Amendment" did not violate *Griffin*, because a reasonable juror would not view this as a comment on defendant's failure to testify).
- *United States. v. Al-Muqsit*, 191 F.3d 928, 937 (8th Cir. 1999) (improper comment by co-defendant's counsel that he would have liked to have cross-examined defendant, but was unable to do so because of defendant's Fifth Amendment privilege, did not deny a fair trial).
- *United States v. Coleman*, 7 F.3d 1500, 1505–06 (10th Cir. 1993) (comment by counsel for co-defendant that defendant's refusal to testify "sets him apart" violated Fifth Amendment, but was harmless error).

A criminal defendant who does not testify has a constitutional right to a cautionary jury instruction that no inference of guilt may be drawn from that choice.

- *Carter v. Kentucky*, 450 U.S. 288, 305 (1981) ("Just as adverse comment on a defendant's silence 'cuts down on the privilege by making its assertion costly,' the failure to limit the jurors' speculation on the meaning of that silence, when the defendant makes a timely request that a prophylactic instruction be given, exacts an impermissible toll on the full and free exercise of the privilege. Accordingly, we hold that a state trial judge has the constitutional obligation, upon proper request, to minimize the danger that the jury will give evidentiary weight to a defendant's failure to testify.") (citation omitted).

- *Woodall v. Simpson*, 685 F.3d 574, 579 (6th Cir. 2012) (defendant entitled to "no adverse inference" instruction at penalty phase despite having pled guilty).

Accordingly, where a trial judge improperly rejects a defendant's request for such a "no adverse inference" instruction, courts generally apply a constitutional harmless error analysis to determine whether reversal is appropriate.

- *United States v. Soto*, 519 F.3d 927, 930 (9th Cir. 2008) (agreeing with First Circuit and holding that failure to give a requested "no adverse inference" instruction requires reversal, unless harmless beyond a reasonable doubt).
- *Beathard v. Johnson*, 177 F.3d 340, 350 (5th Cir. 1999) (court's failure to deliver requested "no adverse inference" instruction may be harmless error).
- *United States v. Burgess*, 175 F.3d 1261, 1267–68 (11th Cir. 1999) (although holding that failure to give no-inference instruction was subject to harmless error analysis, court nonetheless reversed conviction because it was not convinced beyond a reasonable doubt that trial court's failure to give instruction did not contribute to the conviction).
- *United States v. Wagstaff*, No. 86–5585, 1987 WL 37826, at *2 (4th Cir. June 17, 1987) (conviction reversed when trial court rejected defendant's proffered "no adverse inference" instruction and gave one that "failed to tell the jury in plain, unequivocal language that it could not draw an adverse inference from the defendant's failure to take the stand").

- *State v. Mayes*, 63 S.W.3d 615, 638 (Mo. 2001) (failure to give requested "no adverse inference" instruction during death penalty phase not harmless and requires new trial on issue of punishment).
- *State v. Griffin*, 576 N.W.2d 594, 597 (Iowa 1998) (court's failure to give "no adverse inference" instruction was harmless beyond a reasonable doubt in light of overwhelming evidence of defendant's guilt).
- *Commonwealth v. McIntosh*, 646 S.W.2d 43, 44–45 (Ky. 1983) (court's failure to give "no adverse inference" instruction was harmless error due to "overwhelming" evidence of guilt).

A court may give a "no inference of guilt" instruction even though the defendant objects to the instruction for strategic reasons, such as not wishing to emphasize the failure to testify. *Lakeside v. Oregon*, 435 U.S. 333, 340–41 (1978). The Supreme Court noted, however, that states are free to "forbid [their] trial judges from doing so as a matter of state law." *Id.* at 340. Consequently, some state courts require adherence to a defendant's wishes.

- *Commonwealth v. Garcia*, 888 A.2d 633, 634 (Pa. 2005) (in a multi-defendant action, a court must respect the request for a "no adverse inference" instruction by one defendant, even if another defendant waives his right to the instruction).
- *Commonwealth v. Rivera*, 805 N.E.2d 942, 953 n.9 (Mass. 2004) ("We remain of the view that judges should not give the instruction when asked not to do so. We are merely saying that it is not *per se* reversible error to do so.").

See also

- *Commonwealth v. Edwards*, 637 A.2d 259, 261 (Pa. 1993) (it is per se reversible error to give "no inference of guilt" instruction when defendant requests that it not be given).
- *State v. Thompson*, 430 N.W.2d 151, 153 (Minn. 1988) ("[A] trial judge ordinarily should obtain a criminal defendant's permission before giving [the no adverse inference instruction].").

Indeed, at least one federal circuit court has noted that the better practice is for trial judges to respect the tactical decisions of defense counsel, particularly where there are no conflicting wishes expressed by co-defendants.

- *United States v. Williams*, 521 F.2d 950, 955 n.11 (D.C. Cir. 1975) ("Although such a refusal to honor the wishes of defendant [to give a no-inference instruction] has not been held to be reversible error, we believe, as several courts have suggested, that the better practice, in cases where there are no conflicting wishes of codefendants, is for the trial judge to respect the tactical decisions of defense counsel.") (internal citations omitted).

Some states have enacted statutes or rules of evidence that, in the absence of a request that the no-adverse inference charge not be given, require the court to issue such an instruction. *See, e.g.*, Conn. Gen. Stat. Ann. § 54–84(b); Ind. R. Evid. § 501(d)(3).

After the Supreme Court's decision in *Carter v. Kentucky*, the majority of federal and state appellate courts required judges to issue no adverse inference instructions to juries at the penalty phase of the case as well, at least where the defendant remains silent. *See, e.g., Edwards v. Roper*, 688 F.3d 449, 461 (8th Cir. 2012) (assuming that a no-adverse inference instruction was required at the penalty phase, but finding that denial of the instruction was harmless); *State v. Mayes*, 63 S.W.3d 615, 637–38 (Mo. 2001) (en banc) (trial court committed prejudicial error by refusing, over defendant's objection, to instruct the jury that it could not draw an adverse inference on punishment from defendant's failure to testify at the penalty phase, even though the court issued a no-adverse inference instruction at the guilt phase). However, the Supreme Court subsequently held in *White v. Woodall*, 572 U.S. 415 (2014) that refusal to give a no-adverse inference instruction at the penalty phase is not so clearly established as to require relief under the difficult-to-meet standard for issuance of a writ of habeas corpus under 28 U.S.C. § 2254(d).

Fifth Amendment Rights of the Trial Witness

A witness's Fifth Amendment right not to testify generally trumps a defendant's Sixth Amendment rights to compulsory process and to present a defense. Thus, most courts have denied attempts by the defendant to call to the stand a witness who intends to assert the Fifth Amendment privilege against self-incrimination.

- *United States v. Santiago*, 566 F.3d 65, 70 (1st Cir. 2009) (defendant has no right to compel a witness who will legitimately assert the Fifth Amendment to all questions to take the witness stand).
- *United States v. Branch*, 537 F.3d 328, 342 (4th Cir. 2008) (trial court did not abuse its discretion in refusing defendant's request to call to the witness stand a passenger in the car in which drugs were found when the witness would have asserted his Fifth Amendment privilege against self-incrimination).
- *United States v. Reed*, 173 F. App'x 184, 189 (3d Cir. 2006) ("We have held that a criminal defendant may not call a witness for the sole purpose of allowing the jury [to] hear the witness invoke his or her Fifth Amendment privilege. . . . This rule is well grounded as allowing a witness to testify for the purpose of invoking the Fifth Amendment would only invite the jury to make an improper inference.") (internal citations omitted).
- *United States v. Mabrook*, 301 F.3d 503, 507 (7th Cir. 2002) (defendant does not have a right to force a witness to appear before the jury simply to invoke a Fifth Amendment privilege).
- *United States v. Griffin*, 66 F.3d 68, 70 (5th Cir. 1995) ("Once a witness appears in court and refuses to testify, a defendant's compulsory process rights are exhausted.").
- *United States v. Harris*, 542 F.2d 1283, 1298 (7th Cir. 1976) ("The defendants have no right to have the jury draw inferences from the witnesses' exercise of [the Fifth Amendment].").
- *Bowles v. United States*, 439 F.2d 536, 541–42 (D.C. Cir. 1970) (en banc) (explaining that a witness's invocation of the Fifth Amendment

in the presence of the jury will have a disproportionate impact on their deliberations, and that "the probative value of the event is almost entirely undercut by the absence of any requirement that the witness justify his fear of incrimination and by the fact that it is a form of evidence not subject to cross-examination") (citation omitted).

However, a few state courts grant trial judges the discretion to force a witness who will assert his or her privilege against self-incrimination to take the witness stand and to invoke the privilege in front of the jury.

- *Gray v. State*, 796 A.2d 697, 702–14 (Md. 2002) (court has discretion to allow defendant to call non-testifying witness to the witness stand).
- *Porth v. State*, 868 P.2d 236, 240 (Wyo. 1994) ("We hold that the trial court has discretion to allow or disallow the defendant to call a witness to the stand who the court knows will invoke [the] Fifth Amendment privilege against self-incrimination in the presence of the jury.") (citations omitted).

It is well settled that a witness who asserts the Fifth Amendment privilege against self-incrimination is "unavailable" under Federal Rule of Evidence 804(a). *See, e.g., United States v. Salerno*, 505 U.S. 317, 321 (1992); *United States v. Innamorati*, 996 F.2d 456, 474 (1st Cir. 1993). Former testimony by the witness asserting the Fifth Amendment may, if certain conditions are met, be admissible for or against the defendant. *See* Fed. R. Evid. 804(b)(1) (excepting from hearsay rule "[t]estimony that: (A) was given as a witness . . . ; and (B) is now offered against a party who had . . . an opportunity and similar motive to develop it by direct, cross-, or redirect examination").

The concern that the jury will infer a defendant's guilt from a witness's assertion of the Fifth Amendment privilege against self-incrimination applies equally to the government's attempt to call witnesses to the stand at trial. Numerous courts have prevented the government from calling an alleged participant in the crime as a witness, where the government knew or suspected that the witness will assert his Fifth Amendment privilege against self-incrimination, either as a violation of the defendant's Sixth Amendment right to confront his accusers or as an evidentiary violation.

- *United State v. Rivas-Macias*, 537 F.3d 1271, 1275 n.3 (10th Cir. 2008) ("Because a jury may not draw any legitimate inferences from a witness' [sic] decision to exercise his Fifth Amendment privilege, we have repeatedly held that neither the prosecution nor the defense may call a witness to the stand simply to compel him to invoke the privilege against self-incrimination.") (citations omitted).
- *Harmon v. McVicar*, 95 F.3d 620, 624 (7th Cir. 1996) ("[R]eversible error occurs only where the government intentionally forces the witness to invoke the privilege against self-incrimination with the result that an inference unfavorable to the accused is planted in the minds of the jurors.") (citations omitted).
- *United States v. King*, 461 F.2d 53, 56 (8th Cir. 1972) (conviction reversed where prosecution questioned two witnesses who asserted their Fifth Amendment rights regarding the crime in question, and evidence against the defendant was not strong).
- *Robbins v. Small*, 371 F.2d 793, 795 (1st Cir. 1967) (when it became apparent that government's witness was going to assert his Fifth Amendment privilege regarding every question, prosecutor should have ceased questioning the witness).
- *Higgs v. Commonwealth*, 554 S.W.2d 74, 75 (Ky. 1977) (conviction reversed where witness's invocation of her Fifth Amendment rights was unduly prejudicial to defendant).
- *State v. Allen*, 224 N.W.2d 237, 240–41 (Iowa 1974) (reversing conviction where prosecutor questioned witness knowing that he would assert Fifth Amendment privilege).

In *Douglas v. Alabama*, 380 U.S. 415 (1965), the Supreme Court reversed a conviction where the prosecutor questioned a witness who was asserting his right against self-incrimination about the witness's prior confession implicating the defendant, holding that the defendant's Sixth Amendment right to cross-examine was denied. The Supreme Court has, however, rejected the suggestion that it is invariably reversible error for the prosecutor to require a witness to appear before the jury and exercise the Fifth Amendment privilege to some or all questions.

- *Frazier v. Cupp*, 394 U.S. 731, 733 (1969) (no violation of defendant's confrontation rights for prosecutor to call the witness to the stand, knowing that the witness would assert his Fifth Amendment privilege against self-incrimination, because witness's appearance lasted only two to three minutes).
- *Namet v. United States*, 373 U.S. 179, 189 (1963) (because the witness refused to testify only to a few questions and his refusals were merely "cumulative support for an inference already well established by the non-privileged portion of the witnesses' testimony," there was no evidentiary error in prosecutor calling the witness to the stand).

The tension between a defendant's Sixth Amendment right to compulsory process and a witness's Fifth Amendment right to avoid being compelled to incriminate himself could be resolved by allowing a court to grant the defense witness immunity. However, as discussed in Chapter 9, most courts consider themselves powerless to grant immunity to a witness, and prosecutors rarely do so on behalf of a criminal defendant. The judge's obligations to balance a defendant's Confrontation Clause rights against a witness's rights against compulsory self-incrimination are often tested when a witness asserts his self-incrimination privilege on cross-examination, a subject briefly addressed in Chapter 7.

During Post-Trial Proceedings

The Supreme Court has made it clear that convicted defendants may not be compelled to testify against themselves at sentencing hearings. In *Estelle v. Smith*, 451 U.S. 454, 462–63 (1981), the Court rejected the argument that incrimination is complete once guilt has been adjudicated and held the Fifth Amendment applicable to capital sentencing hearings. Because the defendant retains the privilege against self-incrimination through sentencing, the defendant's silence at trial, or thereafter at sentencing, cannot normally be used as a basis for drawing an adverse inference in determining the facts of the offense. *See also Mitchell v. United States*, 526 U.S. 314, 326–27 (1999); *White v. Woodall*, 572 U.S. 415 (2014) (describing *Mitchell* as having "disapproved a trial judge's drawing an adverse inference from the defendant's silence at sentencing with regard to factual determinations respecting the circumstances and details of the crime"). Indeed, neither a defendant's guilty plea nor incriminating statements made at the plea colloquy waive the right to remain silent at sentencing. *Id.* at 316–17.

The Supreme Court in *Mitchell* left open the question whether a court may consider the defendant's refusal to speak at a sentencing hearing (or to a probation officer conducting a pre-sentence investigation for the court) to determine factors relevant to sentencing other than the nature of the crime of conviction. Thus, although the Fifth Amendment right generally applies at sentencing, many courts "have allowed sentencing courts to rely on, or draw inferences from, a defendant's exercise of his Fifth Amendment rights for purposes other than determining the facts of the offense of conviction." *Lee v. Crouse*, 451 F.3d 598, 605 n.3 (10th Cir. 2006) (citation omitted).

- *United States v. Caro*, 597 F.3d 608, 629 (4th Cir. 2010) (collecting cases on use of defendant's refusal to testify as an aggravating sentencing factor on the lack of remorse).
- *United States v. Kennedy*, 499 F.3d 547, 551–52 (6th Cir. 2007) (court could consider defendant's refusal to submit to post-trial psychosexual examination at sentencing, because inference drawn from refusal related solely to future dangerousness and not to facts regarding the seriousness of the offense of conviction).
- *United States v. Bolden*, 479 F.3d 455, 466 (6th Cir. 2007) (conditioning reduced sentence on willingness to disclose disposition of robbery proceeds does not violate Fifth Amendment).
- *United States v. Warren*, 338 F.3d 258, 264 (3d Cir. 2003) (the denial of a sentencing reduction for acceptance of responsibility based on a defendant's post-guilty plea silence constituted a "denied benefit

rather than a penalty" and thus did not violate the defendant's Fifth Amendment rights).

- *United States v. Constantine*, 263 F.3d 1122, 1128–29 (10th Cir. 2001) (conditioning sentence reduction on defendant's willingness to discuss prior robberies did not violate Fifth Amendment).
- *State v. Burgess*, 943 A.2d 727, 758 (N.H. 2008) (citing federal circuit decisions since *Mitchell* holding that it is not a Fifth Amendment violation to deny a reduction of sentence under the acceptance of responsibility provision of the federal sentencing guidelines to a defendant who remains silent at sentencing).
- *State v. Blunt*, 71 P.3d 657, 662 & n.13 (Wash. 2003) (stating that "most courts have generally declined to extend *Mitchell* to prohibit inferences from silence in the context of sentence enhancements that do not involve factual details of the underlying crime" and collecting cases).

But cf. United States v. Cabrera, 811 F.3d 801, 807 (6th Cir. 2016) (sentencing judge violated defendant's Fifth and Sixth Amendment rights by issuing a harsher sentence because the defendant offered a "fantastical" defense and had not testified at trial); *and State v. Washington*, 832 N.W.2d 650, 660–61 (Iowa 2013) (deciding that sentencing judge had violated defendant's Fifth Amendment right when he issued harsher sentence based on defendant's refusal to answer a question about whether he was on drugs the day of sentencing).

A defendant awaiting sentencing, who is called to testify as a witness at another person's trial, may invoke his Fifth Amendment privilege against compelled self-incrimination.

- *United States v. Londono*, 175 F. App'x 370, 372 (2d Cir. 2006) (defendant who had pled guilty, but had not yet been sentenced, could not be compelled to testify at a co-defendant's trial).
- *United States v. Stewart*, 129 F. App'x 758, 766–67 (4th Cir. 2005) (recognizing that *Mitchell v. United States* suggested that a defendant who awaits sentencing after having pled guilty may assert the

privilege against self-incrimination if called as a witness in the trial of a co-defendant).

- *United States v. Hernandez*, 962 F.2d 1152, 1161 (5th Cir. 1992) ("[I]mpending sentencing may furnish grounds for a legitimate fear of incurring additional criminal liability from testifying, in which case the [Fifth Amendment] privilege should remain in effect.") (citations omitted).
- *United States v. Lugg*, 892 F.2d 101, 102–03 (D.C. Cir. 1989) (agreeing with other circuits that convicted, but yet-to-be sentenced, defendants retain their Fifth Amendment rights not to testify regarding incriminating matters that may affect their sentence).
- *United States v. Paris*, 827 F.2d 395, 399 (9th Cir. 1987) ("A convicted but unsentenced defendant retains his Fifth Amendment rights.") (citations omitted).
- *United States v. Tindle*, 808 F.2d 319, 325 (4th Cir. 1986) (witness allowed to invoke his Fifth Amendment privilege at trial of co-defendant, when plea agreement "specifically provided that nothing in the agreement would be construed to protect [witness] in any way from prosecution for perjury").

See also

- *United States v. Rivas-Macias*, 537 F.3d 1271, 1281 (10th Cir. 2008) (defendant's rights to compulsory process were not violated when co-defendant, who had not yet been sentenced, was not compelled to testify on defendant's behalf).

Most courts do not view sentencing as eliminating potential incrimination for the crime of conviction, at least where the opportunity for direct appellate review and, therefore, a possible reversal of the conviction remains.

- *United States v. Kennedy*, 372 F.3d 686, 691 (4th Cir. 2004) ("We have held in no uncertain terms that a defendant's right to invoke the Fifth Amendment as to events for which he has been convicted extends to the period during which the conviction is pending appeal.") (citations omitted).

- *Graham v. Durr*, 433 P.3d 1098 (Alaska 2018) (defendant in civil litigation could assert the privilege against self-incrimination in response to plaintiff's discovery requests where his criminal sentence was still on appeal).
- *People v. Cantave*, 993 N.E.2d 1257 (N.Y. 2013) (court violated defendant's Fifth Amendment privilege when it granted prosecutor's request to cross-examine him about the underlying facts of a rape conviction that was on direct appeal).
- *Ellison v. State*, 528 A.2d 1271, 1278 (Md. 1987) (holding that Fifth Amendment and Article 22 of Maryland Declaration of Rights entitled convicted defendant to invoke privilege against self-incrimination during pendency of direct appeal and sentence review proceedings).
- *State v. Linscott*, 521 A.2d 701, 703–04 (Me. 1987) (finding that defendant had a Fifth Amendment right not to testify at another's trial when he had an appeal pending on the same set of circumstances).

However, where no direct appeals remain pending, the courts generally find that compelling the defendant to make incriminating admissions regarding the crime of conviction poses no Fifth Amendment problem, because there "is no more than a remote or speculative possibility" of incrimination.

- *Rice v. Mich. Parole Bd.*, No. 1:05-CV-549, 2005 WL 2297463, at *3–4 (W.D. Mich. Sept. 21, 2005) (no Fifth Amendment violation to require defendant whose appeals had been denied to admit information regarding crimes of which he had been convicted).
- *State v. Barone*, 986 P.2d 5, 20 (Or. 1999) (concluding that a witness does not possess a Fifth Amendment privilege against self-incrimination after his direct appeals have been exhausted, and may not refuse to answer questions about the crime of conviction

simply because he intends to attack the conviction through habeas corpus proceedings).

But cf. James v. State, 75 P.3d 1065, 1072 (Alaska Ct. App. 2003) (defendant had Fifth Amendment right not to admit guilt during mandated sex offender treatment program because such admissions could still be used against him if he obtained post-conviction relief); *State ex rel. Henderson v. Fabian*, 735 N.W.2d 295, 310–11 (Minn. 2007) (holding that an inmate who had exhausted his right to direct appeal still had a Fifth Amendment privilege not to answer questions concerning his offense of conviction during a state-mandated sex offender treatment program because he testified at trial that he did not commit the offense, and making any admission to the contrary in the sex offender treatment program would have supported a conviction for perjury; the court did not reach the defendant's separate argument that because his conviction could have been overturned in his federal habeas proceeding, any admissions he might have made could have been used against him in a new trial).

During Probation and Parole

A probationer's or parolee's right to exercise the Fifth Amendment privilege in connection with his probation/parole supervision was addressed by the Supreme Court in *Minnesota v. Murphy*, 465 U.S. 420 (1984). There, the defendant was placed on probation for a sex-related crime and ordered to be truthful to his probation officer in all matters. As a result of admitting a past crime to his probation officer, the defendant was later convicted of murder. He challenged his conviction on the basis that his incriminating statement was impermissibly compelled and should not have been admitted into evidence in the subsequent prosecution. The Minnesota Supreme Court ruled that because Murphy had been ordered by the sentencing court to respond truthfully to the probation officer's questions and the probation officer had substantial reason to believe that Murphy's answers would be incriminating, the officer should have warned Murphy of his privilege against self-incrimination, and that her failure to do so barred the use of Murphy's confession at his subsequent trial.

The U.S. Supreme Court reversed. It ruled that the general obligation to answer a probation officer's questions truthfully did not render Murphy's admissions "compelled" statements, and that Murphy had a choice to either assert the privilege or respond, as he was neither in "custody" under *Miranda* nor was he threatened with an impermissible penalty if he exercised his right not to answer. The Court considered whether to excuse Murphy's failure to assert his privilege because the probation officer's actions threatened to impose sanctions that would force Murphy to forgo asserting his right against self-incrimination, which would have brought the case within the "penalty exception" the Court has long ruled the Fifth Amendment forbids. But the Court found that the applicable conditions of probation merely forbade false statements and contained "no suggestion that [Murphy's] probation was conditioned on his waiving his Fifth Amendment privilege with respect to further criminal prosecution." *Id.* at 437.

The *Murphy* Court did suggest, however, that "if the questions put to the probationer . . . call for answers that would incriminate him in a pending or later criminal prosecution," and the state, "either expressly or by implication, asserts that invocation of the privilege would lead to revocation of probation, it would have created the classic penalty situation." "[T]he failure to assert the privilege would be excused, and the probationer's answers would be deemed compelled and inadmissible in a criminal prosecution." *Id.* at 435.

Thus, a probationer or parolee's Fifth Amendment rights appear to turn on the consequence of remaining silent in the face of questioning. If revocation follows from invocation of a probationer's or parolee's Fifth Amendment privilege, the incriminating statements are deemed compelled and cannot be used in a subsequent prosecution. If threat of revocation is not the consequence of silence, a probationer can be forced to speak and have his self-incriminating statements used against him in a criminal prosecution. Accordingly, courts have reached different results depending on whether a probationer or parolee was required to surrender his Fifth Amendment privilege in order to remain on probation or parole.

- *United States v. Lara*, 850 F.3d 686 (4th Cir. 2017) (because revocation of probation was not automatic upon assertion of Fifth Amendment privilege at sex offender treatment program intake interview, defendant's incriminating statements were deemed voluntary and not compelled and district court could consider them at sentencing hearing).
- *People v. Roberson*, 377 P.3d 1039 (Colo. 2016) (concluding that Fifth Amendment privilege against self-incrimination precluded judge from revoking a sex offender's probation based on his refusal to answer a polygraph examiner's question concerning his use or viewing of child pornography while on probation, and remanding for further fact-finding on other questions).
- *United States v. Von Behren*, 822 F.3d 1139, 1145 (10th Cir. 2016) (where probationer was required to submit to polygraph testing over questions that required admission to past crimes and was told that his refusal to answer would lead to revocation of his supervised release and return to prison, the government's threat amounted to unconstitutional compulsion within the meaning of the Fifth Amendment and defendant's petition to modify the polygraph requirement must be granted).
- *United States v. Ramos*, 685 F.3d 120, 128–29 (2d Cir. 2012) (upholding denial of motion to suppress incriminating statements made to parole officer in subsequent prosecution for making false statements, where Ramos was not explicitly or implicitly threatened with parole revocation for invoking his Fifth Amendment privilege, and instead failed to invoke his right against self-incrimination).
- *United States v. Vreeland*, 684 F.3d 653, 660 (6th Cir. 2012) (conviction for making false statements upheld and no Fifth Amendment violation found where evidence established that Vreeland was neither explicitly nor implicitly threatened with revocation when speaking to his probation officer under general condition to be truthful).

- *United States v. York*, 357 F.3d 14, 24–25 (1st Cir. 2004) (interpreting mandatory polygraph testing condition of supervised release as not threatening revocation upon refusal, and granting probationer a right to a hearing before imposition of a penalty upon refusal to answer questions that could implicate him in crimes other than those for which he stood convicted).
- *United States v. Lee*, 315 F.3d 206, 212 (3d Cir. 2003) (Fifth Amendment right against self-incrimination not violated by polygraph condition of probation supervision when probationer could end exam and was not required to answer incriminating questions).
- *Bennett v. Bigelow*, 387 P.3d 1016 (Utah 2016) (ruling that state was not entitled to summary judgment, where parolee had raised genuine issue of fact about whether his parole was conditioned on his waiver of the Fifth Amendment).
- *State v. Van Komen*, 376 P.3d 738, 744 (Idaho 2016) (where judge revoked defendant's probation specifically because defendant asserted his Fifth Amendment right to remain silent and refused to take a polygraph examination about this participation in a sex crime while on probation, the court violated defendant's Fifth Amendment rights).
- *Commonwealth v. Knoble*, 42 A.3d 976, 983 (Pa. 2012) (refusing to suppress incriminating statements made during mandatory polygraph examination, where probation would not have been automatically revoked for refusing to answer).

Some state courts have solved the tension created by *Minnesota v. Murphy* by preventing responses to a probation officer's questions concerning the probationer's participation in a crime before or during probation from being used in any subsequent prosecution. *See People v. Garcia*, 2 Cal. 5th 792 (Cal. 2017) (holding constitutional a state statutory requirement that convicted sex offenders waive privilege against self-incrimination and participate in polygraph examinations as part of sex offender management program, provided state is precluded from using compelled answers to commence or continue subsequent criminal prosecution); *State v. Cate*, 683 A.2d 1010, 1019 (Vt. 1996) (court vacated a condition of probation requiring the defendant to acknowledge culpability for conduct for which he was convicted, and ruled that courts should grant probationer judicial use immunity "that makes any statements required for successful completion of rehabilitative probation inadmissible against the probationer at a subsequent criminal proceeding"); *State v. Evans*, 252 N.W.2d 664 (Wis. 1977) (granting probationer use and derivative use immunity for any statements made about prior crimes and preventing use of his refusal to answer at a subsequent revocation hearing without his having first been advised of the immunity). Similarly, at least one state court has invoked its supervisory powers to adopt a rule that prevents incriminating statements a probationer made at a revocation hearing from being used against him in a subsequent criminal prosecution. *See Cooper v. State*, 422 P.3d 722 (Nev. 2018). In contrast, several federal courts have gone in the opposite direction, holding that the privilege is not violated as long as the probationer or parolee retains the right to move to suppress incriminating statements made in a required sex offender treatment program should the government seek to use them in a subsequent prosecution.

- *United States v. Johnson*, 446 F.3d 272, 279–80 (2d Cir. 2006) (because the parolee retained the right to challenge subsequent use in court of incriminating statements produced by a compelled polygraph examination, he could be required to take the polygraph exam or have his parole revoked).
- *United States v. Morgan*, 44 F. App'x 881, 886–87 (10th Cir. 2002) (condition requiring defendant to self-report any violation of his supervised release upheld because defendant could later assert his Fifth Amendment right if he were subsequently penalized for reporting the violation).
- *Piña v. Vail*, No. 08-CV-0511-MJP-JPD, 2009 WL 1320962, at *9 (W.D. Wash. May 11, 2009) (a parolee's Fifth Amendment right was not violated by the requirement that he submit to periodic polygraph testing as a condition of supervised release, in part because he had "not made any showing . . . that he could not challenge the admission of such statements in a future criminal proceeding").

- *United States v. Porter*, No. 03-CR-0129 (CPS), 2008 WL 117839, at *7 (E.D.N.Y. Jan. 3, 2008) (requirement that a parolee submit to polygraph examinations as a condition of supervised release did not violate his Fifth Amendment rights "because he can challenge the use of any incriminating statements made during the course of the polygraph examination in any court proceeding") (citation omitted).

The reasoning of these federal cases is inconsistent with the Supreme Court decision in *Maness v. Myers*, 419 U.S. 449 (1975), which held that subsequent suppression of compelled self-incriminating testimony is inadequate protection of a person's Fifth Amendment privilege. The *Maness* decision is considered further in Chapter 4.

It is important to note that *Minnesota v. Murphy* considered that the revocation of probation or parole does not constitute a criminal proceeding for purposes of the Self-Incrimination Clause, and hence "there can be no valid claim of the privilege on the ground that the information sought can be used in revocation proceedings." *Minnesota v. Murphy*, 465 U.S. 420, 435 n.7 (1984). Thus, the use of statements made during probation supervision to revoke probation is generally not a violation of the privilege against self-incrimination. *See, e.g.*, *United States v. Hulen*, 879 F.3d 1015, 1020–21 (9th Cir. 2018) (because revocation of probation or supervised release does not constitute a criminal case under the Self-Incrimination Clause, the government may use statements made in a sex offender treatment program in a proceeding to revoke supervised release).

Distinguishing Non-Criminal from Criminal Proceedings

Because the words of the Fifth Amendment prohibit the use of compelled self-incriminating testimony only in criminal cases, assertions of the privilege in non-criminal settings are treated differently. For instance, although no adverse inference can be drawn against a criminal defendant from invocation of the Fifth Amendment in a criminal case, an adverse inference against a party who asserts the Fifth Amendment may be drawn by the fact-finder in a civil case. Similarly, although a defendant cannot be compelled to take the witness stand in his own criminal trial, a party can be compelled by the opposing party to take the witness stand and either testify or assert the Fifth in a purely civil case, at least where the testimony is used only to impose civil sanctions.

As Chapter 2 discussed, the Supreme Court has not decided when a criminal case begins, or when it ends, for purposes of the Self-Incrimination Clause. Whether a proceeding is criminal or civil for the purposes of applying the Fifth Amendment is similarly undecided. The Supreme Court has been deferential to Congress's or a state legislature's definition of a proceeding as civil and remedial, but recognizes that despite the label applied by the legislature, a statute may contain sanctions so punitive that they turn a designated civil remedy into a criminal penalty. *See generally Kennedy v. Mendoza-Martinez*, 372 U.S. 144, 168 (1963) (setting forth a multifactor test to be used in determining whether an act of Congress is "penal or regulatory in character" where conclusive evidence of congressional intent is absent). Nonetheless, distinguishing criminal from civil cases is difficult. On the one hand, an ostensibly civil proceeding may involve sanctions sufficiently severe as to be considered criminal for purposes of the Fifth Amendment. For example, in *Boyd v. United States*, 116 U.S. 616, 633–34 (1886), the Supreme Court indicated that a proceeding involving the forfeiture of certain property based on the commission of a criminal offense was "quasi criminal" and "within . . . criminal proceedings for . . . that portion of the [F]ifth [A]mendment which declares that no person shall be compelled in any criminal case to be a witness against himself." On the other hand, a century later, the Supreme Court held that proceedings under a state's Sexually Dangerous Persons Act were not criminal, despite the fact that proof beyond a reasonable doubt was required and the respondent risked indefinite incarceration in a maximum security institution. *Allen v. Illinois*, 478 U.S. 364, 374 (1986). According to the five-member majority, a proceeding that appears criminal may sufficiently serve non-punitive interests and eliminate the need to apply self-incrimination prohibitions as they are applied in criminal cases, especially if it is labeled "civil." *Id.* at 369.

Proceedings or requirements that have been held to fall on the civil side of the imprecise line between criminal and civil proceedings include the following:

Deportation proceedings:

- *I.N.S. v. Lopez-Mendoza*, 468 U.S. 1032, 1038–39 (1984) (*Miranda* exclusionary rule not applicable to deportation proceedings).
- *United States ex rel. Bilokumsky v. Tod*, 263 U.S. 149, 157 (1923) (certain involuntary confessions are admissible in deportation hearings).
- *Fong Yue Ting v. United States*, 149 U.S. 698, 730 (1893) (expulsion of non-citizens is a civil proceeding that does not involve protections required by the Constitution in criminal cases).
- *But cf. Padilla v. Kentucky*, 559 U.S. 356 (2010) (holding that criminal defense attorneys must advise non-citizen clients about deportation risks of a guilty plea and suggesting that deportation is "uniquely difficult to classify").

Mental health involuntary commitment proceedings:

- *Kansas v. Hendricks*, 521 U.S. 346 (1997) (upholding the constitutionality of the Kansas Sexually Violent Predator Act and characterizing confinement as civil rather than criminal for purpose of both the Double Jeopardy Clause and the Ex Post Facto Clause).
- *State v. Williams*, 930 N.E.2d 770, 777–78 (Ohio 2010) (involuntary commitment for accused felon found permanently incompetent to stand trial is a civil proceeding for purposes of the Self-Incrimination Clause).
- *In re Beverly*, 342 So. 2d 481, 488–89 (Fla. 1977) ("The Fifth Amendment privilege is not designed to protect any disclosures which are made by a mental patient during a psychiatric examination and which will lead [o]nly to an assessment of his mental or emotional condition. The privilege has no application in commitment proceedings so long as the proceedings do not entangle him in any criminal prosecution.") (citations omitted).
- *People ex rel. Keith v. Keith*, 231 N.E.2d 387, 390 (Ill. 1967) (person to be committed to a psychiatric hospital may be called to testify in his own commitment hearing because the proceeding is civil rather than criminal, and testimony revealing a psychiatric condition requiring confinement does not bring it within the privilege).

But cf. McNeil v. Dir., Patuxent Inst., 407 U.S. 254, 257 (1972) (Douglas, J., concurring) (asserting that the privilege against self-incrimination was applicable to involuntary commitment proceedings, even though they were normally labeled civil proceedings).

Most proceedings involving the imposition of civil monetary penalties:

- *United States v. Ward*, 448 U.S. 242, 251 (1980) (statute imposing civil monetary penalty for failure to file oil spill report was not criminal for purpose of the Self-Incrimination Clause of the Fifth Amendment).
- *Duncan v. Norton*, 974 F. Supp. 1328, 1331 (D. Colo. 1997) (refusing to find that proceeding to impose civil money penalties necessarily violated defendant's Fifth Amendment rights, reasoning that so long as penalties are rationally related to the statute's remedial purposes, they do not constitute an impermissible criminal sanction that threatens defendant's Fifth Amendment protections).

Professional disciplinary proceedings:

- *Roach v. Nat'l Transp. Safety Bd.*, 804 F.2d 1147, 1153–54 (10th Cir. 1986) (finding that proceeding involving revocation of a pilot's license is civil, stating, "[r]evocation of a pilot certificate is not an affirmative disability or restraint, but merely revocation of a privilege conditioned on compliance with the safety regulations of the FAA. Revocation of a privilege voluntarily granted is characteristically free of the punitive criminal element") (citation omitted).
- *In re Pressman*, 658 N.E.2d 156, 159 (Mass. 1995) (attorney may be disciplined solely on basis of testimony given under a federal grant of immunity because disciplinary case is civil, not criminal).
- *In re Anonymous Attorneys*, 362 N.E.2d 592, 596–97 (N.Y. 1977) (immunity granted to attorneys before grand jury did not preclude use of their grand jury testimony at attorney disciplinary hearings).

Proceedings found to constitute criminal proceedings or quasi-criminal proceedings for purposes of the Fifth Amendment include the following:

Juvenile delinquency commitment proceedings:

- *In re Gault*, 387 U.S. 1, 49 (1967) ("[P]roceedings to determine 'delinquency,' which may lead to commitment to a state institution, must be regarded as 'criminal' for purposes of the privilege against self-incrimination.").

Certain civil forfeiture proceedings:

- *Austin v. United States*, 509 U.S. 602, 608 n.4 (1993) (Self-Incrimination Clause, which is "limited to 'criminal cases,' has been applied in civil forfeiture proceedings, but only where the forfeiture statute has made the culpability of the owner relevant . . . or where the owner faced the possibility of subsequent criminal proceedings") (citations omitted).
- *See also Leonard v. Texas*, 137 S. Ct. 847 (2017) (Thomas, J., disagreeing with the denial of certiorari and suggesting that Texas civil forfeiture law, despite being intended as remedial, is in fact criminal in effect and subject to due process).
- *See also Bajakajian v. United States*, 524 U.S. 321, 334 (1998) (holding that forfeiture of $357,144, in connection with a conviction for illegally transporting cash out of the United States, violated the Excessive Fines Clause).
- *See also United States v. Ursery*, 518 U.S. 267 (1996) (*in rem* civil forfeiture is neither punishment nor criminal for purpose of Double Jeopardy Clause).
- *In the Matter of Property Seized from Jean Carlos Herrera and Fernando Rodrigues*, 912 N.W.2d 454 (Iowa 2018) (ruling that Fifth Amendment right against compelled self-incrimination applied in Iowa civil forfeiture proceedings).

Sex registration requirements:

Courts have struggled over whether certain states-sex offender registration laws are civil or criminal for the purpose of various constitutional protections. Although the Supreme Court held that Alaska's Sex Offender Registration Act was a civil remedy for purpose of the Ex Post Facto Clause in *Smith v. Doe*, 538 U.S. 84, 92 (2003), other courts have found other state's sex offender registration laws to be punitive in effect. *See, e.g.*, *Doe v. Snyder*, 834 F.3d 696, 705–06 (6th Cir. 2016) (holding that Michigan's Sex Offender Registration Act is punitive and violates the Ex Post Facto Clause); *Doe v. State*, 111 A.3d 1077, 1100 (N.H. 2015) (same as to New Hampshire law).

Certain guardianship proceedings:

- *In re A.G.*, 785 N.Y.S.2d 313, 315, 6 Misc. 3d 447, 450 (2004) (in an Article 81 proceeding to appoint a guardian for an allegedly incapacitated person, the Fifth Amendment prevented the state from compelling the respondent to testify as a witness).

Assertions of the Fifth Amendment Right Against Self-Incrimination in Non-Criminal Proceedings and the Consequences of Invoking and/or Remaining Silent

During Civil Cases

It has long been held that the Fifth Amendment privilege against self-incrimination may be invoked by parties (and witnesses) in civil proceedings. *See United States v. Saline Bank of Va.*, 26 U.S. 100, 104 (1828) ("The rule clearly is, that a party is not bound to make any discovery [in a civil case] which would expose him to penalties."). As long as the person can demonstrate that the testimony (or the act of producing documents) might incriminate the person in pending or future criminal proceedings, the invocation of the Fifth Amendment in civil proceedings is valid. *Pillsbury Co. v. Conboy*, 459 U.S. 248, 263–64 (1983) (self-incriminating testimony given in a civil deposition may not be compelled over a valid assertion of the Fifth Amendment privilege, unless such testimony has been immunized). The consequences of asserting one's Fifth Amendment right in a civil case are reviewed later in this chapter.

In a standard civil case filed and litigated pursuant to the Federal Rules of Civil Procedure or its state counterparts, a party may assert the privilege against self-incrimination at any stage of the proceedings. A party may refuse to answer specific allegations in a civil complaint (or counterclaims and other claims for affirmative relief) on the basis of the Fifth Amendment and have the assertion, if unchallenged or deemed proper, treated as a denial.

- *Rogers v. Webster*, 776 F.2d 607, 609 (6th Cir. 1985) (per curiam) (properly invoked claim of Fifth Amendment privilege in response to allegations in civil complaint should be treated as a denial).
- *de Antonio v. Solomon*, 42 F.R.D. 320, 322 (D. Mass. 1967) (court allowed defendant to assert Fifth Amendment privilege in his answer and treated it, and his subsequent similar invocations of the right, as a denial).

Courts usually deny a party in a civil case the right to assert the Fifth Amendment in a blanket fashion, requiring the asserting party to parse the allegations and differentiate between those that require the invocation of the Fifth Amendment and those that do not.

- *Mohamed v. Jeppesen Dataplan, Inc.*, 614 F.3d 1070, 1098 (9th Cir. 2010) (defendant was obliged to answer those allegations that he can and claim self-incrimination privilege to the rest).
- *United States v. Castro*, 129 F.3d 226, 229 (1st Cir. 1997) ("[t]he privilege cannot be invoked on a blanket basis" and the district court must conduct "a particularized inquiry" into each claim of privilege) (citations omitted).
- *North River Ins. Co. v. Stefanou*, 831 F.2d 484, 486 (4th Cir. 1987) ("[A] proper invocation of the [Fifth Amendment] privilege [does not] mean that a defendant is excused from the requirement to file a responsive pleading; he is obliged to answer those allegations that he can and to make a specific claim of the privilege as to the rest.") (citation omitted).
- *In re Livent, Inc. Noteholders Secs. Litig.*, 151 F. Supp. 2d 371, 443–44 (S.D.N.Y. 2001) (granting plaintiff's motion to strike defendant's blanket Fifth Amendment answer, but allowing defendant to provide supplemental answer that parsed allegations individually).
- *Indus. Indem. Co. v. Niebling*, 844 F. Supp. 1374, 1378 (D. Ariz. 1994) (requiring the defendant to file an amended answer after defendant's first answer contained only a blanket assertion of his Fifth Amendment right).

A party may refuse to answer questions posed in written discovery, such as interrogatories or requests for admission, on the basis of the Fifth Amendment.

- *United States v. Kordel*, 397 U.S. 1 (1970) (holding that a corporate vice president simultaneously prosecuted and sued by the Food and Drug Administration (FDA) in a civil enforcement action for the same events could have invoked his individual Fifth Amendment privilege against self-incrimination in response to FDA-propounded interrogatories).
- *Campbell v. Gerrans*, 592 F.2d 1054, 1057 (9th Cir. 1979) (upholding assertions of Fifth Amendment privilege against self-incrimination in response to interrogatories).
- *Gordon v. FDIC*, 427 F.2d 578, 581 (D.C. Cir. 1970) (reversing district court's denial of defendant's motion to strike the FDIC's request for admission and mentioning that while Federal Rule of Civil Procedure 36 "prevents the use of a response as evidence in a criminal case," court must determine on remand if defendant had proper basis to invoke privilege against self-incrimination).
- *Adelphia Commc'ns Corp. v. Rigas (In re Adelphia Commc'ns Corp.)*, 317 B.R. 612, 623–24 (Bankr. S.D.N.Y. 2004) ("[A] civil litigant may legitimately use the Fifth Amendment to avoid having to answer inquiries during any phase of the discovery process.").

As is the case in responding to factual allegations in pleadings, a party cannot generally refuse to answer all interrogatories or requests for admission, but must invoke the Fifth Amendment privilege only to those inquiries calling for self-incriminating answers and must be prepared to demonstrate how a response could constitute Fifth Amendment-protected information.

- *Davis v. Fendler*, 650 F.2d 1154, 1160 (9th Cir. 1981) (party must offer an explanation of why interrogatories could be incriminating).
- *SEC v. Zimmerman*, 854 F. Supp. 896, 898 (N.D. Ga. 1993) (approving defendant's specific claims of his Fifth Amendment privilege and

denying government's claim that defendant had improperly invoked a blanket privilege).

- *Guy v. Abdulla*, 58 F.R.D. 1, 2 (N.D. Ohio 1973) (defendant required to "make answers to interrogatories until there is a reasonable danger that continuing to answer will tend to incriminate him") (citations omitted).

There are cases in which courts have refused to accept an invocation of the Fifth Amendment privilege in civil pleadings or discovery responses signed only by counsel—on the basis that the Fifth Amendment is a personal right. However, such personal verification should not be required in federal courts. Federal Rule of Civil Procedure 11 authorizes an attorney to sign pleadings for matters asserted in good faith, and there is no exception for pleadings asserting the Fifth Amendment.

- *Garcia-Quintero v. Gonzales*, 455 F.3d 1006, 1019 n.10 (9th Cir. 2006) (recognizing circumstances in which an attorney's invocation of the Fifth on behalf of a client would be appropriate).
- *United States v. Johnson*, 752 F.2d 206, 210–11 (6th Cir. 1985) (recognizing in dicta that an attorney may assert a Fifth Amendment privilege on behalf of a client).

On the other hand, some defendants have successfully argued that they cannot be held to have waived their privilege against self-incrimination where their counsel signed a pleading containing potentially incriminating admissions.

- *ACLI Int'l Commodity Servs., Inc. v. Banque Populaire Suisse*, 110 F.R.D. 278, 287 (S.D.N.Y. 1986) (refusing to find that a party had waived the privilege against self-incrimination based upon averments contained in an answer that had not been verified by the party and instead had been signed only by counsel).

Where a corporation is a party to a civil case and its executives who have sufficient knowledge to answer interrogatories or request for admissions are asserting their personal Fifth Amendment rights, courts have required the corporation to appoint an agent, who, upon review of the corporate records, can respond as best as possible to the opposing party's inquiries. *See SEC v. A Chicago Convention Center LLC*, Memorandum Opinion and Order dated August 5, 2013 (N.D. Illinois, Judge Amy J. St. Eve) (denying SEC's motion to compel corporate defendant to require former employees living abroad to answer interrogatories for a corporate defendant whose primary officers were asserting the Fifth Amendment, but agreeing that corporation should appoint someone else to review records for purpose of answering SEC discovery requests).

As discussed in Chapter 8, the act of producing documents may incriminate. Therefore, a party may assert the Fifth Amendment in response to a request for the production of documents in a civil case and, correspondingly, a non-party may assert the Fifth Amendment in response to a civil subpoena calling for the production of documents.

- *SEC v. Waltzer & Assocs.*, No. 96–6261, 1997 WL 561062, at *3 (2d Cir. Sept. 10, 1997) (overruling third party's objection to producing documents in response to SEC subpoena on basis that act of production was not sufficiently incriminating in this case).
- *de Antonio v. Solomon*, 42 F.R.D. 320, 323–24 (D. Mass. 1967) (granting deposition witness's motion to quash subpoena for production of her passport based on her privilege against self-incrimination).

However, courts are reluctant to grant a motion to quash a subpoena directed to a third party in its entirety on the basis of a blanket Fifth Amendment assertion, or to allow a blanket objection on the basis of the Fifth Amendment privilege to a request for documents to a party. Rather, the court may require a log justifying the assertion of the Fifth Amendment act of production privilege for each document or category of documents.

- *Waymo LLC v. Uber Technologies, Inc.*, Order Denying Motion to Modify Privilege Log Requirements Based on Fifth Amendment, N.D. Cal., Apr. 10, 2017 (corporation required to serve detailed privilege log despite objection of a third-party individual who was asserting his Fifth Amendment rights).

- *United States v. Grable*, 98 F.3d 251, 257 (6th Cir. 1996) (district court should individually review *in camera* any documents to which a summoned party raises a Fifth Amendment objection).
- *SEC v. Caramadre*, 717 F. Supp. 2d 217, 224 (D.R.I. 2010) (denying respondents' refusal to respond to SEC request for production of documents and requiring them to provide a privilege log listing documents they would withhold on Fifth Amendment grounds).
- *United States v. Carlin*, No. 06–1906, 2006 WL 2619800, at *1 (E.D. Pa. Sept. 11, 2006) (endorsing use of a privilege log to establish application of Fifth Amendment).
- *Toler v. United States*, No. 2:01-MS-004, 2003 WL 21255039, at *6 (S.D. Ohio Apr. 29, 2003) (denying motion to quash IRS subpoena when party refused to produce privilege log).
- *United States v. Bell*, 217 F.R.D. 335, 337–38 (M.D. Pa. 2003) (utilizing *in camera* review to determine whether documents to be produced pursuant to government summons were subject to Fifth Amendment protection).
- *Starlight Int'l, Inc. v. Herlihy*, 181 F.R.D. 494, 498 (D. Kan. 1998) (rejecting defendants' blanket objection in response to all document requests and directing them to produce a privilege log).
- *In re Astor*, 62 A.D.3d 867, 870 (N.Y. App. Div. 2009) (proper procedure is for the party asserting that the Fifth Amendment protects the production of documents "to establish a factual predicate" by completing a privilege log).
- *Tona, Inc. v. Evans*, 590 A.2d 873, 876–77 (R.I. 1991) (requiring witness to provide sufficient factual basis for the invocation of the Fifth Amendment privilege as it applies to each document request).

Because such a document-by-document description risks revealing Fifth Amendment-protected information, parties or witnesses should consider requesting that the court enter a protective order restricting access to the privilege log.

- *In re Syncor ERISA Litig.*, 229 F.R.D. 636, 649 (C.D. Cal. 2005) (denying motion to compel production of privilege log where defendant argued that "the mere production of the log would violate his privilege against self-incrimination in light of the Government's ongoing investigation of his actions").

Indeed, where the demand for document production is broad and seeks to require the responding party to identify which documents might be responsive, instead of merely seeking the production of documents specifically identified in the demand for production, parties should consider requesting that no privilege log be required. The creation in these cases of the privilege log itself admits both to the existence and the possession of the documents by the respondent, admissions that, as Chapter 8 notes, are protected by the Fifth Amendment. The Supreme Court reasoned in *United States v. Hubbell*, 530 U.S. 27, 41 (2000), that "the collection and production of the materials demanded was tantamount to answering a series of interrogatories" that turns the creation of the privilege log into protected Fifth Amendment testimony. A judge may even grant a motion to avoid creating a Fifth Amendment privilege log. *See, e.g.*, Report & Recommendations of Magistrate Judge at 11–17, *SEC v. Chin*, Civil Action No. 12-cv-01336-PAB-BNB, 2012 (D. Colo. Nov. 29, 2012) and *In re Fustolo*, No. 13–12692-JNF, 2015 WL 9595421, at *5 (Bankr. D. Mass. Dec. 31, 2015).

A party or a witness may refuse to respond to questions at a deposition on the basis of the Fifth Amendment privilege against self-incrimination.

- *Pillsbury Co. v. Conboy*, 459 U.S. 248, 263–64 (1983) (a deponent's civil deposition testimony, which closely tracks his prior immunized testimony, may not be compelled over a valid claim of his Fifth Amendment right).
- *West Virginia ex. Rel. Wright v. Honorable James C. Stucky*, 517 S.E.2d 36 (W. Va. 1999) (Court of Appeals reversed district court order that required deponent to answer questions by virtue of being granted use without derivative use immunity and that imposed a protective order, neither of which was deemed adequate).
- *Andover Data Servs., Inc. v. Statistical Tabulating Corp.*, 876 F.2d 1080, 1084–85 (2d Cir. 1989) (reversing district court order that sought to compel witness to testify in civil case by imposing protective order that prevented government from obtaining deposition

testimony, holding that a protective order did not adequately shield the witness from prosecution's potential use of testimony).

- *Anton v. Prospect Café Milano, Inc.*, 233 F.R.D. 216, 219–20 (D.D.C. 2006) (defendant who was under investigation had a legitimate fear of prosecution and could invoke his Fifth Amendment privilege during his deposition).
- *In re J.M.V., Inc.*, 90 B.R. 737, 741–42 (Bankr. E.D. Pa. 1988) (president of debtor corporation properly asserted Fifth Amendment at deposition taken by trustee).

Again, the deponent must generally appear and refuse to answer those specific questions posing a danger of incrimination and, if challenged, demonstrate to a court the reasonable basis for fearing incrimination from the answers.

- *District Title v. Warren*, 265 F. Supp. 3d 17 (D.D.C. 2017) (requiring witness to appear for deposition and assert self-incrimination privilege on question-by-question basis).
- *Hansen v. Wwebnet*, 2017 WL 1032268 (S.D.N.Y. Mar. 16, 2017) (Carter, J.) (denying motion to compel further deposition testimony after reviewing transcript in which witness declined to answer specific questions based on valid Fifth Amendment claim).
- *United States v. Highgate*, 521 F.3d 590, 594 (6th Cir. 2008) (finding that the district court "erred by not inquiring into the legitimacy or scope of [a witness's] claimed privilege," where the witness made a blanket assertion of his privilege).
- *Nat'l Life Ins. Co. v. Hartford Accident & Indem. Co.*, 615 F.2d 595, 596 (3d Cir. 1980) (holding that "a witness in a civil proceeding may not invoke a blanket fifth amendment privilege prior to the propounding of questions").
- *Coushatta Tribe of La. v. Abramoff*, No. 07–1886, 2009 WL 2406303, at *3–5 (E.D. La. July 31, 2009) (finding witness had properly invoked his Fifth Amendment rights in a deposition concerning insurance coverage, even though he had been granted immunity by certain federal authorities and had pled guilty, when he was still subject to state prosecution and was awaiting sentencing).

- *United States v. Hansen*, 233 F.R.D. 665, 667–68 (S.D. Cal. 2005) (defendant cannot refuse to attend a deposition by invoking a blanket Fifth Amendment privilege).
- *Francis v. Wynn Las Vegas, LLC*, 262 P.3d 705, 709–10 (Nev. 2011) (upholding lower court's grant of summary judgment against a defendant on all claims based on the defendant's blanket and overbroad assertion of the Fifth Amendment during his deposition, and warning that parties must first seek alternative means of protecting their client's rights against self-incrimination before using a broad-brush approach to assertions of the privilege).

Although *Griffin v. California*, 380 U.S. 609 (1965), determined it would be improper to call a criminal defendant to the stand or to comment on a defendant's refusal to testify, the courts are divided on whether it is proper in a civil case for a party to require the opposing party to invoke the privilege against self-incrimination in front of the jury. *Compare Fisher v. Hooper*, 732 A.2d 396, 404–05 (N.H. 1999) (error for trial court to have allowed party to call her husband to take the stand and invoke his privilege against self-incrimination in front of the jury) *with Cerro Gordo Charity v. Fireman's Fund Am. Life Ins. Co.*, 819 F.2d 1471, 1482 (8th Cir. 1987) (not improper for plaintiff to call defendant to stand for purposes of having him invoke his Fifth Amendment privilege). Similarly, the case law does not support a claim that the witness's intent to assert his Fifth Amendment right against self-incrimination automatically justifies the witness not taking the stand and responding to examination in a civil case.

- *FDIC v. Fid. & Deposit Co. of Md.*, 45 F.3d 969, 978 (5th Cir. 1995) ("[R]efus[ing] to adopt a rule that would categorically bar a party from calling, as a witness, a non-party who had no special relationship to the party, for the purpose of having that witness exercise his Fifth Amendment right.").
- *Rosebud Sioux Tribe v. A & P Steel, Inc.*, 733 F.2d 509, 522 (8th Cir. 1984) (In a civil case, "a party may call a witness to the stand even when that witness has made known an intention to invoke the Fifth Amendment.").

- *SEC v. MacElvain*, 417 F.2d 1134, 1137–38 (5th Cir. 1969) (witness's right against self-incrimination is not violated by forcing him to take the stand as an adverse witness in an enforcement action).

During Administrative Proceedings and Agency Investigations
The Supreme Court has applied the privilege against self-incrimination to administrative proceedings before both state and federal agencies. In *Murphy v. Waterfront Commissioner of New York Harbor*, 378 U.S. 52 (1964), for instance, a state administrative body propounded questions to a witness regarding certain labor activities. After the witness refused to answer on the basis of the Fifth Amendment privilege, the agency sought to hold the witness in contempt. The Supreme Court vacated the resulting contempt judgment, holding that the privilege against self-incrimination applied in the administrative proceeding. Other Supreme Court cases have upheld the assertion of the Fifth Amendment privilege in response to agency subpoenas or during administrative hearings.

- *Ohio Adult Parole Auth. v. Woodard*, 523 U.S. 272, 285–86 (1998) (applying Fifth Amendment to testimony before clemency board).
- *Garrity v. New Jersey*, 385 U.S. 493, 494–95 (1967) (applying Fifth Amendment to testimony before a state attorney general).
- *Petition for Groban*, 352 U.S. 330, 333 (1957) (deciding that the Fifth Amendment privilege is available in administrative investigations).
- *Smith v. United States*, 337 U.S. 137, 141–45 (1949) (applying Fifth Amendment to testimony before the federal Office of Price Administration).

The law regarding the assertion of the Fifth Amendment in administrative proceedings is similar to the law regarding assertions of the Fifth Amendment in civil litigation. For instance, a respondent may not assert a blanket privilege to avoid appearing at an administrative proceeding or to avoid responding to proper discovery in an administrative adjudicative hearing, at least not without suffering adverse consequences.

- *United States v. Drollinger*, 80 F.3d 389, 392 (9th Cir. 1996) (per curiam) (taxpayer confronted with a summons to appear for examination and to produce documents must present himself for questioning and elect to raise the Fifth Amendment on a question-by-question basis).

- *United States v. Lazar*, No. 04–20017-DV, 2006 WL 3761803, at *9–11 (W.D. Tenn. Dec. 20, 2006) (denying Fifth Amendment challenge to federal health care fraud statute authorizing prosecutors to issue administrative subpoena seeking documents).
- *United States v. Garza*, No. 94A00011, 1994 WL 479265, at *10 (O.C.A.H.O. 1994) (in an administrative proceeding alleging respondent knowingly hired undocumented workers, judge required respondent to file statements supporting each Fifth Amendment-based objection to each request for admission and interrogatory, explaining how a response might have a tendency to incriminate her).

During Legislative Proceedings

Numerous commentators have questioned whether the Fifth Amendment should apply in congressional hearings and investigations. For example, after Enron executives invoked the Fifth Amendment privilege in congressional hearings not to answer questions about the company's collapse, Yale constitutional law professor Akhil Reed Amar wrote that the privilege should not be available in congressional proceedings. Akhil Reed Amar, *Taking the Fifth Too Often*, N.Y. Times (Feb. 18, 2002), http://www.nytimes.com/2002/02/18/opinion/taking-the-fifth-too-often.html. Professor Amar argued that "[t]he Fifth Amendment prohibits a person from being compelled to be a witness against himself in any 'criminal case,' but a congressional hearing is hardly a criminal case." *Id.*

Professor Amar's position notwithstanding, it is well established that the Fifth Amendment applies to congressional proceedings whenever the witness may reasonably fear that compelled congressional testimony will subsequently be used in a criminal case. In the companion cases *Quinn v. United States*, 349 U.S. 155, 162–64 (1955), *Emspak v. United States*, 349 U.S. 190, 202 (1955), and *Bart v. United States*, 349 U.S. 219, 221–22 (1955), each of which involved contempt prosecutions of labor leaders who invoked the Fifth Amendment and refused to answer various questions posed by the House Un-American Activities Committee, the Supreme Court upheld the right to assert the privilege in questioning before congressional committees. In *Quinn*, the Supreme Court addressed whether the Fifth Amendment applies to congressional proceedings, stating that "limitations on [Congress's] power to investigate are found in the specific individual guarantees of the Bill of Rights, such as the Fifth Amendment's privilege against self-incrimination." 349 U.S. at 161. The Court then held that because the congressional witness may have incriminated himself by answering the committee's questions about his alleged membership in the Communist Party, he "was entitled to claim the privilege." *Id.* at 162. A few years later, in *Watkins v. United States*, 354 U.S. 178, 188 (1957), the Supreme Court reiterated that the "Bill of Rights is applicable to [congressional] investigations as to all forms of governmental action," and that "[w]itnesses cannot be compelled to give evidence against themselves." The Court also pointed out that in *Quinn*, *Emspak*, and *Bart*, "the Government did not chellenge [*sic*] in any way that the Fifth Amendment protection was available to the witness[es], and such a challenge could not have prevailed." *Id.* at 196.

Indeed, in *Adams v. Maryland*, 347 U.S. 179 (1954), the Supreme Court reversed a defendant's conviction where testimony he gave before a Senate committee was used to convict him. The Court reasoned that his Senate testimony was compelled by an immunity statute that failed to grant him "complete immunity" under the then-applicable requirements of *Counselman v. Hitchcock*. Inherent in the Court's decision was the recognition that the Fifth Amendment applied in congressional proceedings.

Not only have the Supreme Court and lower courts allowed the Fifth Amendment privilege against self-incrimination to be asserted in congressional proceedings, but, since at least 1857, Congress has also passed immunity statutes protecting witnesses from the use of their incriminating testimony against them in criminal cases. The current immunity statute contains a provision for the granting of immunity for testimony before both Houses of Congress and their committees as follows.

> (a) In the case of any individual who has been or may be called to testify or provide other information at any proceeding before or ancillary to either House of Congress, or any committee, or any subcommittee of either House, or any joint committee of the two

Houses, a United States district court shall issue, in accordance with subsection (b) of this section, upon the request of a duly authorized representative of the House of Congress or the committee concerned, an order requiring such individual to give testimony or provide other information which he refuses to give or provide on the basis of his privilege against self-incrimination, such order to become effective as provided in section 6002 of this title.

(b) Before issuing an order under subsection (a) of this section, a United States district court shall find that—

(1) in the case of a proceeding before or ancillary to either House of Congress, the request for such an order has been approved by an affirmative vote of a majority of the Members present of that House;

(2) in the case of a proceeding before or ancillary to a committee or a subcommittee of either House of Congress or a joint committee of both Houses, the request for such an order has been approved by an affirmative vote of two-thirds of the members of the full committee; and

(3) ten days or more prior to the day on which the request for such an order was made, the Attorney General was served with notice of an intention to request the order.

18 U.S.C. § 6005.

Both federal and state courts have long recognized the applicability of the Fifth Amendment privilege, or analogous state constitutional provisions, to state and local legislative inquiries.

- *Raley v. Ohio*, 360 U.S. 423, 426–27 (1959) (recognizing the right to assert Fifth Amendment by witnesses appearing before Ohio Un-American Activities Commission).
- *Doyle v. Hofstader*, 177 N.E. 489, 496, 257 N.Y. 244, 263–64 (1931) (Cardozo, J.) (New York has recognized that the privilege against self-incrimination is applicable in legislative proceedings, despite its non-application in the British House of Commons).
- *In re Emery*, 107 Mass. 172, 185–86 (1871) (Massachusetts Declaration of Rights provision against compelled self-incrimination

prevented prosecution of witness for refusing to give answers to legislative committee's questions regarding alleged bribery among state police).

The method of invoking the privilege against self-incrimination during legislative proceedings and the congressional remedies for seeking to hold the person invoking the privilege in contempt are discussed in Chapter 4.

During Responses to Government Reporting Demands

In our highly regulated society, persons are required to file forms and to answer questions posed by government officials in numerous contexts. The remark of Justice Frankfurter in 1948, dissenting in *Shapiro v. United States*, 335 U.S. 1, 51 (1948), that "virtually every major public law enactment . . . has record-keeping provisions" is even more true today. Although the Fifth Amendment will rarely form a basis for refusing either to file a form altogether or to answer all questions posed by the government for legitimate regulatory purposes, one may appropriately assert the privilege in response to government inquiries and demands in the same manner as in judicial proceedings, if the answer would constitute compelled self-incrimination.

For instance, while the requirement that citizens file annual tax returns does not itself violate the privilege against self-incrimination (even if all or part of the income was derived from criminal activity), *United States v. Sullivan*, 274 U.S. 259, 263–64 (1927), an objection based on the Fifth Amendment may be upheld to specific inquiries on a tax return.

- *Garner v. United States*, 424 U.S. 648, 660–61 (1976) (although the defendant could have asserted his Fifth Amendment privilege when asked his occupation, having failed to do so the tax return in which the defendant identified himself as a professional gambler was properly admitted into evidence).
- *Grosso v. United States*, 390 U.S. 62, 67 (1968) (reversing a conviction for willful failure to pay a wagering excise tax and willful failure to file with the IRS a form reporting wagering income because the

"petitioner's submission of an excise tax payment, and his replies to questions on the attendant [form], would directly and unavoidably have served to incriminate him").

Interestingly, the assertion of a Fifth Amendment privilege on a tax return cannot subject the taxpayer to a frivolous return penalty. *See, e.g., Youssefzadeh v. Commissioner*, No. 14868–14-L (T.C. Nov. 6, 2015) (granting defendant summary judgment in action by IRS seeking to impose frivolous tax return penalty under section 6702(a) where defendant selectively asserted self-incrimination privilege).

There is a disagreement about whether a taxpayer may refuse to disclose not only the source of his income but also the amount, if the amount alone would be incriminatory.

Compare

- *United States v. Edwards*, 777 F.2d 644, 651 (11th Cir. 1985) (a taxpayer may decline to state the amount of his income in "the limited circumstances . . . when the amount alone might have incriminated him").
- *United States v. Barnes*, 604 F.2d 121, 148 (2d Cir. 1979) ("[T]he right to make a [v]alid claim of privilege is available even as to amount of a taxpayer's income, as well as any other item on the return which could legitimately cause self-incrimination.").
- *United States v. Paepke*, 550 F.2d 385, 394 (7th Cir. 1977) (Tone, J., concurring) (stating that the defendant could "have declined to state even the amount of his income if that fact alone might have tended to incriminate him") (citations omitted).

with

- *United States v. Shivers*, 788 F.2d 1046, 1049 (5th Cir. 1986) ("[T]he *amount* of a taxpayer's income is not privileged even though the *source* of income may be.") (quoting *United States v. Wade*, 585 F.2d 573, 574 (5th Cir. 1978)).

- *United States v. Pilcher*, 672 F.2d 875, 877 (11th Cir. 1982) ("Although the source of income might be privileged, the amount must be reported.") (citing *Wade*, 585 F.2d at 574).
- *United States v. Brown*, 600 F.2d 248, 252 (10th Cir. 1979) ("A careful reading of *Sullivan* and *Garner*, therefore, is that the self-incrimination privilege can be employed to protect the taxpayer from revealing the information as to an illegal source of income, but does not protect him from disclosing the amount of his income.") (citation omitted).

The Supreme Court does not apply a "liberal construction" of the Fifth Amendment to regulatory reporting enactments directed to the public at large, such as tax returns. Instead, the Court has upheld many types of regulatory reporting statutes against Fifth Amendment challenges, despite the hazards the statutes pose for compelling self-incriminating disclosures.

In *California v. Byers*, 402 U.S. 424, 433–34 (1971), for instance, a divided Court sustained the constitutionality of a statute that required the driver of an automobile involved in an accident to stop and give his name and address. Four members of the Court determined that, because the purpose of the statute was to promote the satisfaction of civil liabilities resulting from automobile accidents and not criminal prosecutions, the possibility of incrimination was slight. The four dissenters, in two separate opinions, argued that while neither stopping nor providing identification were incriminating per se, compliance with the statute required drivers to disclose that they were the driver of an automobile involved in an accident, which disclosure could provide "a link in the chain of testimony" in a later prosecution. *Id.* at 459 (citation omitted). Justice Harlan, whose concurrence supplied the crucial fifth vote for upholding the statute, disagreed with the plurality's conclusion that the stop and identification requirement did not compel incrimination. However, he reasoned that because the government was pursuing legitimate regulatory interests rather than seeking to enforce a criminal law, it was permissible to apply a balancing test between the government's interest and the interest protected by the Fifth Amendment. Based on the balancing test, Justice Harlan reasoned that the mere possibility of incrimination was "insufficient to defeat the strong policies in favor of disclosure called for by the statutes like the one challenged here." *Id.* at 428.

Other Supreme Court decisions apply a similar reasoning.

- *Hiibel v. Sixth Jud. Dist. Ct. of Nev.*, 542 U.S. 177, 190–91 (2004) (Self-Incrimination Clause did not apply to Nevada's "stop and identify" statute, because there was not sufficient showing of reasonable fear of incrimination given the regulatory purposes involved for individuals to identify themselves when asked to do so by the police).
- *Balt. City Dep't of Soc. Servs. v. Bouknight*, 493 U.S. 549, 555–56 (1990) (mother who refused to produce child at demand of Department of Social Services, even though the production might incriminate her, "may not invoke the privilege . . . because production is required as part of a non-criminal regulatory regime").
- *Shapiro v. United States*, 335 U.S. 1, 32–33 (1948) (upholding statute that compelled potentially self-incriminating product pricing information be provided to the government because of the essentially non-criminal and regulatory purposes promoted).

On the other hand, where the government reporting requirement compelling a self-incriminating disclosure is "directed at a highly selective group inherently suspect of criminal activities," the Supreme Court has struck such requirements as violative of the Fifth Amendment, on the theory that the purpose of the reporting requirement is simply to entrap individuals into making self-incriminatory admissions. *Byers*, 402 U.S. at 429.

- *Albertson v. Subversive Activities Control Bd.*, 382 U.S. 70, 78 (1965) (an order pursuant to a statute requiring registration by individual members of the Communist Party violated the Fifth Amendment, because responding to any of the form's questions would involve the party in admitting to an element of a crime).
- *Marchetti v. United States*, 390 U.S. 39, 42 (1968) (striking down a gambling tax reporting statute as violative of the Fifth Amendment

because the obligation to register and pay the occupational tax would necessarily compel a self-incriminating statement).

- *Haynes v. United States*, 390 U.S. 85, 101 (1968) (reversing a conviction for failing to register a firearm that was illegal to possess on the grounds that the Fifth Amendment protected such compelled self-incrimination).
- *Leary v. United States*, 395 U.S. 6, 29 (1969) (finding that plea of self-incrimination provided a complete defense to charge of noncompliance with transfer tax provisions of the Marihuana Tax Act).

See also

- *Dep't of Revenue v. Kurth Ranch*, 511 U.S. 767, 805 (1994) (affirming decision that Montana's efforts "to collect a tax on the possession of drugs was the functional equivalent of a successive criminal prosecution" barred by the Double Jeopardy Clause of the Fifth Amendment).

To determine which reporting requirements fall on the side of the line offending the Fifth Amendment right against self-incrimination and those that do not, the Supreme Court established a three-factor test in *Albertson v. Subversive Activities Control Board*, 382 U.S. 70 (1965). This test requires courts to evaluate whether the reporting requirement (1) is aimed at "a highly selective group inherently suspect of criminal activit[y]"; (2) is "asserted in an essentially . . . regulatory area of inquiry"; and (3) "create[s] a substantial likelihood of prosecution." *See, e.g.*, *United States v. Adair*, No. 88–1264, 1988 WL 114791, at *2 (6th Cir. Oct. 31, 1988) (citation omitted).

Although the test may be criticized as arbitrary and unworkable, the following decisions illustrate the application of this three-factor test by lower courts:

- *United States v. Juvenile Male*, 670 F.3d 999, 1011 (9th Cir. 2012) (citing cases from other circuits, court rejected Fifth Amendment challenge to sex offender registration requirement on basis that having already pled guilty to the sex offense, the registration requirement did not require incrimination).

- *United States v. Garcia-Cordero*, 610 F.3d 613, 615 (11th Cir. 2010) (ruling that an immigration law requiring that persons transporting undocumented aliens into the United States immediately report to immigration officials did not violate the privilege against self-incrimination).
- *Bionic Auto Parts & Sales Inc. v. Fahner*, 721 F.2d 1072, 1083 (7th Cir. 1983) (statute requiring auto parts dealers to keep records of altered, defaced, or removed serial numbers violated the Fifth Amendment rights of sole proprietors).
- *In re Grand Jury Subpoena Duces Tecum*, 368 F. Supp. 2d 846, 856–57 (W.D. Tenn. 2005) (quashing grand jury subpoena requiring production of records pertaining to performers in sexually explicit films, on basis that statute requiring records to be kept of every model or performer, including his or her date of birth, was part of a criminal enforcement scheme directed at persons suspected of criminal activities involving child pornography).

The so-called required records doctrine, described by the foregoing cases and further discussed in Chapter 8, is a particularly slippery doctrine in which the end results appear to be driven more by policy than by the Fifth Amendment. Despite the argument that the Fifth Amendment does not authorize courts to craft exceptions based on their evaluation of the usefulness of the government demands in promoting law enforcement, the required records doctrine shows no signs of losing its strength.

Legal Consequences of Asserting the Fifth Amendment in Non-Criminal Cases

The Adverse Inference

In *Baxter v. Palmigiano*, 425 U.S. 308, 318–20 (1976), the Supreme Court upheld the use of an adverse inference based on a prisoner's Fifth Amendment refusal to testify in a prison disciplinary hearing. While recognizing that neither a judge nor a jury can consider a defendant's

Fifth Amendment assertion in criminal cases in reaching their verdicts, *Baxter* held that prison officials could infer from the inmate's Fifth Amendment assertion that he had committed the disciplinary infraction charged, as long as that was not the sole basis upon which the discipline was imposed. *See also Ohio Adult Parole Auth. v. Woodard*, 523 U.S. 272 (1998) (adverse inference permissible from silence in clemency proceeding, which is not part of the criminal case).

Because *Baxter* arose in the context of a proceeding concerning the internal administration of prisons, an arena in which the Supreme Court has consistently shown decision makers substantial deference, the decision could be viewed as a very narrow one. However, the Supreme Court supported its decision by referencing the "prevailing rule" that the Fifth Amendment does not forbid adverse inferences against parties when they refuse to testify in non-criminal cases. *Baxter*, 425 U.S. at 318 ("Our conclusion is consistent with the prevailing rule that the Fifth Amendment does not forbid adverse inferences against parties to civil actions when they refuse to testify in response to probative evidence offered against them. . . ."). Therefore, *Baxter v. Palmigiano* has become the leading case cited for allowing the use of an adverse inference in any proceeding other than a criminal case. Almost every federal circuit has recognized the ability of a fact-finder to draw from a Fifth Amendment-based refusal to testify (or to produce documents over which the party has control) the inference that, had the invoking party testified, the testimony would have been unfavorable to that party. *See also LiButti v. United States*, 178 F.3d 114, 120 (2d Cir. 1999) ("[A]n adverse inference may be given significant weight because silence when one would be expected to speak is a powerful persuader.") (citing *United States ex rel. Bilokumsky v. Tod*, 263 U.S. 149, 153–54 (1923)). But an adverse inference is always subject to exclusion under Federal Rule of Evidence 403, and failure to conduct an analysis of whether the probative value of the advance inference is outweighed by the danger of unfair prejudice can itself be reversible error. *See, e.g., Woods v. START Treatment & Recovery Ctrs., Inc.*, 864 F.3d 158, 171 (2d Cir. 2017). Whether to allow an adverse inference is, therefore, always subject to judicial discretion.

- *Hinojosa v. Butler*, 547 F.3d 285, 291–92 (5th Cir. 2008) (holding that the lower court abused its discretion in excluding evidence of a party's invocation of the Fifth Amendment during discovery).
- *United States v. Stein*, 233 F.3d 6, 16 (1st Cir. 2000) (noting, in dicta, that the Massachusetts Board of Bar Overseers was allowed to draw an adverse inference from defendant's Fifth Amendment-based silence).
- *Curtis v. M&S Petroleum, Inc.*, 174 F.3d 661, 674 (5th Cir. 1999) (plaintiffs were entitled to an adverse inference instruction against the defendant corporation based on the corporate representative's invocation of his Fifth Amendment privilege).
- *LaSalle Bank Lake View v. Seguban*, 54 F.3d 387, 390 (7th Cir. 1995) ("The rule that adverse inferences may be drawn from Fifth Amendment silence in civil proceedings has been widely recognized by the circuit courts of appeals, including our own, in the two decades since *Baxter* was decided.") (citations omitted).
- *Evans v. Robbins*, 897 F.2d 966, 970 (8th Cir. 1990) (finding that a negative inference may be allowed when the defendant refuses to produce documents known to be in his possession on the basis of the Fifth Amendment).
- *RAD Servs., Inc. v. Aetna Cas. & Sur. Co.*, 808 F.2d 271, 277–78 (3d Cir. 1986) (no error for court to allow jury to draw adverse inference against parties who refuse to answer based on the Fifth Amendment when faced with probative evidence against them).

Most state courts agree that neither the Fifth Amendment nor their equivalent state constitutional provisions forbid the use of an adverse inference in non-criminal cases, and many states have enacted rules of evidence or statutes allowing it in civil cases generally or in specific types of actions.

- *Lentz v. Metro. Prop. & Cas. Ins. Co.*, 768 N.E.2d 538, 541–45 (Mass. 2002) (where court finds the witness is acting on behalf of and to further the interests of one of the parties, his assertion of the privilege against self-incrimination may be used as an adverse inference).

- *Olin Corp. v. Castells*, 428 A.2d 319, 321 (Conn. 1980) (the Fifth Amendment privilege against self-incrimination does not "forbid the drawing of adverse inferences against parties to civil actions. . . .").
- *See also* Alaska R. Evid. § 512(d); Minn. Stat. § 518c.316(g); Pa. Stat. § 23–7316(g); Maine Rev. Stat. § 19–3016.7.

However, some states forbid the adverse inference in civil cases. *People v. Holloway*, 33 Cal. 4th 96, 131, 91 P.3d 164 (Cal. App. 2004) ("California law, then, makes no distinction between civil and criminal litigation concerning adverse inferences from a witness's invocation of the privilege against self-incrimination. . . .").

The adverse inference is available in civil cases in which the government is a party in the same fashion as it is between private litigants, there being no requirement that the government extend immunity to the opposing party with a valid Fifth Amendment privilege in order to obtain his or her testimony in a civil case.

- *SEC v. Jasper*, 678 F.3d 1116, 1126 (9th Cir. 2012) ("As properly instructed, the jury could have concluded that the sum total of [Jasper's] Fifth Amendment invocations supported the adverse inference against him.").
- *SEC v. Cherif*, 933 F.2d 403, 417 (7th Cir. 1991) (allowing the trial judge to draw an adverse inference from defendant's refusal to submit to an accounting that would allegedly show misuse of funds).
- *SEC v. DiBella*, No. 3:04 CV 1342 (EBB), 2007 WL 1395105, at *5 (D. Conn. May 8, 2007) (permitting plaintiff's counsel in an enforcement action to read to the jury the questions defendant refused to answer during an investigative deposition taken seven years earlier, and instructing the jury that it may, but need not, draw an adverse inference from the assertions).
- *United States v. Bonanno Organized Crime Family of La Cosa Nostra*, 683 F. Supp. 1411, 1451 (E.D.N.Y. 1988) (denying the defense argument that adverse inferences should not be drawn because the

government is a party and has the power to grant immunity against future prosecutions).

The adverse inference may even be used against a party in a civil case based on a non-party's exercise of the Fifth Amendment privilege against self-incrimination. Where the court finds that the witness asserting the Fifth Amendment privilege is acting on behalf of or to further the interests of another party—often in the case of former employees of a corporate party—courts will generally, but not always, allow an adverse inference against the party.

- *Coquina Investments v. TD Bank, N.A.*, 760 F.3d 1300 (11th Cir. 2014) (trial court did not abuse its discretion by allowing plaintiff to call a non-party, a former bank employee, as a witness in order to have him exercise his Fifth Amendment right and permitting the jury to draw an adverse inference from his assertion).
- *LiButti v. United States*, 107 F.3d 110, 122–23 (2d Cir. 1997) (suggesting relevant factors to consider in deciding admissibility of non-party's invocation of Fifth Amendment privilege and whether adverse inferences may consequently be drawn against the party).
- *Brink's Inc. v. City of N.Y.*, 717 F.2d 700, 710 (2d Cir. 1983) (refusal of past and present employees to answer questions based on their Fifth Amendment privilege supports an adverse inference against the corporation for which they worked).
- *In re Urethane Antitrust Litig.*, No. 04–1616-JWL, 2013 WL 100250, at *1–3 (D. Kan. Jan. 8, 2013) (court applied the factors from *LiButti* and determined that the adverse inference was not appropriate in a case where seven former Bayer employees had asserted the Fifth Amendment privilege in a case against Dow Chemical for price-fixing concerning urethane chemical products).
- *Brookridge Funding Corp. v. Aquamarine, Inc.*, 675 F. Supp. 2d 227, 234 (D. Mass. 2009) (although court recognized that an adverse inference may be drawn against a party based on the assertion of the Fifth Amendment privilege of a person who was neither an officer, employee, nor former employee of the corporate

party, the court reasoned that the plausible inferences from the witness's assertion of privilege are too varied to allow an adverse inference in the case).

- *In re Tableware Antitrust Litig.*, No. C-04–3514 VRW, 2007 WL 781960, at *5 (N.D. Cal. Mar. 13, 2007) (denying company motion to exclude reference to former CEO's testimony in which he invoked his Fifth Amendment right).

Although the Fifth Amendment does not prohibit an adverse inference against a party asserting the privilege in a non-criminal proceeding, there is no requirement that the fact-finder accept the adverse inference. Indeed, the standard adverse inference jury instruction informs the jury that it may, but need not, infer that a refusal to answer on the basis of the Fifth Amendment means that the answers would have been adverse to the asserting party's position.

- *Pyles v. Johnson*, 136 F.3d 986, 997 (5th Cir. 1998) ("However, the fact that the Fifth Amendment does not prohibit such inferences does not imply that the fact-finder is required to make them.").
- *Farace v. Indep. Fire Ins. Co.*, 699 F.2d 204, 210–11 (5th Cir. 1983) (refusing to reverse trial judge's decision to exclude evidence regarding a prior invocation of the Fifth Amendment because it had limited probative value).

Given that an innocent person can legitimately invoke the Fifth Amendment privilege, the prejudicial effect of the adverse inference may often exceed its probative value, thereby justifying a court rejecting the ability of a party to either reference the witness's Fifth Amendment invocation or attempt to argue the adverse inference to the jury, as an evidentiary matter.

- *Mitchell v. United States*, 562 U.S. 314, 329 (1999) (in holding that drawing an adverse inference against a defendant at sentencing was an impermissible burden on the exercise of the right against self-incrimination, the Court commented that laymen "too readily assume that those who invoke [the privilege against self-incrimination] are either guilty of crime or commit perjury in claiming the privilege").

- *Harrell v. DCS Equip. Leasing Co.*, 951 F.2d 1453, 1464–65 (5th Cir. 1992) (recognizing that "the potential prejudice in revealing [a prior] invocation of the Fifth Amendment is high, because the jury may attach undue weight" given the legitimate reasons for an innocent person to decline to testify).
- *United States ex rel. DRC, Inc. v. Custer Battles, LLC*, 415 F. Supp. 2d 628, 634 (E.D. Va. 2006) (rejecting adverse inference as to the Fifth Amendment assertion to numerous questions as cumulative and unfairly prejudicial, but permitting the adverse inference as to Fifth Amendment assertions to three specific questions).
- *In re WorldCom, Inc. Secs. Litig.*, No. 02 CIV 3288 DLC, 2005 WL 375315, at *5 (S.D.N.Y. Feb. 17, 2005) (warning against "potential for lawyer abuse when the examining attorney effectively testifies for the witness who is invoking the [Fifth Amendment] privilege" by posing fact-specific questions that would invite jurors to give weight to the questions based on the adverse inference from the refusal to answer).
- *In re Citric Acid Litig.*, 996 F. Supp. 951, 961 (N.D. Cal. 1998) (where witness invoked his Fifth Amendment right to every question asked during deposition, the "testimony" was irrelevant pursuant to Federal Rule of Civil Procedure 403).
- *Pereira v. Aetna Cas. & Sur. Co. (In re Payroll Express Corp.)*, 216 B.R. 344, 364–65 (S.D.N.Y. 1997) (relative youth of witness and lack of evidence of relationship with plaintiff precluded adverse inference from witness's assertion of the Fifth Amendment).
- *Ullman-Briggs, Inc. v. Salton/Maxim Housewares, Inc.*, Nos. 92 C 680, 92 C 2394, 1996 WL 535083, at *17 (N.D. Ill. Sept. 17, 1996) (refusing to allow an adverse inference to be drawn from a blanket invocation of the Fifth Amendment during a deposition because it was "impossible" to draw a negative inference in regard to any particular question).
- *Cavalier Clothes, Inc. v. Major Coat Co.*, No. CIV.A. 89–3325, 1995 WL 314511, at *6 (E.D. Pa. May 18, 1995) (finding the use of an

adverse inference to be constitutionally impermissible when counsel deposed witness, knowing that he would invoke the Fifth Amendment, and there was no independent evidence of fraud).

- *In re Handy & Harman Refining Grp., Inc.*, 266 B.R. 32, 34–35 (Bankr. D. Conn. 2001) (finding that a non-party—corporation's former comptroller—did not have sufficiently close relationship with corporation to justify adverse inference from his assertion of the Fifth Amendment privilege).
- *Lentz v. Metropolitan Property & Casualty Ins. Co.*, 437 Mass. 23, 28, 768 N.E.2d 538 (2002) ("Ultimately the test is whether any adverse inference sought is reasonable, reliable, relevant to the dispute, and fairly advanced against a party.").

Two criminal cases addressing the use of a defendant's prior silence to impeach subsequent testimony provide support for the exclusion (particularly in a civil enforcement action brought by the government) of an adverse inference based on a Fifth Amendment assertion. In *Grunewald v. United States*, 353 U.S. 391, 416 (1957), one of the defendants (Halperin) asserted his Fifth Amendment privilege when called before the grand jury, despite insisting on his innocence. Halperin was subsequently indicted and testified in his own defense. The government then cross-examined him on his prior assertions of the privilege to impeach his credibility. After the jury convicted, Halperin appealed on the basis that the cross-examination was improper. The Supreme Court agreed with Halperin and ruled that his previous silence was not a prior inconsistent statement. While acknowledging that "the question whether a prior statement is sufficiently inconsistent . . . is usually within the discretion of the trial judge," the Supreme Court explained that the potential for unfair prejudice from a jury's consideration of prior silence "far outweighed" the probative value of the assertion. *Id.* at 423–24. The Court thus elected to exercise its supervisory power to reverse the conviction.

Similarly, in *United States v. Hale*, 422 U.S. 171, 180–81 (1975), applying *Grunewald*, the Supreme Court held that the defendant's silence in the face of police questioning was not probative and carried significant potential for prejudice, thereby warranting the reversal of conviction where the defendant was cross-examined about his prior silence. The Court reasoned:

> Not only is evidence of silence at the time of arrest generally not very probative of a defendant's credibility, but it also has a significant potential for prejudice. The danger is that the jury is likely to assign much more weight to the defendant's previous silence than is warranted. And permitting the defendant to explain the reasons for his silence is unlikely to overcome the strong negative inference that the jury is likely to draw from the fact that the defendant remained silent at the time of his arrest.

Id. at 180. The Court considered the evidentiary error made by the lower court to have "grave constitutional overtones" and thereby exercised its supervisory power to reverse the conviction. *Id.* at n.7 (citation omitted). *See also United States v. Zaccaria*, 240 F.3d 75, 79 (1st Cir. 2001) (relying on *Hale*'s discussion of the inadmissibility of the defendant's silence in deciding that district judge did not abuse his discretion in excluding evidence that a witness had been silent after having been advised of his constitutional rights).

The reasoning in these cases demonstrates that the refusal to testify often has little probative value and that its use—whether to impeach or to support an adverse inference—must be carefully evaluated. Even when the adverse inference is allowed, it is usually an insufficient basis upon which to enter judgment against a party. Most courts require independent evidence of liability before deciding the case against the party asserting a Fifth Amendment right.

- *In re Marrana*, 445 F.3d 518, 522–23 (1st Cir. 2006) (expressing reservations, but declining to decide whether an adverse inference may be taken on summary judgment, where the standard requires the court to take all reasonable inferences in the non-moving party's favor).
- *Stichting Ter Behartiging Van de Belangen v. Schreiber*, 407 F.3d 34, 55 (2d Cir. 2005) ("Even assuming that a jury might draw [an adverse inference], however, we are required at summary judgment to draw all reasonable inferences in favor of the non-moving party. . . .").

- *Doe ex rel. Glanzer v. Glanzer*, 232 F.3d 1258, 1264 (9th Cir. 2000) ("[L]ower courts interpreting *Baxter* have been uniform in suggesting that the key to the *Baxter* holding is that such adverse inference can only be drawn when independent evidence exists of the fact to which the party refuses to answer.") (citations omitted).
- *United States v. Stelmokas*, 100 F.3d 302, 311 (3d Cir. 1996) (silence alone, without other evidence, is insufficient to support a decision against the defendant).
- *LaSalle Bank Lake View v. Seguban*, 54 F.3d 387, 394 (7th Cir. 1995) (court may not enter summary judgment solely on adverse inferences drawn from Fifth Amendment privilege asserted in response to discovery).
- *In re McCormick*, 49 F.3d 1524, 1527 (11th Cir. 1995) (a bankruptcy court may not deny confirmation of reorganization plan solely because debtor asserted Fifth Amendment privilege against self-incrimination in discovery).
- *Koester v. Am. Republic Invs., Inc.*, 11 F.3d 818, 823–24 (8th Cir. 1993) (overturning award of punitive damages because the award was based only on defendant's invocation of his Fifth Amendment rights, and had no other supporting evidence).
- *Nat'l Acceptance Co. of Am. v. Bathalter*, 705 F.2d 924, 932 (7th Cir. 1983) (reversing district court's entry of judgment on pleadings after defendant asserted the Fifth Amendment to several averments in complaint, holding that Fifth Amendment claim was not an admission and that judgment could not rest solely on constitutionally protected silence).
- *Anderson v. City of Rockford*, 2018 WL 2332066 at *15 (N.D. Ill. May 23, 2018) (ruling that the adverse inference drawn against a police officer who asserted the privilege against self-incrimination about fabricating a defendant's statement was not enough, in the absence of other evidence, to support summary judgment).
- *Parsons & Whittemore Enters. Corp. v. Schwartz*, 387 F. Supp. 2d 368, 371–72 (S.D.N.Y. 2005) (court declined to draw adverse inference from defendant's assertion of Fifth Amendment privilege for

purposes of summary judgment, where it was required to draw all reasonable inferences in favor of the defendant).

- *Fid. Funding of Cal., Inc. v. Reinhold*, 79 F. Supp. 2d 110, 116–17 (E.D.N.Y. 1997) ("The propriety of drawing an inference against the defendants . . . is especially problematic in the context of a motion for summary judgment, where a court is admonished to construe all evidence, including the defendants' silence, in a light most favorable to the non-moving party.") (citation omitted).
- *Akers v. Prime Succession of Tenn., Inc.*, 387 S.W.3d 495, 506 (Tenn. 2012) ("[I]n instances when there is no corroborating evidence to support the fact under inquiry, no negative inference is permitted.").

Interestingly, at least one court has required that a party receive advance notice that an adverse inference may be drawn from the exercise of the right to remain silent, although the decision was based on policy, rather than constitutional, considerations.

- *In re Samatha C.*, 847 A.2d 883, 920–21 (Conn. 2004) (trial court is required to give advance notice to parents facing termination of their parental rights of the prospect that an adverse inference might be drawn from their refusal to testify on Fifth Amendment grounds at the termination hearing).

One area where an adverse inference is particularly problematic is in asset forfeiture proceedings, which have been held in some circumstances to be quasi-criminal for Fifth Amendment purposes. Thus, some courts have been reluctant to allow the United States an adverse inference from a forfeiture claimant's invocation of the Fifth Amendment privilege against self-incrimination.

- *United States v. Real Prop. Known & Numbered as Rural Route 1, Box 137-B*, 24 F.3d 845, 851 (6th Cir. 1994) (per curiam) (ruling that adverse inferences from assertion of Fifth Amendment right is unwarranted in asset forfeiture cases, reasoning that such cases are more closely related to criminal sanctions).

- *United States v. Prop. Located at 15 Black Ledge Drive*, 897 F.2d 97, 103 (2d Cir. 1990) (expressing concern about allowing use of adverse inference in case involving forfeiture of a home).
- *United States v. $57,790.00 in U.S. Currency*, No. 01cv414 BTM (NLS), 2007 WL 433198, at *10 (S.D. Cal. Jan. 29, 2007) (expressing concern about allowing use of adverse inference in case involving forfeiture of cash).

However, some courts have imposed consequences even more burdensome than an adverse inference on a claimant in an asset forfeiture proceeding who asserts the Fifth Amendment privilege. Given that forfeiture proceedings often accompany criminal investigations, these decisions appear to penalize the Fifth Amendment assertions unnecessarily.

- *United States v. $133,420.00 in U.S. Currency*, 672 F.3d 629, 641 (9th Cir. 2012) (upholding the striking of claimant's interrogatory response asserting ownership and possession of seized currency, where claimant asserted her privilege against self-incrimination in response to questions regarding details of ownership).
- *United States v. $148,840 in U.S. Currency*, 521 F.3d 1268, 1277 (10th Cir. 2008) (approving grant of summary judgment to government where claimant failed to offer evidence on a matter on which he had the burden of proof by virtue of asserting the Fifth Amendment).
- *United States v. Two Parcels of Real Prop. Located in Russell County, Ala.*, 92 F.3d 1123, 1129 (11th Cir. 1996) (granting summary judgment of forfeiture of several pieces of property, and denying argument that rules regarding invocation of the Fifth Amendment in criminal cases should apply).
- *United States v. Certain Real Prop. & Premises Known as 4003–4005 5th Ave., Brooklyn, N.Y.*, 55 F.3d 78, 83 (2d Cir. 1995) (affirming order barring submission of evidence offered in forfeiture action by claimants who asserted Fifth Amendment in discovery).

- *In re 650 Fifth Avenue & Related Properties*, 2017 WL 2214869 (S.D.N.Y. May 18, 2017) (refusing to allow former members of claimant's board to retract invocations of the Fifth Amendment during discovery and permitting government to call the invoking witnesses at trial or to play their videotaped depositions in order to permit the jury to assess their demeanor in deciding whether or not to draw the adverse inference).
- *United States v. $11,500.00 in U.S. Currency*, 797 F. Supp. 2d 1092, 1099 (D. Or. 2011) (granting motion to strike declaration of claimant's wife, offered to explain an innocent source of funds, where wife invoked the Fifth Amendment privilege on that issue in her deposition), *aff'd in part on other grounds, rev'd in part on other grounds* 710 F.3d 1006 (9th Cir. 2013).

In 2000, the federal civil forfeiture statute, 18 U.S.C. § 981, was amended to grant a court the authority to stay a civil forfeiture proceeding at the request of the claimant if "(A) the claimant is the subject of a related criminal investigation or case, (B) the claimant has standing to assert a claim in the civil forfeiture proceeding, and (C) continuation of the forfeiture proceeding will burden the right of the claimant against self-incrimination in the related [criminal] investigation or case." The stay of the civil forfeiture case is mandatory if the claimant has satisfied the elements of section 981, and stays in civil forfeiture actions are now more common. *See, e.g.*, *United States v. The Real Property Known as 212 East 47th Street, Apt. 4E, New York, New York*, 2017 WL 1496931, at *5 (D.N.J. Apr. 25, 2017).

It is worth noting here that courts have struggled over the issue of whether a party may assert the Fifth Amendment privilege in a non-criminal proceeding without having an adverse inference used against him if he subsequently testifies. The "easy" case is where the proceedings are separate proceedings—a doctrine discussed in Chapter 8.

- *Fujisawa Pharms. Co. v. Kapoor*, No. 92 C 5508, 1999 WL 543166, at *9 (N.D. Ill. July 21, 1999) (assertion of the privilege against self-incrimination in a congressional hearing did not warrant an adverse inference in a later civil case in which the defendant testified).

The harder case is where a person invokes the privilege against self-incrimination at one stage of a proceeding but later waives the privilege and testifies—presumably eliminating the probative value of the adverse inference. Nonetheless, some courts have allowed an adverse inference to be drawn in a civil action where the defendant who testified at a later stage had earlier asserted his Fifth Amendment privilege against self-incrimination. In *SEC v. DiBella*, No. 3:04 CV 1342 (EBB), 2007 WL 1395105 (D. Conn. May 8, 2007), for instance, the court granted the motion by the Securities and Exchange Commission (SEC) for an adverse inference instruction based on DiBella's assertion of the Fifth Amendment at the investigative stage deposition, even though he testified at the subsequent civil enforcement deposition. In that case, the court found that the SEC had been prejudiced by the inability to gather the facts earlier, especially because, at his civil case deposition, DiBella consistently testified that he did not recall the answers to questions due to the passage of time. The fact that DiBella testified in the subsequent civil proceeding did not protect him from an adverse inference being drawn from his Fifth Amendment assertion in the prior investigative stage of the case. *See also SEC v. Herman*, No. 00 Civ. 5575 (PKC) (MHD), 2004 WL 964104, at *7 (S.D.N.Y. May 5, 2004) (drawing a negative inference from the defendants' assertion of the Fifth Amendment "during the course of the SEC's investigation" even though they "later testified in deposition in this case" because "their prior use of the Fifth Amendment privilege . . . is relevant to our inquiry and lends further support to the evidentiary case presented by the SEC"); *SEC v. Cassano*, No. 99 Civ. 3822 (LAK), 2000 WL 1512617, at *2 n.1 (S.D.N.Y. Oct. 11, 2000) (in drawing a negative inference from the defendants' assertion of the Fifth Amendment during an SEC investigation, the court explained that the defendants' subsequent waiver of the privilege "in this action goes to the weight of the inference, not to the propriety of drawing it"); *but cf. SEC v. BIH Corp.*, 5 F. Supp. 3d 1342, 1347 (M.D. Fla. 2014) (the court declines to draw the requested adverse inference where the defendant took the Fifth in the investigation stage, but subsequently submitted to being deposed); *SEC v. Freiberg*, No. 2:05-CV-00233 PGC, 2007 WL 2692041, at *2 & n.1 (D. Utah Sept. 12, 2007) (declining to draw an adverse inference from the defendant's assertion of the privilege against self-incrimination during the SEC investigative stage).

Other Consequences of Asserting the Fifth Amendment in Non-Criminal Proceedings

The adverse inference is only one consequence that courts have applied to a party's assertion of the privilege against self-incrimination in a non-criminal proceeding. Numerous courts have imposed more serious sanctions, particularly where the Fifth Amendment appears to have been used for tactical advantage. These sanctions include dismissing the asserting party's claims for affirmative relief, precluding the asserting party from submitting evidence related to subjects for which the privilege has been raised, or striking testimony given by the asserting party. While courts rarely impose such harsh sanctions on parties asserting common law privileges that deprive their adversaries of otherwise relevant evidence, few courts appear to question the legitimacy of imposing such sanctions on a civil litigant whose otherwise valid assertion of the Fifth Amendment similarly deprives the opposing party of relevant evidence. Rather, courts express the following concern: "[T]he protective shield of the Fifth Amendment should [not] be converted into a sword. . . ." *United States v. Hastings*, 461 U.S. 499, 515 (1983) (Stevens, J., concurring). *See also United States v. Rylander*, 460 U.S. 752, 758 (1983) (noting that the lower court had converted the privilege "from the shield against compelled self-incrimination which it was intended to be into a sword whereby a claimant asserting the privilege would be freed from adducing proof in support of a burden which otherwise would have been his. None of our cases support this view.").

Similarly colorful language appears in other cases.

- *Gutierrez-Rodriguez v. Cartagena*, 882 F.2d 553, 577 (1st Cir. 1989) ("A defendant may not use the fifth amendment to shield herself from the opposition's inquiries during discovery only to impale her accusers with surprise testimony at trial.") (citation omitted).

- *Lyons v. Johnson*, 415 F.2d 540, 542 (9th Cir. 1969) ("The scales of justice would hardly remain equal in these respects, if a party can assert a claim against another and then be able to block all discovery attempts against him by asserting a Fifth Amendment privilege to any interrogation whatsoever upon his claim.").
- *Jones v. B.C. Christopher & Co.*, 466 F. Supp. 213, 227 (D. Kan. 1979) ("Plaintiff should not be able to have his cake and eat it too.") (internal quotation marks omitted).
- *State v. Terry*, 339 S.C. 352, 529 S.E.2d 274, 277 (2000) (one cannot "use his fifth amendment privilege against self-incrimination as both a sword and a shield").

Dismissal of claims for affirmative relief has long been a judicial response to a party's assertion of the Fifth Amendment. Divorce cases provide a common forum for such decisions.

- *Davis v. Davis*, 357 S.E.2d 495, 498, 233 Va. 452, 457 (1987) (a moving party "who exercises his privilege against self-incrimination to refuse to answer questions pertinent to the issues involved will have his complaint dismissed upon timely motion") (citations omitted).
- *Minor v. Minor*, 240 So. 2d 301, 302 (Fla. 1970) (approving trial court order which "compel[led] the plaintiff wife in a divorce action to answer over objections invoking the Fifth Amendment protection against self-incrimination certain pretrial deposition questions relating to the husband's counterclaim of adultery, or suffer dismissal of her complaint").
- *Christenson v. Christenson*, 162 N.W.2d 194, 204 (Minn. 1968) (ruling that plaintiff wife must either waive her privilege against self-incrimination or have her action dismissed).

The dismissal of claims for affirmative relief is, however, a strong sanction for the invocation of a constitutionally based privilege, and the better-reasoned decisions require courts to consider other alternatives first.

- *McMullan v. Bay Ship Mgmt.*, 335 F.3d 215, 216, 218–19 (3d Cir. 2003) (district court should consider sanctions less severe than dismissal of plaintiff's suit for his refusal to respond to interrogatories and his refusal to respond to request for documents on Fifth Amendment grounds).
- *Wehling v. CBS*, 608 F.2d 1084, 1088 (5th Cir. 1979) ("When plaintiff's silence is constitutionally guaranteed, dismissal is appropriate only where other, less burdensome remedies would be an ineffective means of preventing unfairness to the defendant.").
- *Steiner v. Minn. Life Ins. Co.*, 85 P.3d 135, 143 (Colo. 2004) (en banc) (reversing trial court's dismissal of a doctor's breach of contract suit, where doctor had invoked his privilege against self-incrimination during discovery, and requiring trial judge to engage in analysis to determine if any other remedy short of dismissal could be imposed).
- *Texas Dep't of Pub. Safety Officers Ass'n v. Denton*, 897 S.W.2d 757, 763 (Tex. 1995) (trial court erred by dismissing plaintiff's suit for unlawful termination where, after plaintiff refused to respond to certain discovery requests based on his right against self-incrimination, court failed to consider less burdensome remedies).
- *Wohlstrom v. Buchanan*, 884 P.2d 687, 693 (Ariz. 1994) (error to dismiss claimant's action to contest forfeiture, where claimant refused to answer questions beyond the mere fact that he owned the $127,000 in seized currency).
- *Hackes v. Hackes*, 446 A.2d 396, 399 (D.C. 1982) (when a litigant invokes the Fifth Amendment to prevent discovery, sanctions may be imposed, but striking a pleading should be the last resort).
- *Robinson v. Robinson*, 615 A.2d 1190, 1194–97 (Md. 1992) (wife's invocation of Fifth Amendment right in refusing to answer question about alleged adultery warranted adverse inference, but did not preclude her from testifying or presenting evidence regarding her fitness as parent in custody proceeding, and decision to award her custody was not abuse of discretion).

When a defendant asserts the right against compelled self-incrimination, usually in discovery, courts have imposed various other sanctions short of dismissal, including prohibiting the defendant from asserting affirmative defenses, submitting evidence, or later testifying on matters related to the subjects as to which the privilege was asserted.

- *United States v. $133,420.00 in U.S. Currency*, 672 F.3d 629, 644 (9th Cir. 2012) (court did not err in striking claimant's interrogatory responses where claimant refused on basis of Fifth Amendment privilege to answer questions about the basis for her claim to assets to be forfeited).
- *Nationwide Life Ins. Co. v. Richards*, 541 F.3d 903, 911 (9th Cir. 2008) (district court properly precluded the defendant wife from testifying about her lack of involvement in the murder of her husband because she had asserted her privilege against self-incrimination during her deposition).
- *United States v. Certain Real Prop.*, 55 F.3d 78, 86–87 (2d Cir. 1995) (district court did not abuse discretion in ruling that claimant to property subject to forfeiture was barred from submitting material previously withheld on basis of Fifth Amendment privilege).
- *In re Vitamins Antitrust Litig.*, 120 F. Supp. 2d 58, 72 (D.D.C. 2000) (striking affidavit in support of defendant's motion to dismiss for lack of jurisdiction, where defendant asserted the Fifth in response to jurisdictional discovery).
- *Meyer v. Second Jud. Dist. Ct. of Nev.*, 591 P.2d 259, 263 (Nev. 1979) (ex-wife was prohibited from testifying at custody hearing after asserting Fifth Amendment in response to questions at deposition about her purchase of drugs and her use of drugs at home).

The SEC has been a particularly aggressive proponent of sanctioning defendants who assert the privilege against self-incrimination during discovery in civil injunctive actions brought by the SEC. Although the federal securities laws also carry criminal sanctions, courts have imposed preclusion orders against defendants who invoke the Fifth Amendment during SEC civil enforcement proceedings.

- *SEC v. Benson*, 657 F. Supp. 1122, 1129 (S.D.N.Y. 1987) (precluding defendant from "offering evidence in support of . . . positions on which he has declined to furnish disclosure" because he claimed his privilege under the Fifth Amendment).

- *SEC v. Cymaticolor Corp.*, 106 F.R.D. 545, 550 (S.D.N.Y. 1985) (issuing an order precluding the defendant from offering into evidence any matter relating to the factual basis for his denials and defenses as to which he had asserted his Fifth Amendment rights).

These remedies, however, are also subject to question. For instance, in *SEC v. Greystone Nash, Inc.*, 25 F.3d 187, 192 (3d Cir. 1994), the court reversed a district judge who prevented defendants from submitting any evidence to contest summary judgment after they had asserted their Fifth Amendment right during discovery depositions. While recognizing that a belated assertion of the privilege on the eve of trial could justify such harsh sanctions, the court reasoned:

> A trial court must carefully balance the interests of the party claiming protection against self-incrimination and the adversary's entitlement to equitable treatment. Because the privilege is constitutionally based, the detriment to the party asserting it should be no more than is necessary to prevent unfair and unnecessary prejudice to the other side.

Id. at 192. *See also Evans v. City of Chi.*, 513 F.3d 735, 743 (7th Cir. 2008) (allowing the defendant to testify at trial despite having asserted the Fifth Amendment at his deposition).

Similarly, in *SEC v. Monterosso*, 746 F. Supp. 2d 1253, 1264 (S.D. Fla. 2010), the court refused to strike a defendant's affirmative defenses, reasoning that the defendant already risked the imposition of an adverse inference from his invocation of the privilege and that striking affirmation defenses was too drastic a sanction.

A practical issue that must often be considered by a party asserting the Fifth Amendment privilege against self-incrimination is the risk to his or her insurance coverage. A carrier that can demonstrate prejudice may be entitled to deny coverage, according to various courts, when an insured invoked the Fifth Amendment in examinations under oath and at trial in violation of the insurance policy's cooperation clause.

- *Med. Protective Co. v. Bubenik*, 594 F.3d 1047, 1053 (8th Cir. 2010) (dentist who was sued for malpractice was properly denied insurance coverage by virtue of his asserting the Fifth Amendment at trial of the malpractice case and refusing to submit to examination by the insurer).
- *United States Fid. & Guar. Co. v. Wigginton*, 964 F.2d 487, 490–91 (5th Cir. 1992) (an insured whose property was destroyed by fire and who was charged with second-degree arson was properly denied fire insurance coverage for refusing to submit to an examination on Fifth Amendment grounds).
- *Aetna Cas. & Sur. Co. v. State Farm Mut. Auto Ins. Co.*, 771 F. Supp. 704 (W.D. Pa. 1991), *aff'd* 961 F.2d 207 (3d Cir. 1992) (requiring the insurer to prove not only that the insured's assertion of the Fifth Amendment privilege violated the cooperation clause but that the insurer suffered substantial prejudice).

Although the general rule is that an individual who asserts a Fifth Amendment right against self-incrimination in response to questions or requests for information from an insurer will be considered in breach of the standard cooperation clause and not entitled to coverage, at least one court has created an exception where the insurer was required by statute to turn over to prosecutors the information it gathered from the insured. In *Weathers v. American Family Mutual Insurance Co.*, 793 F. Supp. 1002, 1022 (D. Kan. 1992), the court held that an insurer could not rely upon an insured's refusal to answer its questions about a mysterious fire at her home to deny coverage, when the insurer was required to provide all arson-related information it obtained to prosecutors.

Ultimately, what, if any, sanctions should be imposed on a party asserting the Fifth Amendment privilege in civil litigation is a matter of discretion and depends upon a careful balancing of prejudice to the opposing party and the rights of the invoking party.

- *In re Carp*, 340 F.3d 15, 23 (1st Cir. 2003) ("[I]n a civil proceeding, the drawing of a negative inference is a permissible but not an ineluctable, concomitant of a party's invocation of the Fifth

Amendment. . . . When all is said and done, the trial court has discretion over whether a negative inference is an appropriate response to the invocation of the Fifth Amendment in a particular civil case.") (internal citations omitted).

- *FDIC v. Fid. & Deposit Co. of Md.*, 45 F.3d 969, 977 (5th Cir. 1995) (holding it appropriate for a court to use a balancing test under Federal Rule of Evidence 403 to determine if an adverse inference should properly be drawn against an insurer based on the insured's assertion of the Fifth Amendment privilege).
- *SEC v. Colello*, 139 F.3d 674, 677 (9th Cir. 1988) (holding that the lower courts are free to fashion whatever remedy is required to prevent unfairness when the invocation of the privilege prejudices another party).

Granting Stays in Civil Cases During Parallel Criminal Proceedings

When a party is facing parallel civil and criminal cases, courts may stay the civil proceedings to protect him from having to choose between invoking his Fifth Amendment privilege and suffering an adverse inference or other consequence, or having to testify, exposing him to potential self-incrimination in the criminal case. In the Enron investigation, for instance, former Enron CFO Andrew Fastow asked the district court to shield him from having to testify in any of the civil cases pending against him and others until the parallel criminal proceedings were resolved. The district court granted the motion, and issued a stay postponing discovery directed to Fastow until resolution of his criminal liability. *In re Enron Corp. Secs., Derivative & "ERISA" Litig.*, No. MDL No. 1446, 2003 WL 25508889, at *9 (S.D. Tex. Mar. 25, 2003).

While courts rarely stay an entire case, it is not unusual to stay civil discovery during parallel criminal investigations at the request of the defendant.

- *SEC v. HealthSouth Corp.*, 261 F. Supp. 2d 1298, 1316 (N.D. Ala. 2003) (granting stay of civil proceedings against former CEO Scrushy, noting that the defendant should not be "placed in the precarious position of either waiving his Fifth Amendment rights" or asserting the privilege and losing the civil proceeding).

- *In re Adelphia Commc'ns Secs. Litig.*, No. 02–1781, 2003 WL 22358819, at *3 (E.D. Pa. May 13, 2003) (discussing reasons why criminal proceedings militate in favor of a stay of parallel civil proceedings).
- *Walsh Secs., Inc. v. Cristo Prop. Mgmt., Ltd.*, 7 F. Supp. 2d 523, 529 (D.N.J. 1998) (granting defense motion to stay interrogatory and deposition discovery).
- *Volmar Distribs., Inc. v. N.Y. Post Co.*, 152 F.R.D. 36, 42 (S.D.N.Y. 1993) (staying discovery until criminal case had been resolved).
- *White v. Mapco Gas Prods., Inc.*, 116 F.R.D. 498, 501–03 (E.D. Ark. 1987) (staying discovery until grand jury completed its investigation).
- *Ex parte Rawls*, 953 So. 2d 374, 387 (Ala. 2006) (issuing writ of mandamus granting the husband's motion to stay divorce proceedings until the criminal stalking charge brought by his wife was finally adjudicated).

However, a defendant has no constitutional right to stay a parallel civil proceeding pending the outcome of the related criminal action or investigation. *SEC v. Dresser Indus., Inc.*, 628 F.2d 1368, 1375 (D.C. Cir. 1980) (en banc). Rather, the decision to stay a civil proceeding lies with the discretion of the court, and depends on the particular status of the civil and criminal proceedings. *United States v. Kordel*, 397 U.S. 1, 11–13 (1970).

In determining whether a stay should be entered, federal courts generally employ a balancing test using the following six factors: (1) the extent to which issues in the criminal case overlap those presented in the civil case; (2) the status of the criminal case, including whether the defendant has been indicted; (3) the private interests of the plaintiff in proceeding expeditiously versus the prejudice to the plaintiff caused by the delay; (4) the private interests of, and burden on, the defendant; (5) the interests of the court; and (6) the public's interest.

- *Louis Vuitton Malletier S.A. v. LY USA, Inc.*, 676 F.3d 83, 98–100 (2d Cir. 2012) (collecting cases applying both a six-factor and a five-factor test, deciding that matter of a stay is left to judicial exercise of discretion).

- *Keating v. Office of Thrift Supervision*, 45 F.3d 322, 324–25 (9th Cir. 1995) (discussing five-factor test for determining whether a stay of the civil case is appropriate).
- *In re CFS-Related Secs. Fraud Litig.*, 256 F. Supp. 2d 1227, 1236–37 (N.D. Okla. 2003) (applying a fact-specific examination of the factors to determine that a stay of all discovery was inappropriate).
- *In re Worldcom, Inc. Secs. Litig.*, No. 02 Civ. 3288 (DLC), 2002 WL 31729501, at *3–4 (S.D.N.Y. Dec. 5, 2002) (examining factors to determine that it was appropriate to stay proceedings regarding certain parties).
- *Trs. of Plumbers & Pipefitters Nat'l Pension Fund v. Transworld Mech., Inc.*, 886 F. Supp. 1134, 1139–41 (S.D.N.Y. 1995) (balancing interests to approve stay).
- *Arden Way Assocs. v. Boesky*, 660 F. Supp. 1494, 1496–97 (S.D.N.Y. 1987) ("In weighing these factors the courts are mindful that a policy of issuing stays 'solely because a litigant is defending simultaneous multiple suits would threaten to become a constant source of delay and an interference with judicial administration.' Thus, '[a]bsent a showing of undue prejudice upon defendant or interference with his constitutional rights, there is no reason why plaintiff[s] should be delayed in [their] efforts to diligently proceed to sustain [their] claim.'" (quoting *Paine, Webber, Jackson & Curtis, Inc. v. Malus S. Andrus, Inc.*, 486 F. Supp. 1118, 1119 (S.D.N.Y. 1980)).
- *Golden Quality Ice Cream Co. v. Deerfield Specialty Papers, Inc.*, 87 F.R.D. 53, 56–59 (E.D. Pa. 1980) (denying a stay after considering factors, but refusing to allow "unfettered discovery" until the criminal trial was completed).

State courts and administrative agencies often use the same framework.

- *Aspen Fin. Servs. v. Eighth Judicial Dist. Court*, 289 P.3d 201, 206–08 (Nev. 2012) (refusing stay after applying five-factor test).

- In the Matter of Civil Investigative Demands To Nordic Clinical, Inc. & Encore Plus Solutions, Inc., Dated March 9, 2018, FTC, April 27, 2018 (denying stay after applying five-factor test).

Where the issues in the criminal case significantly overlap those presented in the civil case, a stay is more likely, since the risk of self-incrimination is more obvious.

- *In re Worldcom, Inc. Secs. Litig.*, No. 02 Civ. 3288 (DLC), 2002 WL 31729501, at *4 (S.D.N.Y. Dec. 5, 2002) ("The first question to be resolved is the extent to which the issues in the criminal case overlap with those present in the civil case, since self-incrimination is more likely if there is a significant overlap.") (citations omitted).

But cf.

- *In re CFS-Related Secs. Fraud Litig.*, 256 F. Supp. 2d 1227, 1237, 1242 (N.D. Okla. 2003) (court decided that "less drastic measures" than a stay could adequately protect defendants' interests despite "a complete overlap of issues present in the criminal and civil cases.")

In analyzing the status of the criminal case, courts focus primarily on whether the defendant has been indicted.

- *CFTC v. A.S. Templeton Grp., Inc.*, 297 F. Supp. 2d 531, 534 (E.D.N.Y. 2003) ("Pre-indictment requests for a stay of civil proceedings are generally denied.") (citation omitted).
- *Sterling Nat'l Bank v. A-1 Hotels Int'l, Inc.*, 175 F. Supp. 2d 573, 576 (S.D.N.Y. 2001) ("[D]istrict courts in this Circuit 'generally grant the extraordinary remedy of a stay only after the defendant seeking a stay has been indicted.'").
- *Volmar Distribs., Inc. v. N.Y. Post Co.*, 152 F.R.D. 36, 39 (S.D.N.Y. 1993) ("The strongest case for granting a stay is where a party under criminal indictment is required to defend a civil proceeding involving the same matter.").

- *In re Par Pharm. Inc. Secs. Litig.*, 133 F.R.D. 12, 13–14 (S.D.N.Y. 1990) ("The weight of authority in this Circuit indicates that courts will stay a civil proceeding when the criminal investigation has ripened into an indictment, . . . but will deny a stay of the civil proceeding where no indictment has issued.") (citations omitted).

Pre-indictment requests for a stay of civil proceedings are frequently denied, whereas post-indictment requests for a stay are more frequently granted.

- *Roberts v. Brown*, No. 2–13-CV-07461, 2014 WL 3503094 (C.D. Cal. July 14, 2014) ("[T]here is a strong case in favor of a stay after a grand jury returns a criminal indictment. . . .") (citing cases).
- *Bryer v. Jefferson et al.*, 2013 WL 3753420, at *1 (D. Del. July 8, 2013) (granting motion for stay after defendant was indicted).
- *In re Anicom Inc. Secs. Litig.*, No. 00 C 4391, 2002 WL 31496212, at *2–3 (N.D. Ill. Nov. 8, 2002) (denying stay of proceedings where defendants faced only a threat of indictment).
- *State ex rel. Okla. Bar Ass'n v. Gasaway*, 863 P.2d 1189, 1197–98 (Okla. 1993) (denying respondent's request for a stay of disciplinary proceedings pending resolution of criminal proceeding arising from the same matter, noting that respondent had no constitutional right to prevent the fact-finder from considering his refusal to testify).

The chances of the court issuing a pre-indictment stay increase where the prosecutor seeks the stay. In *In re Worldcom, Inc. Securities Litigation*, a securities fraud case, the government requested a stay as to the officer defendants, arguing that the stay would (1) prevent discovery in the civil case from being used to circumvent discovery limitations in the criminal case; (2) encourage witness cooperation in criminal proceedings; and (3) preserve defendants' assets as a source of payment of potential restitution orders. 2002 WL 31729501, at *8–9. The court granted the government's request. Conversely, the court denied a stay for the underwriter and director defendants, where the government did not join in the request submitted by those defendants.

Similar decisions include the following:

- *SEC v. Chestman*, 861 F.2d 49, 50 (2d Cir. 1988) (denying defendant's petition for a writ of mandamus seeking to overturn stay of civil proceedings granted at government's request).
- *Campbell v. Eastland*, 307 F.2d 478, 480 (5th Cir. 1962) (reversing trial court decision that denied a government request to stay discovery until criminal matter was concluded).
- *SEC v. Downe*, No. 92 Civ. 4092 (PKL), 1993 WL 22126, at *12–14 (S.D.N.Y. Jan. 26, 1993) (granting government application to intervene and to stay discovery).
- *Twenty First Century Corp. v. LaBianca*, 801 F. Supp. 1007, 1009–11 (E.D.N.Y. 1992) (allowing the government to intervene and granting their motion for a stay of discovery).

The timing of the parallel civil proceeding obviously plays a significant role.

- *In re CFS-Related Secs. Fraud Litig.*, 256 F. Supp. 2d 1227, 1238–39 (N.D. Okla. 2003) (denying stay of civil proceedings where securities litigation had been pending for several years).
- *In re Gaming Lottery Secs. Litig.*, No. 96 Civ. 5567 RPP, 2000 WL 322951, at *1–2 (S.D.N.Y. Mar. 28, 2000) (denying stay where securities fraud class action had been pending for four years and discovery was already completed).

Where the timing of the criminal proceedings is uncertain, the court's interest weighs more strongly in declining to stay the civil action.

- *In re Worldcom, Inc. Secs. Litig.*, 2002 WL 31729501, at *8 (S.D.N.Y. Dec. 5, 2002) ("Of greater significance to judicial efficiency is the uncertainty as to when the criminal proceedings will conclude.") (citations omitted).
- *But cf.* Order Granting Defs.' *Ex Parte* Application to Stay Case at 1, *Stephanie Clifford v. Donald J. Trump, Jr., et al.*, No. CV 18–02217

SJO (FFM) (C.D. Cal. Apr. 27, 2018), ECF No. 53 (granting Michael Cohen's application for a stay subsequent to an FBI raid of his law office, but without knowledge of the timing of any indictment).

In addition to seeking a stay, civil defendants who fear parallel criminal investigations may use other methods to preserve their Fifth Amendment rights during discovery without impeding or prejudicing the rights of the plaintiff. Protections less drastic than a complete stay of the civil proceeding include (1) sealing answers to interrogatories or depositions and directing that they not be used for any purpose outside the civil case; (2) imposing protective orders; (3) imposing a stay for only a finite period of time; (4) limiting a stay to a particular subject; or (5) limiting disclosure of compelled testimony to opposing counsel only. *See, e.g.*, *In re CFS-Related Secs. Fraud Litig.*, 256 F. Supp. 2d 1227, 1240 (N.D. Okla. 2003). A number of courts have recognized these remedies.

- *United States v. Parcels of Land*, 903 F.2d 36, 44 (1st Cir. 1990) (entering a protective order that prohibited use of defendant's deposition transcript, interrogatory answers, and affidavit in any potential criminal proceeding brought against him, except in connection with perjury charges or for purposes of impeachment).
- *SEC v. Dresser Indus., Inc.*, 628 F.2d 1368, 1375 (D.C. Cir. 1980) (court may impose protective orders or postpone civil discovery).
- *Green v. Cosby*, Civil Action 14–30211, MGM Memorandum and Order Regarding Defendant's Motion to Stay This Action During the Pendency of His Criminal Case, 4/4/16 (staying discovery addressed to the defendant without issuing general stay of the civil case).
- *Digital Equip. Corp. v. Currie Enters.*, 142 F.R.D. 8, 12 (D. Mass. 1991) ("[T]his court may, in lieu of a general stay, impose protective orders, seal interrogatories, impose a stay for a finite period of time, or limit a stay to a particular subject matter.").

Several courts appear to be reluctant to grant a prosecutor's request to stay civil proceedings brought by other government agencies, such as the SEC, pending the completion of criminal cases, applying "strict scrutiny" to such requests.

- *SEC v. Oakford Corp.*, 181 F.R.D. 269, 273 (S.D.N.Y. 1998) (Rakoff, J.) (putting government on notice that government's desire to obtain a tactical advantage by requesting a stay would "receive strict scrutiny in the future").
- *SEC v. Saad*, 229 F.R.D. 90, 91 (S.D.N.Y 2005) (denying a request by the U.S. Attorney's Office for a general stay of discovery in a parallel SEC civil case).
- *SEC v. Cioffi*, No. 08-CV-2457 (FB) (VVP), 2008 WL 4693320, at *2 (E.D.N.Y. Oct. 23, 2008) (denying prosecutor's request for stay of civil discovery in parallel SEC enforcement case, but allowing prosecutor to object to specific discovery requests).
- *SEC v. Fraser*, No. CV-09–00443-PHX-GMS, 2009 WL 1531854, at *3 (D. Ariz. June 1, 2009) (following *Cioffi*).

These cases recognize that the government's coordination of parallel civil and criminal enforcement cases should not necessarily prevent a defendant from trying to defend himself in the criminal case by taking discovery in the civil case. Thus, rather than seeking a stay of the criminal case, defendants often move expeditiously to take discovery in the parallel civil case.

The denial of a motion for a stay is considered an interlocutory order and is not appealable in federal court as a matter of right. However, 28 U.S.C. § 1292(b) permits a district court to certify an order for interlocutory appellate review in certain circumstances and at least one district judge found exceptional grounds to certify its decision to deny a stay to the federal appeals court. *See, e.g.*, Order Granting Claimant's Mot. for An Order Certifying an Interlocutory Appeal, *United States v. Real Property & Improvements Located at 2441 Mission St., San Francisco, Cal.*, No. 2013cv02062, 2014 WL 1350914 (N.D. Cal. Apr. 4, 2014).

CHAPTER 4

The Process for Determining the Validity of the Assertion

A claim that the Fifth Amendment protects the witness from responding to an inquiry is not generally sufficient—standing alone—to sustain the assertion. A court must make its own evaluation of the assertion. However, for a court to compel the witness to disclose the answer in support of a Fifth Amendment privilege claim, absent an order of immunity, would obviously defeat the privilege. Thus, to sustain the assertion or deny its validity, a court must determine whether the demand for testimony presents a sufficient danger of incrimination—without knowing what the answer will be.

The leading case providing guidance to courts for determining the validity of a Fifth Amendment assertion is *Hoffman v. United States*, 341 U.S. 479 (1951). In *Hoffman*, the defendant was convicted of criminal contempt for refusing to obey a district court order requiring him to answer questions before a grand jury investigating fraud against the federal government. The Supreme Court reversed the defendant's conviction for contempt, holding that under all of the circumstances, the defendant had a reasonable concern that answering the questions posed could incriminate him. In so ruling, the Court made clear that "[t]he witness is not exonerated from answering merely because he declares that in so doing he would incriminate himself" and that it was for the district court to say whether the witness had a valid basis to assert the Fifth Amendment. *Id.* at 486. The Court then went further:

> To sustain the privilege, it need only be evident from the implications of the question, in the setting in which it is asked, that a responsive answer to the question or an explanation of why it cannot be answered might be dangerous because injurious disclosure could result.

Id. at 486–87.

The Court indicated that a judge must accept the witness's Fifth Amendment assertion unless it is '"*perfectly clear* . . . that the witness is mistaken, and that the answer(s) *cannot possibly* have such tendency' to incriminate." *Id.* at 488–89. Thus, *Hoffman* demands substantial deference by the courts to the witness's assertion of the Fifth Amendment privilege.

In a grand jury proceeding, a witness's assertion of the Fifth Amendment privilege is challenged infrequently, for the criminal nature of the inquiry will often make the validity of the person's assertion self-evident. Similarly, in a criminal trial the danger of incrimination will often be obvious, requiring the person invoking the privilege to make little if any independent demonstration of its validity. On the other hand, in settings where the potential incrimination is not self-evident, many courts require the party asserting the privilege to bear the burden of going forward, and bear the burden of proof, to justify the Fifth Amendment assertion.

- *Estate of Fisher v. Comm'r*, 905 F.2d 645, 649–50 (2d Cir. 1990) (noting that while the burden of establishing the existence of the danger of self-incrimination lies with the witness, the witness need not prove the hazard of self-incrimination by a preponderance of the evidence, but need only show "a reasonable possibility that his own testimony will incriminate him").
- *In re Morganroth*, 718 F.2d 161, 169 (6th Cir. 1983) ("Where there is nothing suggestive of incrimination about the setting in which a seemingly innocent question is asked, the burden of establishing a foundation for the assertion of the privilege [but not the burden of proof] should lie with the witness making it.") (citations omitted).
- *Baker v. Limber*, 647 F.2d 912, 917 (9th Cir. 1981) ("The trial court must make this determination from the facts as well as from 'his

personal perception of the peculiarities of the case.' If he decides that no threat of self-incrimination is evident, the defendant then bears the burden of showing the danger of incrimination.") (citations omitted).

- *OSRecovery, Inc. v. One Groupe Int'l, Inc.*, 262 F. Supp. 2d 302, 307, n.23 (S.D.N.Y. 2003) (if the incriminatory nature of the questions is not readily apparent from the setting, the witness bears the burden to show a credible basis for invoking the Fifth Amendment).
- *Jett v. State*, 498 S.E.2d 274, 276 (Ga. Ct. App. 1998) ("The burden is on the individual claiming the privilege 'to state the general reason for his refusal to answer and to specifically establish that a real danger of incrimination existed with respect to each question.'").
- *United States v. Dominguez*, No. 96C00027, 1997 WL 148816, at *2 (O.C.A.H.O. 1997) (in compelling witness to answer certain deposition questions in an administrative proceeding, the judge remarked, "[T]he party invoking the Fifth Amendment privilege against self-incrimination bears the burden of proof the privilege exists.") (citation omitted).

The processes used by the courts in various settings to determine the validity of a Fifth Amendment assertion are reviewed next.

Procedures for Determining the Validity of Fifth Amendment Assertions in Grand Jury Proceedings

When the prosecutor challenges a grand jury witness's assertion of the Fifth Amendment privilege, it is generally sufficient for the witness's counsel to explain to a judge how the dangers of self-incrimination are real rather than imaginary.

- *In re Grand Jury Subpoena to John Doe*, 41 F. Supp. 2d 616, 620 (W.D. Va. 1999) (holding that witness must do more than merely state that the answers would incriminate and applying a two-step inquiry "whether the information is incriminating in nature" and, if so, "whether criminal prosecution is sufficiently a possibility" to determine the applicability of the Fifth Amendment privilege) (citation omitted).

To support the validity of the assertion, counsel should be allowed to present facts that would tend to support the witness's claim, regardless of whether the material satisfies the rules of evidence.

- *In re Atterbury*, 316 F.2d 106, 111 (6th Cir. 1963) (error not to allow defense to call government attorney as witness in order to demonstrate validity of Fifth Amendment assertion).
- *In re Portell*, 245 F.2d 183, 187 (7th Cir. 1957) (error not to receive newspaper clippings showing witness to be a companion of person under investigation in order to demonstrate valid privilege assertion).

See also

- Fed. R. Evid. 104(a): "[T]he court must decide any preliminary question about whether . . . a privilege exists. . . . In so deciding, the court is not bound by evidence rules. . . ."
- *Zicarelli v. N.J. State Comm'n of Investigation*, 406 U.S. 472, 478–79 (1972) (noting without criticism that "appellant introduced numerous newspaper and magazine articles bearing upon his self-incrimination claim").

Because of the secrecy attendant to all federal grand jury proceedings (and most state grand jury proceedings), the determination of the Fifth Amendment assertion's validity must also be held in a non-public proceeding and, most often, *in camera*. Indeed, courts seem unwilling to allow a person asserting the Fifth Amendment privilege before the grand jury to refuse to submit to an *in camera* review for the purpose of deciding whether the invocation, if challenged, is valid.

- *United States v. Myers*, 593 F.3d 338, 348 & n.15 (4th Cir. 2010) (refusing to consider an appeal of a district court order directing witness to produce missing items for the court's *in camera* review, noting that by doing so the witness would not waive her Fifth Amendment privilege).

- *United States v. Drollinger*, 80 F.3d 389, 393 (9th Cir. 1996) (remanding to permit district court to conduct an *in camera* hearing regarding validity of taxpayer's refusal to answer IRS questions on the basis of the Fifth Amendment privilege).
- *In re Three Grand Jury Subpoenas*, 847 F.2d 1024, 1028–29 (2d Cir. 1988) (requiring grand jury witness to produce a tape cassette recording to the court for *in camera* inspection and upholding contempt order where witness refused, reasoning that producing item for *in camera* review was not incriminating).

If the court finds a grand jury witness's invocation of the Fifth Amendment privilege to be invalid and orders the witness to testify (or to produce documents), at least one former justice of the Supreme Court has suggested that the witness can comply and subsequently object at trial to both direct and derivative use of any such testimony on the ground that he was compelled by the court order to reveal the self-incriminating testimony.

- *Maness v. Meyers*, 419 U.S. 449, 474 (1975) (White, J., concurring) (expressing his view that a witness is protected by a constitutionally imposed use immunity if, despite a Fifth Amendment objection, he is required by court order and threat of contempt to answer).

However, Justice White's argument that subsequent suppression is an adequate protection of a witness's Fifth Amendment right was explicitly rejected by the majority of the Supreme Court in *Maness*. For the majority, Chief Justice Burger stated:

> In the present case the City Attorney argued that if petitioner's client produced the magazines he was amply protected because in any ensuing criminal action he could always move to suppress. . . . Laying to one side possible waiver problems that might arise if the witness followed that course, we nevertheless cannot conclude that it would afford adequate protection. Without something more "he would be

> compelled to surrender the very protection which the privilege is designed to guarantee."

Id. at 461–62 (citations omitted). Thus, to preserve the Fifth Amendment privilege claim, the grand jury witness must refuse to testify even after being ordered to do so and appeal the ensuing order of contempt. As Chief Justice Burger recognized, only through pre-compliance appellate review is the witness able to test the validity of the privilege without "le[tting] the cat out [of the bag]." *Id.* at 463.

This was also the lesson of *Pillsbury Co. v. Conboy*, 459 U.S. 248, 262 (1983). In that case, a former executive of a company under investigation for antitrust violations had been given full use and derivative use immunity in exchange for his grand jury testimony. Later, in a civil case pursuing the same antitrust violations, he was asked deposition questions that closely tracked his grand jury testimony. The executive invoked the Fifth Amendment and refused to answer. The U.S. Supreme Court held the trial court could not compel the executive to answer deposition questions over a valid assertion of the Fifth Amendment, "absent a duly authorized assurance of immunity at the time." *Id.* at 257. The Court reasoned that a judge should not

> at the time of the civil testimony, pre-determine the decision of the court in a subsequent criminal prosecution on the question whether the Government has met its burden of proving "that the evidence it proposes to use is derived from a legitimate source wholly independent of the compelled testimony." Yet in holding [the witness] in contempt for his Fifth Amendment silence, the [trial court] essentially predicted that a court in any future criminal prosecution of [the witness] will be obligated to protect against evidentiary use of the deposition testimony petitioners seek. We do not think such a predictive judgment is enough.

Id. at 261 (citation omitted).

See also Balsys, 524 U.S. 666, 683 n.9 (1998) (mentioning that judicial exclusion of compelled self-incriminating testimony merely "functions as a failsafe" and that the general rule "requires a grant of immunity prior to the compelling of any testimony"). Despite the statements in *Maness* and *Pillsbury*, at least one court has decided subsequent to *Chavez* that grand jury proceedings are not a criminal case, an issue subject to debate, and have thereby required that witnesses produce self-incriminating information to a grand jury and move to suppress the admissibility of the compelled statements if subsequently charged. *See*, *e.g*, *In re Misc. 4281*, 149 A.3d 1253 (Md. Ct. Spec. App. 2016). For the reasons identified by Justice Burger in *Maness v. Myers*, this is a dangerous course for the witness to follow. Until more direction is given by the Supreme Court on when a criminal case commences for purposes of the Fifth Amendment Self-Incrimination Clause, a witness is better advised to resist a grand jury subpoena that seeks to compel self-incriminating testimony or document production through contempt, as opposed to making the production and hoping to be able to put the "cat back into the bag" before trial. This was the proper course of action before *Chavez* and remains the proper course today.

Importantly, an order holding a federal grand jury witness in contempt for refusing to relinquish his Fifth Amendment refusal to testify or to produce documents is immediately appealable pursuant to 28 U.S.C. § 1291.

- *United States v. Under Seal*, 737 F.3d 330 (4th Cir. 2013) (reviewing district court order requiring grand jury witnesses to comply with subpoena for documents that court ruled were required records and not protected by act of production doctrine).
- *In re Grand Jury*, 705 F.3d 133, 143 (3d Cir. 2012) (district court's contempt order is immediately appealable because it is a final judgment on the willfully disobedient witness in what is effectively a separate proceeding).
- *In re Sequoia Auto Brokers Ltd.*, 827 F.2d 1281, 1283 (9th Cir. 1987) (bankruptcy court's contempt order against principal of debtor was final and appealable because principal was non-party and because contempt was based on the invocation of Fifth Amendment).
- *In re Special Fed. Grand Jury*, 819 F.2d 56, 57 (3d Cir. 1987) (upholding appellate review of civil contempt issued against grand

jury witness who asserted Fifth Amendment right against compelled self-incrimination).

- *In re Witness Before Special Oct. 1981 Grand Jury*, 722 F.2d 349, 351–52 (7th Cir. 1983) (upholding jurisdiction to hear grand jury witness's appeal from order holding witness in civil contempt for refusing to obey subpoenas for the production of documents on Fifth Amendment grounds).

Most courts will stay the execution of an order holding a party in contempt until the appellate court adjudicates the appeal, when the underlying issue is the party's refusal to comply based on the Self-Incrimination Clause and the claim is not frivolous. Compare *United States v. Under Seal*, 737 F.3d 330 (4th Cir. 2013) (district court stayed contempt order without imposing bond) with *In re Grand Jury Investigation M.H.*, 648 F.3d 1067 (9th Cir. 2011) (district court granted a request for a stay, but required the posting of a $250,000 bond).

Of course, if the witness does not resist the court order and complies, instead of continuing to assert his Fifth Amendment privilege and being held in contempt, he may generally not appeal. *Cobbledick v. United States*, 309 U.S. 323, 328 (1940). As the Supreme Court has explained:

> The necessity for expedition in the administration of the criminal law justifies putting one who seeks to resist the production of desired information to a choice between compliance with a trial court's order to produce prior to any review of that order, and resistance to that order with the concomitant possibility of an adjudication of contempt if his claims are rejected on appeal.

United States v. Ryan, 402 U.S. 530, 533 (1971) (citations omitted). *See also In re Grand Jury Subpoena*, 709 F.3d 1027, 1029 (10th Cir. 2013) (deciding that the circuit court lacks jurisdiction to consider interlocutory appeal of Fifth Amendment privilege claim to documents subpoenaed by grand jury when, after motion to quash was denied, the witness complied with the court's order to produce rather than being held in contempt).

The sole exception is when the person claiming privilege—including the Fifth Amendment privilege—is not the subpoenaed witness. *See Perlman v. United States*, 247 U.S. 7 (1918) (allowing an interlocutory appeal when an intervenor claims an interest in preventing a third party's disclosure of documents or testimony and the party subject to the subpoena is unwilling to risk contempt). Although the *Perlman* doctrine is beyond the scope of this book, it is worth noting that the doctrine may be undergoing revision in light of the Supreme Court's decision in *Mohawk Industries, Inc. v. Carpenter*, 558 U.S. 106 (2009) (reasoning that post-judgment appeals generally suffice to protect rights of litigants in cases involving claimed violations of the attorney-client privilege).

Procedures for Determining the Validity of Fifth Amendment Assertions by Witnesses in a Criminal Trial

Witnesses can often demonstrate that a truthful answer to any question they could possibly be asked during a criminal trial would be incriminating. Trial witnesses, particularly if represented by counsel, will often make a motion not to be required to take the stand to invoke their Fifth Amendment privilege. The court may accept an out-of-court demonstration as to the validity of the witness's Fifth Amendment assertion.

- *United States v. Bates*, 552 F.3d 472, 475–76 (6th Cir. 2009) (trial court's acceptance of witness's blanket refusal to testify not in error when witness had reasonable cause to invoke Fifth Amendment).
- *Davis v. Straub*, 430 F.3d 281, 288–90 (6th Cir. 2005) (state court decision allowing a defense witness to invoke privilege against self-incrimination and thereby avoid taking the witness stand did not involve an unreasonable application of law necessary to support habeas relief).
- *United States v. Mahasin*, 362 F.3d 1071, 1085–86 (8th Cir. 2004) (court did not abuse its discretion by not conducting further inquiry into the basis for a defense witness's assertion of the Fifth Amendment privilege, when the government informed the court that the witness could be charged with a crime and the court was familiar with the witness's statement to the police and the evidence at trial).

- *United States v. Tsui*, 646 F.2d 365, 367–68 (9th Cir. 1981) (district court did not abuse discretion by upholding a trial witness's blanket assertion of the Fifth Amendment, where the court could determine without question-by-question inquiry that witness's assertions were valid).

When determining whether a criminal trial witness's assertion of the privilege against self-incrimination is valid, the proper procedure is to conduct a proceeding outside the presence of the jury.

- *United States v. Mathews*, 997 F.2d 848, 849 (11th Cir. 1993) (witness questioned outside the presence of the jury to determine whether his assertion of Fifth Amendment privilege was valid).
- *United States v. Schaflander*, 719 F.2d 1024, 1026 (9th Cir. 1983) ("If such questioning [regarding Fifth Amendment rights] is to be done to satisfy the court of the defendant's understanding of his rights, it should be done outside the presence of the jury.").
- *State v. King*, 781 A.2d 1002, 1006 (N.H. 2001) (to justifiably exclude testimony of a defense witness based upon the witness's Fifth Amendment right, the court must conduct a hearing outside the presence of the jury to determine if the privilege is being properly invoked).
- *Commonwealth v. Fisher*, 742 N.E.2d 61, 70 (Mass. 2001) ("[W]here there is some advance warning that a witness might refuse to testify, the trial judge should conduct a voir dire of the witness, outside the presence of the jury. . . .").
- *State v. Lashley*, 664 P.2d 1358, 1365 (Kan. 1983) ("[C]laims of privilege should be determined outside the presence of the jury, since undue weight may be given by a jury to a claim of privilege. If the court determines that the prior statement is admissible, then the jury should be told simply *that the witness is not available* before the prior testimony is read into the record.").
- *People v. Poma*, 294 N.W.2d 221, 222–23 (Mich. Ct. App. 1980) (court should conduct hearing outside presence of jury to determine whether witness "intimately related to the criminal episode at issue" will choose to assert self-incrimination privilege and, if so, not allow witness to be called to the stand).

- *See also Jackson v. Denno*, 378 U.S. 368, 400 (1964) (hearing on admissibility of alleged involuntary confession must be heard outside jury's presence).
- Section 5, Invoking the Fifth Amendment, Benchbook for U.S. District Court Judges (March 2013) (suggesting that judges excuse the jury before examining a witness in order to determine the validity of the Fifth Amendment assertion).
- Ind. Code § 37–3-1 (requiring court to remove the jury and hold an immediate hearing if a witness refuses to testify or produce any item based on the privilege).

Although a defendant has the right to be present at every stage of the trial, a judge has the authority to hear a witness's explanation for why the witness has a valid basis to assert the Fifth Amendment privilege outside of the defendant's presence. *See generally Pixley v. Commonwealth*, 906 N.E.2d 320, 326 (Mass. 2009) and *Taylor v. State*, 977 P.3d 123 (Alaska 1999).

If the court rules that a trial witness may not assert the Fifth Amendment privilege, the witness must generally be held in contempt in order to obtain pre-compliance appellate review. As is the case for grand jury witnesses, an order holding a federal trial witness in contempt is immediately appealable under 28 U.S.C. § 1291.

- *In re Askin*, 47 F.3d 100, 102 (4th Cir. 1995) (considering an appeal of a civil contempt order issued against a witness in criminal trial who refused to testify based on Fifth Amendment privilege).
- *United States v. Johnson*, 736 F.2d 358, 359 n.1 (6th Cir. 1984) (order holding trial witness in civil contempt for refusing to testify on basis of Fifth Amendment privilege is immediately appealable under 28 U.S.C. § 1291 because the contempt was a final judgment as to the non-party witness).

The point at which a criminal defendant must take the stand and testify in order to properly present and preserve a Fifth Amendment-based objection to the admission of evidence at trial, such as a prior confession, is unclear. In *New Jersey v. Portash*, 440 U.S. 450, 464–65 (1979), the

Supreme Court considered a case in which the defendant requested, in advance of his taking the stand, that the trial judge rule whether his prior immunized grand jury testimony could be used to impeach him should he testify. The trial judge ruled it could, a decision that the Supreme Court later held was wrong. More importantly for purposes of this discussion, the Supreme Court disagreed with the state's contention that Portash did not properly preserve his Fifth Amendment objection by not taking the stand and testifying. Rather, the Court found nothing wrong with the New Jersey court's "not requiring Portash to take the witness stand in order to raise his constitutional claim." *Id.* at 456. *See also Brooks v. Tennessee*, 406 U.S. 605 (1972) (holding that the right to remain silent is unconstitutionally penalized by a statute requiring a defendant who chooses to testify to be his own first witness, and approving the state court's adjudication of the claim, though the defendant never testified).

However, in *Luce v. United States*, 469 U.S. 38, 43 (1984), the Supreme Court held that a defendant must testify in order to preserve for appeal a challenge to a ruling in limine involving impeachment with prior convictions. The Court distinguished *Portash* and *Brooks* because "[i]n those cases we reviewed Fifth Amendment challenges to state-court rulings that operated to dissuade defendants from testifying. We did not hold that a federal court's preliminary ruling on a question not reaching constitutional dimensions—such as a decision under Rule 609(a)—is reviewable on appeal." *Id.* at 42–43. Nevertheless, the decision in *Luce* has led to disagreement over when a defendant must take the stand to preserve certain Fifth Amendment-based objections to trial evidence.

Compare

- *United States v. Turner*, 675 F.3d 420, 433–34 (5th Cir. 2012) (applying *Luce* to a defendant's claim that the district judge erred when he ruled that the defendant could be cross-examined about a robbery for which he was charged in state court if he took the stand and testified in his defense at his federal criminal trial).
- *United States v. Wilson*, 307 F.3d 596, 598–601 (7th Cir. 2002) (the defendant did not preserve his Fifth Amendment challenge to the trial court's ruling that if he had introduced evidence regarding his alleged

associate, the prosecution could have introduced evidence regarding his refusal to identify the associate to police, because the defendant did not introduce the evidence regarding the associate at trial).

- *United States v. Bond*, 87 F.3d 695, 700–01 (5th Cir. 1996) (holding based on *Luce* that the defendant had to take the stand and testify in order to appeal the trial court's in limine ruling that he would have waived his Fifth Amendment privilege by testifying).
- *Wagner v. State*, 347 P.3d 109 (Alaska 2015) (because defendant did not testify, he failed to preserve his objection to the trial court's in limine ruling that the prosecution could impeach him with his post-*Miranda* invocation of his right to counsel).
- *People v. Boyd*, 682 N.W.2d 459, 460, 463–66 (Mich. 2004) (extending *Luce* to require that a defendant testify to preserve for appellate review his challenge to a trial court's ruling in limine allowing evidence that he exercised his *Miranda* right to remain silent).

With

- *United States v. Chischilly*, 30 F.3d 1144, 1151 (9th Cir. 1994), *overruled on other grounds*, *United States v. Preston*, 751 F.3d 1008 (9th Cir. 2014) (holding that the defendant could appeal the trial court's ruling that his confession was voluntary and could have been introduced by the prosecution to rebut his insanity defense even though the defendant did not present his insanity defense, and the prosecution did introduce his confession, at trial; the court found that *Luce* did "not apply" because "use of an involuntary confession would violate the Constitution," and "*Luce* . . . recognized that its rule dealt with a preliminary ruling 'not reaching constitutional dimensions'") (citations omitted).
- *United States ex rel. Adkins v. Greer*, 791 F.2d 590, 593–94 (7th Cir. 1986) (the defendant did not have to testify in order to preserve for appeal his Fifth Amendment challenge to the trial court's ruling that the prosecution could have introduced a statement that he made to a police officer if he had taken the stand and testified; the court distinguished *Luce* because the in limine ruling in *Luce* did not involve constitutional considerations).

- *State v. Brings Plenty*, 459 N.W.2d 390, 394 (S.D. 1990) ("*Luce* does not stand for the proposition that Fifth Amendment confession issues are waived if a defendant does not take the stand. The Court specifically distinguished its ruling from Fifth Amendment cases because it was dealing with impeachment with a felony conviction under Rule 609 of the Federal Rules of Evidence.") (citation omitted).

Procedures for Determining the Validity of Fifth Amendment Assertions in Non-Criminal Proceedings

The demonstration required to sustain an invocation of the Fifth Amendment privilege in civil proceedings often involves an *in camera* or ex parte examination, as the party making the assertion will most often need to provide some information to show that he has a valid Fifth Amendment claim.

- *United States v. Argomaniz*, 925 F.2d 1349, 1356 (11th Cir. 1991) (reversing district court ruling enforcing IRS summons and requiring district court to conduct *in camera* hearing to determine validity of Fifth Amendment assertion by taxpayer).
- *Estate of Fisher v. Comm'r*, 905 F.2d 645, 651 (2d Cir. 1990) (error to deny taxpayer's request for an *in camera* review of his claimed Fifth Amendment privilege to IRS discovery requests).
- *United States v. Duncan*, 704 F. Supp. 820, 822 (N.D. Ill. 1989) (in IRS summons enforcement action, court requires witness invoking his Fifth Amendment privilege to submit a memorandum *in camera* explaining why each response would be incriminatory).
- *In re Connelly*, 59 B.R. 421, 445 (Bankr. N.D. Ill. 1986) (debtor required to explain under oath *in camera* or by affidavit, either of which would become a sealed record, the underlying factual basis for his fear of incrimination).

But cf.

- *IRS v. Lanoie*, 403 F. App'x 328, 333–34 (10th Cir. 2010) (observing that an *in camera* inspection is not absolutely required, and finding that the taxpayer did not establish a valid Fifth Amendment claim in a transcribed appearance before an IRS agent).

Although a party in a civil case is not normally allowed to appeal a discovery order until the case is concluded, a non-party witness may obtain immediate appellate review after being held in civil contempt for his refusal to testify based on his self-incrimination privilege.

- *U.S. Catholic Conference v. Abortion Rights Mobilization, Inc.*, 487 U.S. 72, 76 (1988) (stating generally that an "order finding a non-party witness in contempt is appealable notwithstanding the absence of a final judgment in the underlying action") (citations omitted).
- *Gen. Ins. Co. of Am. v. E. Consol. Utilities, Inc.*, 126 F.3d 215, 218 (3d Cir. 1997) (stating that an "order for contempt . . . against a nonparty . . . is immediately appealable") (citations omitted).
- *Peterson v. Douglas Cty. Bank & Trust Co.*, 967 F.2d 1186, 1188 (8th Cir. 1992) (stating that an "order finding a nonparty witness in contempt of court is appealable even if final judgment has not been entered in the underlying action") (citation omitted).
- *In re Corrugated Container Antitrust Litig.*, 662 F.2d 875, 877, 879 (D.C. Cir. 1981) (exercising jurisdiction over a non-party deponent's appeal of a civil contempt order that arose out of his refusal to answer deposition questions based on his Fifth Amendment privilege).

Procedures for Determining the Validity of Fifth Amendment Assertions in Legislative Proceedings

A legislative body does not have a convenient procedure for determining the validity of a witness's Fifth Amendment assertion. Any inquiry by a legislative committee into the basis for a witness's fear of incrimination could force the witness to discuss the nature of the conduct in question and thereby waive his privilege. As the Supreme Court has implicitly recognized, "[i]f an objection to a question is made in any language that a [congressional] committee may reasonably be expected to understand as an attempt to invoke the privilege, it must be respected . . . by the committee. . . ." *Quinn v. United States*, 349 U.S. 155, 162–63 (1955).

The only way the United States Congress can challenge the validity of a witness's Fifth Amendment assertion is to hold the witness in contempt and litigate the issue in federal court. Congress has three options for holding a witness in contempt.

Congress's first option is to hold the witness in criminal contempt under 2 U.S.C. § 192, which provides that any witness subpoenaed by Congress who "refuses to answer any question pertinent to the question under inquiry shall be deemed guilty of a misdemeanor." At the outset, the committee conducting the investigation must "clearly apprise" the witness that it "demands his answer notwithstanding" the Fifth Amendment assertion; otherwise, "there can be no conviction under § 192 for refusal to answer that question." *Quinn*, 349 U.S. at 166. To hold the witness in criminal contempt, the chamber of Congress that issued the subpoena must vote to enforce it and then refer the matter to the Department of Justice for prosecution. *See* 2 U.S.C. § 194. While the Department of Justice has a "duty" to bring the matter before a grand jury, *id.*, "the Executive Branch has exclusive authority and absolute discretion to decide whether to prosecute a case." *United States v. Nixon*, 418 U.S. 683, 693 (1974). There have been several instances outside the Fifth Amendment context in which the Department of Justice has not pursued charges against a witness whom Congress voted to hold in criminal contempt (including the Department of Justice's 2006 decision not to seek an indictment against White House Counsel Harriet Miers and White House Chief of Staff Joshua Bolten, and its 2012 decision not to seek an indictment against Attorney General Eric Holder). There have also been instances where the witness was held in contempt for asserting his Fifth Amendment privilege and the Department of Justice refused to prosecute, as was the case with the IRS Director of Exempt Organizations in 2015.

Congress's second option is to hold the witness in civil contempt. This process involves the House, Senate, or one of their committees filing a civil lawsuit against the witness to compel a response. The Senate can file such a lawsuit under 28 U.S.C. § 1365(a), which provides the United States District Court for the District of Columbia with subject matter jurisdiction "over any civil action brought by the Senate or any authorized committee or subcommittee of the Senate to enforce, to secure a declaratory judgment concerning the validity of, or to prevent a threatened refusal or failure to comply with, any subpoena. . . ." Although no corresponding statute confers subject matter jurisdiction over a civil lawsuit filed by the House of Representatives or one of its committees to enforce a subpoena, the U.S. District Court for the District of Columbia has held that it has federal question jurisdiction under 28 U.S.C. § 1331 to decide such a lawsuit.

- *Comm. on Oversight & Gov't Reform v. Holder*, 979 F. Supp. 2d 1, 17 (D.D.C. 2013) (holding that a civil lawsuit filed by the House Committee on Oversight and Government Reform to enforce a subpoena that it had issued to Attorney General Eric Holder "presents a federal question and that therefore, the court has jurisdiction under 28 U.S.C. § 1331").
- *Comm. on Judiciary v. Miers*, 558 F. Supp. 2d 53, 64 (D.D.C. 2008) ("Both sides concede, and the Court agrees, that 28 U.S.C. § 1331 provides subject matter jurisdiction over this lawsuit. Because this dispute concerns an allegation that Ms. Miers and Mr. Bolten failed to comply with duly issued congressional subpoenas, and such subpoena power derives implicitly from Article I of the Constitution, this case arises under the Constitution for purposes of § 1331.").

The remedy available to Congress in a civil contempt lawsuit is an order directing the witness to comply with the subpoena. *See* 28 U.S.C. § 1365(b) ("Upon application by the Senate or any authorized committee or subcommittee of the Senate, the district court shall issue an order to an entity or person refusing, or failing to comply with, or threatening to refuse or not to comply with, a subpoena . . . requiring such entity or person to comply forthwith."); *Miers*, 558 F. Supp. 2d at 55 ("The Committee on the Judiciary . . . asks the Court to declare that former White House Counsel Harriet Miers must comply with a subpoena and appear before the Committee to testify. . . ."). Accordingly, if a court considering such a lawsuit finds that a witness's Fifth Amendment assertion was not valid, then the witness must give up his privilege and testify before Congress or risk being held in contempt of court. *See* 28 U.S.C. § 1365(b) ("Any refusal or failure to obey a lawful order of the district court issued pursuant to this section may be held by such court to be a contempt thereof.").

Congress's third and final option is to use its inherent contempt power. Under this procedure, the witness asserting the Fifth Amendment privilege is tried before the chamber of Congress that issued the subpoena and, if the assertion is deemed invalid and the individual is convicted for refusing to testify, he can be detained at the Capitol (or possibly the District of Columbia jail) until he agrees to testify. *See Watkins v. United States*, 354 U.S. 178, 207 n.45 (1957) (noting the "historical procedure of summoning the recalcitrant witness before the bar of either House of Congress and ordering him held in custody until he agreed to testify"); *United States v. Fort*, 443 F.2d 670, 676 (D.C. Cir. 1971) (explaining that, when Congress relies on its "inherent powers of civil contempt," the witness is "committed to the Sergeant-at-Arms of the respective House until he was willing to 'purge' himself of his contempt by supplying the requested information") (citations omitted). Because this inherent contempt power has not been used since 1935, it is unlikely that Congress would use the power today to challenge a witness's Fifth Amendment assertion. In the unlikely event that Congress uses its inherent contempt power, the witness could seek prompt judicial review by filing a petition for a writ of habeas corpus and put the validity of his Fifth Amendment assertion before a federal court. *See Fort*, 443 F.2d at 676 (confinement under Congress's inherent contempt power can "always be challenged by *habeas corpus*") (citations omitted).

If Congress pursues any of these options and a federal court is faced with deciding the validity of the witness's Fifth Amendment assertion, the test in *Hoffman* will apply.

- *Emspak v. United States*, 349 U.S. 190, 198–99 (1955) ("'To sustain the privilege,' this Court has recently held, 'it need only be evident from the implications of the question, in the setting in which it is asked, that a responsive answer to the question or an explanation of why it cannot be answered might be dangerous because injurious disclosure could result.' [quoting *Hoffman*, 341 U.S. at 486–87.] . . . Applying this test to the instant case, we have no doubt that the eight questions concerning petitioner's alleged membership in the Communist Party fell within the scope of the privilege.").

- *Aiuppa v. United States*, 201 F.2d 287, 297 (6th Cir. 1952) (upholding a witness's Fifth Amendment assertion before a Senate committee investigating organized crime because "it [wa]s perfectly clear from a careful consideration of all the circumstances that the witness was not mistaken in thinking that answers to the questions asked him could possibly have a tendency to incriminate him") (citation omitted).
- *Jackins v. United States*, 231 F.2d 405, 409–10 (9th Cir. 1956) (in upholding a witness's Fifth Amendment assertion before the House Committee on Un-American Activities, the court stated that "[w]hen a witness called before a committee or other hearing body, is told by his interrogators that he is suspected of wrongdoing, or of association with wrongdoers, those accusations are a part of the setting in which must be judged his right to claim the privilege against self-incrimination").

If a witness is asserting the Fifth Amendment privilege at a congressional hearing, it may not be necessary for the witness to appear at the hearing to make the assertion. It is customary for counsel for the witness to inform the committee by letter that the witness will assert the Fifth Amendment and to request that the witness be excused from appearing. Though the committee often will insist that the witness appear at the hearing to assert the privilege, that course of action is discouraged. In D.C. Legal Ethics Opinion 31 (1977), the Legal Ethics Committee opined that it is unprofessional conduct for congressional committee lawyers to compel a witness to appear at a public hearing to assert the Fifth Amendment when the witness has notified the committee that he or she will invoke the privilege. In D.C. Legal Ethics Opinion 358 (2011), the Committee clarified that its 1977 opinion applies only where compelling the witness to appear at a public hearing to assert the privilege "serves no substantial purpose 'other than to embarrass, delay, or burden' the witness" (citations omitted).

Procedures for Determining the Validity of Fifth Amendment Assertions with Regard to Document Production

As discussed in Chapter 8, subject to certain exceptions, the Fifth Amendment protects against the compelled act of producing documents, as long as the act of production would "testify" to the existence, possession, custody, or authenticity of the documents. Because the act of production privilege can apply to the production of specific documents, and courts generally discourage blanket assertions of the Fifth Amendment privilege, the court will commonly conduct an *in camera* review of the documents during which the resisting party should explain—presumably on a privilege log submitted ex parte to the court—why the act of producing the documents would be incriminating. Chapter 3 cites cases where witnesses asserting the act of production privilege were required to provide either a detailed privilege log or the documents for *in camera* review, or both.

Although there are few published opinions on the subject, Judge Young's careful ruling in *United States v. Chen*, 952 F. Supp. 2d 321 (D. Mass. July 3, 2013), is instructive. In this case, the IRS sought to enforce an administrative summons directing a taxpayer to produce certain records. Among other objections, the taxpayer objected to doing so on the basis of his privilege against self-incrimination. Judge Young agreed that the act of production privilege was implicated in documents the Bank Secrecy Act does not require be kept. However, recognizing that a blanket assertion was not acceptable, the Judge ordered the taxpayer to "submit under seal . . . a document-by-document explanation of his Fifth Amendment assertions and the documents which substantiate those assertions," adding that "[s]uch submissions shall not constitute a waiver of (the taxpayer's) Fifth Amendment privilege. . . ." *Id.* at 334. Although the First Circuit remanded Judge Young's subsequent order granting the IRS summons for further explanation of his reasons, the

Court of Appeals expressed no disapproval of Judge Young's *in camera* inspection order. *United States v. Chen*, 815 F.3d 72 (1st Cir. 2016). *See also SEC v. Farmer*, 560 Fed. App'x 324 (5th Cir. 2014) (per curium) (unpublished opinion) (remanding to district court to allow ex parte submission of documents and act of production privilege log for court to determine *in camera* which documents were protected by the act of production privilege); *Matter of Astor*, 21 Misc. 3d 400 (Westchester Cty., N.Y. 2008) (in an action regarding a contested estate, a previously indicted party was required to produce a privilege log to the court ex parte, explaining why documents he sought to withhold were protected by the act of production privilege).

CHAPTER 5

How the Right Should Be Asserted

The Supreme Court has repeatedly indicated, and in its most recent cases stressed, that the privilege against self-incrimination is not self-executing. To invoke its protections, the witness must make some affirmative declaration or objection at the time the incriminating response is called for. To preserve a claim that the right against self-incrimination has been violated, the witness must claim the privilege "unequivocally." Only when the government attaches a penalty to the assertion of the privilege itself is the claim subject to an exception. In *Garner v. United States*, 424 U.S. 648 (1976), the Supreme Court upheld the admission into evidence disclosures made on the defendant's tax return that he was a professional gambler. The Court remarked:

> Unless a witness objects, a government ordinarily may assume that its compulsory processes are not eliciting testimony that he deems to be incriminating. Only the witness knows whether the apparently innocent disclosure sought may incriminate him, and the burden appropriately lies with him to make a timely assertion of the privilege.... [S]ince Garner made disclosures instead of claiming the privilege on his tax returns, [h]e ... was foreclosed from invoking the privilege when such information was later introduced as evidence against him in a criminal prosecution.

Id. at 655, 665.

Similarly, in *Minnesota v. Murphy*, 465 U.S. 420 (1984), the Court remarked:

> The [Fifth] Amendment speaks of compulsion. It does not preclude a witness from testifying voluntarily in matters which may incriminate him. If, therefore, he desires the protection of the privilege, he must claim it or he will not be considered to have been "compelled" within the meaning of the Amendment.

Id. at 427 (quoting *United States v. Monia*, 317 U.S. 424, 427 (1943)).

If the witness simply refuses to answer the question without giving a reason, the witness is subject to punishment for contempt regardless of whether a proper claim of privilege would have been valid. As the Supreme Court stated in the congressional investigation context, "if the witness refuses a committee request to state whether he relies on the Self-Incrimination Clause, he cannot later invoke its protection in a prosecution for contempt for refusing to answer that question." *Quinn v. United States*, 349 U.S. 155, 164–65 (1955).

In *Salinas v. Texas*, 570 U.S. 178 (2013), the Supreme Court required that a witness invoke the Fifth Amendment in order to preserve the claim that his incriminating statements were compelled. The Court held that the Fifth Amendment does not protect a witness's silence during a voluntary non-custodial police interview from being used against him in a criminal prosecution. Salinas was a possible witness to a double murder, and he answered police questions both at his home and later at the police station, where he agreed to go for further questioning. Police asked him if the shotgun shells recovered from the crime scene would match the shotgun he handed over to police from his house, at which point Salinas remained silent, looked down at the floor, shuffled his feet, and bit his lip. He later answered other questions and left the police station. After Salinas was charged with double murder, the prosecution introduced evidence in its case-in-chief of Salinas's silence and demeanor to the police questions about the shell casings, and argued it was evidence of guilt.

The Supreme Court held that because Salinas did not unequivocally invoke his privilege against self-incrimination during the voluntary police interview, he had no right to have his silence excluded from use against him at trial. The plurality reaffirmed the principle that "a witness who desires [the protection of the privilege] must claim it." *Id.* at 181 (citations omitted). The plurality further held that the Fifth Amendment does not establish an unqualified right to remain silent and, absent certain exceptions where a witness was excused from affirmatively asserting the privilege—circumstances where the cost of silence is so great as to be coercive—silence was generally not a substitute for expressly invoking the privilege.

Although the witness must claim the privilege against self-incrimination, no "ritualistic formula or talismanic phrase" is necessary to properly invoke the privilege. *Emspak v. United States*, 349 U.S. 190, 194 (1955). In ruling on the adequacy of Fifth Amendment assertions Emspak made before a congressional committee, the Supreme Court remarked, "[a]ll that is necessary is an objection stated in language that a committee may reasonably be expected to understand as an attempt to invoke the privilege." *Id. See also Davis v. United States*, 512 U.S. 452, 459 (1994) (noting that while "a suspect need not 'speak with the discrimination of an Oxford don,'" he must make a statement that a reasonable police officer would understand as a request for an attorney in order to invoke his *Miranda* right to counsel). The words that courts have found adequate to assert the privilege in various settings are reviewed below.

How Little Can or Should One Say?

Although the Supreme Court in *Miranda* indicated, at least for suspects in custody, that "[i]f the individual indicates *in any manner*, at any time prior to or during questioning, that he wishes to remain silent, the interrogation must cease," *Miranda*, 384 U.S. at 473–74 (emphasis added), the Court has thereafter repeatedly demanded that the invocation be "clear" and "unambiguous." *See Davis*, 512 U.S. at 459 (holding that to invoke the right to counsel during a custodial interrogation, the suspect must "articulate his desire . . . sufficiently clearly that a reasonable police officer in the circumstances would understand the statement to be a request for an attorney"); *Berghuis v. Thompkins*, 560 U.S. 370, 381 (2010) (ruling that a suspect in custody must invoke his right to remain silent unambiguously, adopting the standard in *Davis v. United States*). The law, at least in federal courts, is clear that muteness or silence is not an unambiguous announcement of the right to remain silent, even after a suspect receives *Miranda* warnings that he has a right to remain silent. In *Berghuis*, for instance, the defendant's two hours and 45 minutes of near-total silence was held to be insufficient to meet this requirement of an "unambiguous" invocation of his *Miranda* right to remain silent. *Berghuis*, 560 U.S. at 381. *See also Hiibel v. Sixth Judicial Dist. Court of Nev.*, 542 U.S. 177, 188–91 (2004) (Court declined to consider certain aspects of petitioner's Fifth Amendment challenge because he gave no indication at the time the police officer requested his name that his refusal to answer was predicated on the Fifth Amendment).

Since *Berghuis*, however, it remains unclear whether the suspect in custody must speak in order to invoke the right to remain silent or whether some other nonverbal expressive conduct will suffice. In *Commonwealth v. Clarke*, 960 N.E.2d 306, 315 (Mass. 2012), the Supreme Judicial Court of Massachusetts disagreed with the prosecution's contentions that *Berghuis* requires a suspect to speak in order to invoke the right to remain silent. It found that "an explicit headshake in response to a direct question—is sufficiently communicative so as to invoke his right to remain silent." 960 N.E.2d at 315 (citation omitted). The Supreme Judicial Court also made a distinction between what action or speech is sufficient to invoke the right to remain silent made at the outset of custodial interrogation and after the suspect has initially waived his *Miranda* rights, noting that "it makes sense to expect heightened clarity from a suspect who wants to change course and cease interrogation after having already indicated a desire" to talk. 960 N.E.2d at 319. *See also State v. I.B.*, 348 P.3d 1250 (Wash. Ct. App. 2015) (shake of head in the negative after police asked a juvenile held for custodial interrogation whether he wanted to talk was unequivocal invocation of his right to remain silent); *State v. Nash*, 619 S.E.2d 684 (Ga. 2005) (in pre-*Berghuis* case, court held that shaking of head to indicate "no" in response to question about whether suspect wanted to talk to police was unequivocal invocation). But these cases are by no means a unanimous view of the law.

In determining whether a statement is sufficiently unambiguous to invoke a suspect's right to remain silent during custodial interrogation, courts consider the statement in context, considering the totality of the surrounding circumstances. The cases—of which there are hundreds, both pre-*Berghuis* and post-*Berghuis*—are very fact specific, and no hard-and-fast rules can be articulated. But the following cases provide a flavor of how courts treat various statements.

- *Sessoms v. Grounds*, 776 F.3d 615, 621 (9th Cir. 2015) (en banc) ("Get me a lawyer" was an unequivocal assertion in totality of the circumstances and sufficient basis for circuit court to rule that subsequent admission of incriminating statements was not harmless error).
- *Garcia v. Long*, 808 F.3d 771, 776–784 (9th Cir. 2015) (when defendant answered with a simple "no" when asked if he wished to talk to the detective after being advised of his *Miranda* rights, all interrogation should have ceased and defendant's subsequent confession was improperly admitted into evidence).
- *Anderson v. Terhune*, 516 F.3d 781, 784 (9th Cir. 2008) (en banc) (suspect's statement "I plead the Fifth" was sufficiently unambiguous to prevent further interrogation and entitle defendant to habeas corpus relief).
- *Sechrest v. Ignacio*, 549 F.3d 789, 806 (9th Cir. 2008) (no unambiguous invocation where suspect, who had initially invoked his *Miranda* rights, stated, "[Y]ou ask some questions, and if I want to answer them I will answer them, and if not, I won't.").
- *United States v. Drapeau*, 414 F.3d 869, 874 (8th Cir. 2005) (statement from suspect that he "did not want to talk to agents" after being advised of his *Miranda* rights was ambiguous when he thereafter made an unprompted offer to cooperate).

- *Burket v. Angelone*, 208 F.3d 172, 199 (4th Cir. 2000) (statements "I just don't think that I should say anything" and "I need somebody that I can talk to" were held too ambiguous to constitute valid assertions of the *Miranda* rights to remain silent and to have counsel present).
- *State v. Nichols*, 390 P.3d 1001, 1010 (Or. 2017) (en banc) (after initially waiving his *Miranda* rights, the statement "It's not something I want to talk about" was deemed an unambiguous assertion of the right to remain silent, given the entire content of the police questioning, rendering subsequent admissions inadmissible).
- *People v. Martinez*, 224 P.3d 877, 9059 (Cal. 2010) (no proper invocation of right to remain silent when suspect, having been asked why he would be accused on an assault he did not commit, stated, "That's all I can tell you.").

Before *Salinas*, it appeared that the language or gestures used to invoke the Fifth Amendment privilege in non-custodial interactions with police could be imprecise. For instance, in *Coppola v. Powell*, 878 F.2d 1562, 1567 (1st Cir. 1989), the defendant told police who questioned him at his home: "Let me tell you something. I'm not one of your country bumpkins. I grew up on the streets of Providence, Rhode Island. And if you think I am going to confess to you, you're crazy." This statement was deemed a sufficient invocation of Fifth Amendment privilege against self-incrimination. *Id.*

However, after *Salinas*, what a person must say to properly invoke his or her right to remain silent is unclear. The safest manner of asserting the Fifth Amendment privilege is by being exceptionally clear about the basis for not responding. In a grand jury, for instance, the statement "I refuse to answer on the grounds that my response may be self-incriminating" is clear and precise. Yet given the stigma that a person may reasonably fear is attached to such an assertion—a subject discussed in Chapter 6—clients often ask lawyers whether they can invoke the privilege without referring to a concern that the answer may be "self-incriminating."

The answer is yes. In both *Emspak v. United States*, 349 U.S. 190, 193 (1955) and *Quinn v. United States*, 349 U.S. 155, 157 (1955), the witnesses invoked the privilege simply by citing the First and Fifth Amendments. The Supreme Court found the invocation sufficient, reasoning that a witness may invoke the privilege simply by citing the Fifth Amendment because, in the context of our time and modern parlance, the "Fifth Amendment" is "synonymous with the privilege against self-incrimination." *Quinn*, 349 U.S. at 163.

The Supreme Court was not concerned by the somewhat unorthodox method of invoking the privilege, despite the government's objection and the lower court's ruling that such a plea was inadequate. The Court in *Emspak* reasoned:

> The answer to this contention is threefold. First, an objection that is sufficiently clear to reveal a probable intention to invoke the privilege cannot be ignored merely because it is not phrased in an orthodox manner. Second, if it is true that in these times a stigma may somehow result from a witness' [sic] reliance on the Self-Incrimination Clause, a committee should be all the more ready to recognize a veiled claim of the privilege. Otherwise, the great right which the Clause was intended to secure might be effectively frustrated by private pressures. Third, it should be noted that a committee is not obliged to either accept or reject an ambiguous constitutional claim the very moment it is first presented. The way is always open for the committee to inquire into the nature of the claim before making a ruling. If the witness intelligently and unequivocally waives any objection based on the Self-Incrimination Clause, or if the witness refuses a committee request to state whether he relies on the Self-Incrimination Clause, he cannot later invoke its protection in a prosecution for contempt for refusing to answer that question.

349 U.S. at 194–95.

See also

- *Lerner v. Casey*, 357 U.S. 468, 471 n.5 (1958) (witness before state commission, who explained his silence by reference to "Fifth Amendment," asserted claim of possible self-incrimination).

It is important not to be too fancy. Courts have not been willing to uphold the application of the Fifth Amendment privilege against self-incrimination to assertions in which the maker gives a reason other than the constitutional privilege against self-incrimination, particularly if the witness is represented by counsel.

- *Hutcheson v. United States*, 369 U.S. 599, 610–11 (1962) (refusing to treat as tantamount to a claim of Fifth Amendment privilege an assertion that congressional questioning violated due process).
- *Rogers v. United States*, 340 U.S. 367, 374–75 (1951) (invalidating a claim of the Fifth Amendment privilege, where the grand jury witness gave a different reason upon her refusal to answer and properly claimed the privilege against self-incrimination only as an afterthought when seeking to purge herself of contempt).
- *United States ex rel. Vajtauer v. Comm'r of Immigration at Port of N.Y.*, 273 U.S. 103, 111–12 (1927) (a respondent's refusal to testify at a deportation hearing on the basis of the "supposed right of the witness not to be called upon to testify until all the evidence in support of the warrant was presented" was insufficient to invoke Fifth Amendment privilege against self-incrimination).

In the context of interactions with the police, any reference to the Fifth Amendment or even *Miranda* should suffice, given the unequivocal implications that such words hold in our lexicon. *See Dickerson v. United States*, 530 U.S. 428, 448 (2000) (noting that *Miranda* warnings have become part of our national culture).

How Much Can or Should One Say?

In *Ohio v. Reiner*, 532 U.S. 17, 21 (2001), the Supreme Court reminded everyone that "one of the Fifth Amendment's basic functions . . . is to protect *innocent* men . . . 'who otherwise might be ensnared by ambiguous circumstances'" (citations omitted). The Court's admonition quoted *Grunewald v. United States*, 353 U.S. 391, 421 (1957), which, in turn, quoted *Slochower v. Board of Higher Education of New York*, 350 U.S. 551, 557–58 (1956). Persons who invoke the Fifth

Amendment privilege may include just such a statement of innocence in their invocation.

It is not uncommon today for witnesses, particularly in highly publicized proceedings before congressional committees, to make broad statements of their innocence in conjunction with their refusal to testify. Such statements may serve to reduce the stigma associated with the assertion. Although it has been argued by commentators that the witnesses in each of the excerpts below waived their privilege by saying too much, the legal basis for such claims is weak.

Statement of Kenneth L. Lay before the Senate Committee on Commerce, Science, and Transportation

Mr. Chairman, I come here today with a profound sadness about what has happened to Enron, its current and former employees, retirees, shareholders and other stakeholders. I also wanted to respond to the best of my knowledge and recollection to the questions you and your colleagues have about the collapse of Enron. I have, however, been instructed by my counsel not to testify based upon my Fifth Amendment constitutional rights.

I am deeply troubled about asserting these rights, because it may be perceived by some that I have something to hide, but after agonizing consideration I cannot disregard my counsel's instructions. Therefore, I must respectfully decline to answer on Fifth Amendment grounds all the questions of this Committee and Subcommittee and of those of any other congressional committee and subcommittee.

When providing their instruction, my counsel referred me to an excerpt from a unanimous Supreme Court decision of less than a year ago. Quote: "One of the Fifth Amendment's basic functions is to protect innocent men." I respectfully ask you not to draw a negative inference because I am asserting my Fifth Amendment constitutional protection on instruction of counsel.

Collapse of Enron: Hearing Before the S. Comm. on Commerce, Science, & Transp., 107th Cong. 25–26 (2002) (statement of Kenneth L. Lay, former Chairman and Chief Executive Officer, Enron).

Statement of Bernard J. Ebbers before the House Financial Services Committee

Good afternoon, Mr. Chairman and members of the committee.

I served as CEO of WorldCom for 17 years. During that time I helped a small company rise to one of America's largest corporations. I am proud of the work that I did at WorldCom, and I believe that despite its recent problems WorldCom continues to be a valuable company that provides important services to many Americans and to the United States Government.

Within the last 2 weeks, following a restatement of earnings by WorldCom, officials at the Department of Justice, the SEC, various congressional committees, and other law enforcement agencies have launched a number of investigations and proceedings relating to WorldCom.

Countless reports in the media have suggested that my conduct as a WorldCom CEO may be examined in these inquiries. During the last week I retained counsel to represent me in connection with these proceedings. Although I would like, more than you know, to answer the questions that you and your colleagues have about WorldCom, I have been instructed by my counsel not to testify based on my fifth amendment constitutional rights.

After careful consideration I have decided to follow my counsel's instructions, even though I do not believe I have anything to hide in these or any other proceedings. I have reached this decision because, one, the investigations appear to be open-ended examinations of a variety of activities at WorldCom, details of which have not been provided to me.

Second, I have not been advised of the specific conduct of mine that is being called into question, and, third, I understand that preliminary statements can be taken out of context, as inquiries such as these become focused over time.

I hope the committee will not draw a negative inference based on my assertion of these constitutional protections on the instruction of my counsel or attempt to subject me to ridicule by asking inflammatory questions, knowing that I will not answer them.

I do not believe that I should be subject to legal harm as a result of my exercise of a basic constitutional protection found in the Bill of Rights. When all of the activities at WorldCom are fairly aired, and when I get the opportunity, and I am very much looking forward to it, to explain my actions in a setting that will not compromise my ability to defend myself in the legal proceedings arising out of the recent events, I believe that no one will conclude that I engaged in any criminal or fraudulent conduct during my tenure at WorldCom.

Until that time, however, I must respectfully decline to answer the questions of this committee on the basis of my fifth amendment privilege.

Wrong Numbers: The Accounting Problems at WorldCom: Hearing Before the H. Fin. Servs. Comm., 107th Cong. 20–21 (2002) (statement of Bernard J. Ebbers, former Chief Executive Officer, Worldcom).

Statement of Lois G. Lerner before the House Oversight and Government Reform Committee

On May 14, the Treasury IGs released a report finding that the Exempt Organizations field office in Cincinnati, Ohio, used inappropriate criteria to identify for further review applications from organizations that planned to engage in political activity which may mean that they did not qualify for tax exemption. On that same day, the Department of Justice launched an investigation into the matters described in the inspector general's report. In addition, members of this committee have accused me of providing false information when I responded to questions about the IRS processing of applications for tax exemption.

I have not done anything wrong. I have not broken any laws. I have not violated any IRS rules or regulations, and I have not provided false information to this or any other congressional committee.

And while I would very much like to answer the committee's questions today, I've been advised by my counsel to assert my constitutional right not to testify or answer questions related to the subject matter of this hearing. After very careful consideration, I have decided to follow my counsel's advice and not testify or answer any of the questions today.

> Because I'm asserting my right not to testify, I know that some people will assume that I've done something wrong. I have not. One of the basic functions of the Fifth Amendment is to protect innocent individuals, and that is the protection I'm invoking today. Thank you.

The IRS: Targeting Americans for Their Political Beliefs: Hearing Before the H. Comm. on Oversight & Gov't Reform, 113th Cong. 22 (2013) (statement Lois G. Lerner, former Director of Exempt Organizations, IRS).

It is important that assertions of innocence that accompany Fifth Amendment-privilege invocations do not contain factual admissions supporting the assertion of innocence. Otherwise, the witness risks waiving the privilege, a subject addressed in Chapter 7. Indeed, because 18 U.S.C. § 1001(a) now criminalizes the making of any knowing and willful false statement "within the jurisdiction of the executive, legislative, or judicial branch of the Government of the United States," it is not advisable for invocation of the Fifth Amendment privilege to be accompanied by factual assertions that could subject the speaker to separate false statement liability. Claiming the Fifth would not automatically protect a speaker from such prosecution for accompanying assertions of fact.

In congressional investigations, a client may commonly make a simple assertion of the privilege before the body posing questions and have counsel provide a more detailed explanation of the assertion outside of the hearing room in written or oral statements to the media. It is important to note, however, the prosecutor or other parties may later seek to admit counsel's statements into evidence, on the basis that the lawyer's statements are admissions of the client under Federal Rule of Evidence §§ 801(d)(2)(C) and (D), and their state counterparts. The ability of an opposing party to use statements made by counsel in any arguments concerning waiver of the Fifth Amendment right—which is undoubtedly personal to the maker—is a subject beyond the scope of this book.

CHAPTER 6

Stigma and the Fifth Amendment

Because the Fifth Amendment protects only against disclosures that could incriminate, the invocation of the privilege carries a stigma that the individual acted in contravention of the criminal law. Fear of this reputational damage often deters witnesses from asserting the privilege. While perceptions of the Fifth Amendment as a refuge for the guilty may never be totally erased, the stigma associated with asserting the Fifth Amendment privilege against self-incrimination is often exaggerated because the amendment also protects the innocent.

The Supreme Court's decision in *Ohio v. Reiner*, 532 U.S. 17 (2001), is instructive. There, the Ohio Supreme Court "held that a witness who denies all culpability does not have a valid Fifth Amendment privilege against self-incrimination." *Id.* at 18. The U.S. Supreme Court, in a rare grant of certiorari "when a state court's interpretation of state law has been influenced by an accompanying interpretation of federal law," disagreed. *Id.* at 20 (citation omitted). In a per curiam decision, the Court reminded Ohio that "truthful responses of an innocent witness, as well as those of a wrongdoer, may provide the government with incriminating evidence from the speaker's own mouth," and are thereby protected by the Fifth Amendment. *Id.* at 21 (citation omitted).

Ohio v. Reiner concerned a father's prosecution for involuntary manslaughter of his two-year-old child as a result of child abuse. The father's defense theory was that the child's babysitter was the culpable party. The babysitter, according to the Court, had reasonable cause to apprehend danger from her answers if she was questioned at the father's trial because she had spent extended periods of time alone with the baby in the weeks before his death. Given this fact—which the Court referred to as "ambiguous circumstances"—the Court ruled unanimously that the babysitter had a valid Fifth Amendment privilege not to testify despite her claimed innocence. *Id.* (citation omitted).

Subsequent decisions demonstrate the vitality of this point.

- *In re Proceedings Before a Grand Jury*, 768 N.E.2d 1102, 1107 (Mass. App. Ct. 2002) (reversing contempt order against grand jury witness for asserting Fifth Amendment privilege in arson investigation, where witness was one of only two people working in the store shortly before fire was set).
- *Begner v. State Ethics Comm'n*, 552 S.E.2d 431, 434–35 (Ga. Ct. App. 2001) (reversing order holding attorney in contempt, after attorney refused to disclose the name of his client for whom he had delivered an anonymous contribution to a political candidate, reasoning that the answers to questions posed by the Georgia State Ethics Commission could incriminate the lawyer even if he was innocent of violating a Georgia law prohibiting anonymous political donations).

The right of an innocent individual to assert the Fifth Amendment has a long historical pedigree. In *Bram v. United States*, 168 U.S. 532 (1897), the Supreme Court reversed the conviction of a sailor accused of murdering the ship's captain where the sailor, insisting he was innocent, nevertheless made a statement that was introduced against him at trial. The Court famously remarked that the Fifth Amendment protects everyone from giving an explanation of their conduct, reasoning that

> If an accused person be asked to explain his apparent connection with a crime under investigation, the ease with which the questions put to him may assume an inquisitorial character, the temptation to press the witness unduly, to browbeat him if he be timid or reluctant, to push him into a corner, and to entrap him into fatal contradictions, which is so painfully evident in many of the earlier [English] trials . . . made the system so odious as to give rise to a demand for its total abolition.

Id. at 544. Other Supreme Court decisions have echoed similar concerns:

- *Brown v. Walker*, 161 U.S. 591, 608 (1896) (despite upholding contempt citation for refusing to testify after being granted transactional immunity, the Court nonetheless remarked: "There is a possibility that any citizen, however innocent, may be subjected to a civil or criminal prosecution, and put to the expense of defending himself. . . . He may be even be convicted of a crime, and suffer imprisonment or other punishment before his innocence is discovered. . . .").
- *Griffin v. California*, 380 U.S. 609, 613 (1965) (in preventing prosecutorial comments on a defendant's decision not to testify, the Court remarked: "It is not every one who can safely venture on the witness stand, though entirely innocent. . . . Excessive timidity, nervousness when facing others and attempting to explain transactions of a suspicious character . . . will often confuse and embarrass him to such a degree as to increase rather than remove prejudices against him").

As noted in Chapter 2, the Self-Incrimination Clause does not protect only potential answers to questions that may directly support a conviction but any answer that could form a "link in the chain of evidence *needed to prosecute.*" *Hoffman v. United States*, 341 U.S. at 486 (emphasis added). The Supreme Court's admonition in *Hoffman* and other cases that the answer may lead merely to prosecution and not to conviction means that the Fifth Amendment need not be viewed as a refuge for scoundrels. Given the ambiguities that attend most complex criminal investigations and the low threshold for commencing a prosecution, a lawyer may reasonably feel that the client has little choice but to invoke the Fifth Amendment privilege, even if the truth will eventually exonerate the client. Clients may be less reluctant to use the privilege if they understand that it protects the innocent and guilty alike.

CHAPTER 7

Waiver and Risk of Waiver

There is no aspect of the Fifth Amendment privilege against self-incrimination as confusing as the law regarding waiver. Much of the confusion stems from the use of the vague term "waiver" to describe two different situations: first, the situation in which the witness forfeits his right to complain about the admissibility into evidence of self-incriminating statements by voluntarily making them, and second, the situation in which a court decides that the witness must, by having provided some self-incriminating testimony, continue to make further self-incriminating disclosures.

Even if we were to limit our consideration of waiver to the second circumstance, it would be difficult to discern clear patterns in court rulings, thereby often leaving witnesses at their peril in determining how to proceed. As with the Fifth Amendment generally, it is best to evaluate waiver in the varying contexts in which the issue has arisen, as only a few general principles can be reliably described.

General Principles

Waiver Is Proceeding-Specific

When a witness "forfeits" his privilege against self-incrimination in one proceeding by voluntarily testifying to self-incriminating facts, the witness may reassert the privilege against self-incrimination in subsequent separate proceedings.

In re Neff, 206 F.2d 149 (3d Cir. 1953), a leading case, explained this proposition as follows:

> The privilege attaches to the witness in each particular case in which he may be called on to testify, and whether or not he may claim it is to be determined without reference to what he said when testifying as a witness on some other trial, or on a former trial of the same case, and without reference to his declarations at some other time or place.

Id. at 152 (citations omitted). *Neff* is a correct statement of the law.

- *United States v. Allmon*, 594 F.3d 981, 985 (8th Cir. 2010) ("there is ample precedent for the rule that waiver of the Fifth Amendment privilege in one proceeding does not waive that privilege in a subsequent proceeding . . .") (citing cases).
- *United States v. Fortin*, 685 F.2d 1297, 1298–99 (11th Cir. 1982) (quoting *Neff* approvingly).
- *United States v. Yurasovich*, 580 F.2d 1212, 1220 (3d Cir. 1978) ("It is well settled by the overwhelming weight of authority that a person who has waived his privilege of silence in one trial or proceeding is not estopped to assert [the privilege] as to the same matter in a subsequent trial or proceeding.").
- *United States v. Cain*, 544 F.2d 1113, 1117 (1st Cir. 1976) ("It is hornbook law that the waiver is limited to the particular proceeding in which the witness appears.") (citation omitted).
- *In re Vitamins Antitrust Litig.*, 120 F. Supp. 2d 58, 66 (D.D.C. 2000) ("[M]ost courts that have considered this issue have held that the waiver of the privilege against self-incrimination in one proceeding does not affect the right of a witness or accused to invoke the privilege as to the same subject matter in another independent proceeding, but is limited to the proceeding in which it occurs.") (citations omitted).
- *Austin v. Nagareddy*, 811 S.E.2d 68 (Ga. Ct. App. 2018) (holding that the judge, in exercising his discretion, erred when he granted a stay based on his view that if the civil defendant testified in a deposition he would waive his right to assert his privilege against self-incrimination in a pending criminal case).

- *Martin v. Flanagan*, 789 A.2d 979, 985–86 (Conn. 2002) (collecting cases from six federal circuits and 17 states holding that a person who testifies in a trial is "not estopped from asserting the [Fifth Amendment] privilege in a subsequent proceeding") (citations omitted).
- *State v. Roberts*, 622 A.2d 1225, 1235 (N.H. 1993) ("[I]t is hornbook law that the waiver [of the privilege] is limited to the particular proceeding in which the witness appears.") (citation omitted).
- *In re Knapp*, 536 So. 2d 1330, 1336 (Miss. 1988) ("[W]aiver of the privilege [against self-incrimination] in one proceeding is limited to a waiver for that proceeding and that proceeding only.").
- *Hummell v. Superior Court*, 211 A.2d 272, 274 (R.I. 1965) ("Substantial authority supports the proposition that one who testifies before a grand jury does not thereby waive the privilege of refusing to testify in some subsequent proceeding on the ground of self-incrimination.").
- *See also Pillsbury Co. v. Conboy*, 459 U.S. 248, 263–64 (1983) (witness who previously testified under grant of immunity before grand jury had right to refuse to answer questions during a civil deposition on same subject).

The rationale for the "separate proceedings" rule is a sensible one: that conditions may change over time, creating new grounds for apprehension by the witness that compelled disclosures would be self-incriminating, or that repetition of testimony in an independent proceeding could constitute an independent source of self-incriminating evidence against the witness. Indeed, the separate proceedings rule does not implicate the danger that courts are generally concerned about when discussing partial waiver—that is, that the fact-finding process will be distorted or that opposing parties will be unfairly prejudiced.

- *In re Corrugated Container Antitrust Litig.*, 661 F.2d 1145, 1155 (7th Cir. 1981) ("[R]epetition of testimony in an independent proceeding may itself be viewed as incriminating. Thus, [non-party deponent's] deposition, even if it merely repeated or acknowledged his earlier testimony, could constitute an independent source of evidence against him."), *aff'd*, *Pillsbury Co. v. Conboy*, 459 U.S. 248 (1983).

- *In re Morganroth*, 718 F.2d 161, 165 (6th Cir. 1983) (recognizing that the privilege is "not waived in a subsequent proceeding by waiver in an earlier one" because circumstances can change).
- *United States v. Miranti*, 253 F.2d 135, 140 (2d Cir. 1958) (ruling that passage of time and events occurring between two appearances before the grand jury rendered the grand jury proceedings separate for purposes of the waiver rule and allowing the witness to assert the Fifth Amendment before the grand jury, after previously testifying before the same grand jury).
- *Heffington v. Moser*, 192 A.3d 900, 911–12 (Md. Ct. Spec. App. 2018) (in holding that a plaintiff in a civil case was entitled to a stay after her indictment, court ruled that her testimony in the civil case deposition did not waive her Fifth Amendment privilege not to testify at the civil trial when she was indicted between the deposition and the trial and circumstances had thereby changed).

The distinction between various proceedings is not always crystal clear. The dominant view is that a grand jury proceeding is a separate proceeding from the subsequent criminal trial. A person who voluntarily testifies before a grand jury may assert his Fifth Amendment privilege and remain silent at pretrial hearings or a trial held on an indictment returned by the grand jury, or vice versa.

- *United States v. James*, 609 F.2d 36, 44 (2d Cir. 1979) (although defendant failed to invoke privilege before the grand jury, he was entitled to invoke it at trial).
- *United States v. Licavoli*, 604 F.2d 613, 623 (9th Cir. 1979) (affirming trial court decision that witness who testified at the grand jury properly invoked his Fifth Amendment rights at trial).
- *United States v. Cain*, 544 F.2d 1113, 1117 (1st Cir. 1976) (affirming trial court ruling that co-defendant, who had previously testified in a deposition in other proceedings, could not be called to testify in defendant's trial).

- *Commonwealth v. Martin*, 668 N.E.2d 825, 829 (Mass. 1996) (holding that the witness had not waived his ability to invoke the privilege against self-incrimination at a subsequent trial by testifying before the grand jury).
- *See also United States v. Williams*, 504 U.S. 36, 46 (1992) (noting prior decisions in which the Court treated grand jury proceedings "as other than a constituent element of a 'criminal prosecution'") (citation omitted).

The rule in the federal courts in the District of Columbia, however, is to the contrary.

- *Ellis v. United States*, 416 F.2d 791, 800 (D.C. Cir. 1969) (witness was required to testify at trial to same matters as to which he testified voluntarily before the grand jury that returned the indictment on which the defendant was being tried).
- *United States v. Miller*, 904 F.2d 65, 67 (D.C. Cir. 1990) (although recognizing decisions that call into question the continuing validity of its prior decision in *Ellis*, the court remarked that it was still good law).

See also

- *United States v. Basciano*, 430 F. Supp. 2d 87, 94–95 (E.D.N.Y. 2006) (having testified in grand jury, witness was deemed unable to assert Fifth Amendment privilege against self-incrimination at subsequent trial and therefore was not unavailable for purpose of allowing defendant to use grand jury testimony in lieu of calling witness to the stand).
- *Harris v. United States*, 614 A.2d 1277, 1282 (D.C. 1992) (acknowledging that in the District of Columbia, a defense witness who testified voluntarily at a pretrial suppression hearing may not invoke the privilege against self-incrimination to avoid testifying on the same issues at the ensuing trial in which he was called as a witness).

An initial criminal trial and a retrial are usually separate proceedings.

- *Kirane v. City of Lowell*, 622 F. Supp. 262, 265 (D. Mass. 1985) ("[A] person who waives his privilege of silence in one trial [is not] estopped from asserting the privilege as to the same matter in a subsequent trial or proceeding.") (citations omitted).
- *State v. Knowles*, 395 So. 2d 678, 680 (La. 1981) ("One can waive silence at one trial and assert the right as to the same matter in a subsequent [separate] trial.") (citation omitted).

Although not based on the application of the separate proceeding doctrine, the testimony given by the defendant at the first trial may be admissible in the second trial without violating the defendant's Fifth Amendment right to remain silent in the second trial, should the initial conviction be reversed on appeal. *See, e.g.*, *Commonwealth v. Rosen*, 42 A.3d 988 (Pa. 2012) (Pennsylvania Supreme Court upheld trial court decision that defendant had waived his Fifth Amendment privilege by presenting a mental capacity defense at his first trial, thereby permitting state to introduce his inculpatory statements during the government expert's evaluation of his mental capacity at his retrial, even though he did not utilize such a defense during the retrial); *Commonwealth v. Beauchamp*, 732 N.E.2d 311, 325–26, (Mass. App. Ct. 2000) (at retrial of murder case, the defendant's testimony of the first trial was admissible as prior recorded testimony). *See also Oku v. Maryland*, 72 A.3d 538, 546–47 (Md. 2013) (state did not violate defendant's Fifth Amendment rights by using testimony he gave in district court at de novo trial in circuit court).

An exception exists when the original testimony was offered to rebut evidence later determined to have been improperly admitted. Thus in *Harrison v. United States*, 392 U.S. 219, 226 (1968), the Supreme Court reversed a conviction where the defendant was induced to testify at his first trial by the improper admission of his prior confessions and that prior testimony was admitted into evidence at his retrial, where the defendant remained silent.

Most courts have ruled that a defendant who invokes his right to remain silent at his second trial may not have the testimony he gave at his first trial admitted into evidence, on the basis that his assertion of his Fifth Amendment right makes him unavailable under the rules of evidence. Most courts read the hearsay rules regarding the admissibility of prior statements from unavailable witnesses as not applicable to criminal defendants asserting their Fifth Amendment rights. *See, e.g.*, *New Jersey v. McInerney*, 163 A.3d 935 (N.J. Super. Ct. 2017) (citing other federal and state cases).

Trials of co-defendants are separate for purposes of the Fifth Amendment, allowing a defendant to testify in his own trial and still exercise his privilege against self-incrimination when called as a witness in the trial of his alleged accomplice.

- *Ottomano v. United States*, 468 F.2d 269, 273–74 (1st Cir. 1972) (reversing contempt judgment that was issued to convicted defendant who refused to testify at a co-defendant's trial while his own motion to vacate was still pending, and thus he was still in possession of his Fifth Amendment privilege as to the crime of conviction).

As previously discussed, sentencing is a separate proceeding from a criminal trial. The Supreme Court has decided that a defendant does not waive his privilege to remain silent at sentencing by making incriminating statements when he enters a guilty plea. See Chapter 3 discussion of *Mitchell v. United States*, 526 U.S. 314, 321 (1999). Although the defendant's trial testimony may be used against him at his sentencing, *Mitchell* would seem to guarantee the testifying defendant a right to remain silent at sentencing.

Although fewer reported cases concern the "separate proceeding doctrine" in the context of purely civil cases, arguments are often made that civil actions involve separate component parts for purposes of the Fifth Amendment, particularly if there are long delays between initial proceedings and trial.

- *FDIC v. Mahajan*, 2014 WL 3359333 (N.D. Ill. 2014) (disclosure of incriminating information by bank officer during FDIC investigation did not prevent officer from relying on Fifth Amendment at her deposition in the FDIC suit against other officers).

- *Krasney v. Nam (In re Gi Yeong Nam)*, 245 B.R. 216, 232, 235 (Bankr. E.D. Pa. 2000) (denying trustee's motion to compel responses to discovery requests in an adversary proceeding, where debtor had testified at Section 341 initial meeting of creditors).
- *State v. Roberts*, 622 A.2d 1225, 1235 (N.H. 1993) (citing to the "majority rule" that "preserves a witness's right to assert the privilege in subsequent, distinct stages of a single proceeding") (citations omitted).

A witness's previous testimony in a civil deposition in one case should not waive the privilege in a later civil suit deposition, if for no other reason than that the new testimony could subject the witness to danger of making new incriminating admissions or admitting to past perjury. *See, e.g., In re Morganroth*, 718 F.2d 161, 165 (6th Cir. 1983); *Carter-Wallace, Inc. v. Hartz Mountain Indus., Inc.*, 553 F. Supp. 45, 49 (S.D.N.Y. 1982) (executive's assertion of the Fifth in deposition was valid, even though he had testified about the same subject in a prior deposition in a separate case).

The "separate proceedings doctrine" also applies to events other than formal court proceedings. Statements made in informal settings and not under oath should not waive the privilege against self-incrimination in a subsequent formal proceeding involving the witness.

- *Nationwide Life Ins. Co. v. Richards*, 541 F.3d 903, 911 (9th Cir. 2008) (witness's statement to investigating officer after murder did not waive her privilege against self-incrimination with respect to later criminal proceeding or with respect to later civil proceeding).
- *Slutzker v. Johnson*, 393 F.3d 373, 389 (3d Cir. 2004) (testimony at coroner inquest did not waive right against self-incrimination in later criminal case).
- *Ellis v. United States*, 416 F.2d 791, 805 n.37 (D.C. Cir. 1969) (noting that "a statement made to investigators" does not constitute a waiver of the right against self-incrimination for purposes of a subsequent trial of the witness).

- *United States v. Miranti*, 253 F.2d 135, 139 (2d Cir. 1958) (FBI interview and second grand jury were separate proceedings for purposes of alleged waiver of Fifth Amendment).
- *United States v. Maikovskis*, No. M18–304, 1978 U.S. Dist. LEXIS 19113, at *7 (S.D.N.Y. Mar. 10, 1978) (prior testimony in depositions conducted by INS personnel over a period of 12 years did not preclude subject of deportation from asserting the Fifth Amendment privilege against self-incrimination at his deportation hearing).
- *Carter v. United States*, 791 A.2d 23, 25 (D.C. 2001) (defense witness properly invoked Fifth Amendment privilege against self-incrimination at trial, despite prior statements made to his probation officer during a pre-sentence interview).

Waiver Must Be Voluntary

To be effective, waiver of the Fifth Amendment privilege must be freely and voluntarily given, in the sense that it was the product of a free and deliberate choice rather than the result of intimidation, coercion, or deception. Importantly, although only a reasonable fear of criminal sanctions can normally form a basis for invoking the privilege against self-incrimination, the threat of penalties and costs other than criminal prosecution can render an asserted waiver involuntary, and therefore ineffective.

- *Garrity v. New Jersey*, 385 U.S. 493, 500 (1967) (holding that a statement obtained from police officers, who had been threatened with termination if they refused to answer questions during a ticket-fixing investigation, could not be used against them in a subsequent criminal prosecution and that the purported waiver was ineffective).
- *Pentlarge v. Murphy*, 541 F. Supp. 2d 421, 427–28 (D. Mass. 2008) (individuals who were civilly committed as sexually dangerous persons had stated a Fifth Amendment violation by alleging that they were denied treatment if they refused to sign form waiving confidentiality for all admissions made during their civil commitment).
- *Raphael v. Conrad*, 371 F. Supp. 256, 258–59 (S.D. Ind. 1974) (finding a statute that required registered lobbyists of the Indiana

legislature to declare that they were not members of the Communist Party or lose their ability to lobby violated the Fifth Amendment privilege against self-incrimination).

- *State v. Fuller*, 915 P.2d 809, 816, 276 Mont. 155, 167 (1996) (defendant's Fifth Amendment rights were violated when he was told he had to honestly disclose his sexual offense history before receiving treatment, and if he did not honestly disclose, his probation would be revoked). *See also United States v. Von Behren*, 822 F.3d 1139 (10th Cir. 2016) (same).

However, where the pressure is not specifically directed at the exercise of the Fifth Amendment privilege, courts are less likely to find the waiver to have been involuntary.

- *United States v. Ferguson*, No. 3:06-CR-137, 2007 WL 4240782, at *7 (D. Conn. Nov. 30, 2007) (no sufficient economic pressure to find involuntary waiver where employee received letter from company informing him that (1) company would consider disciplining employees who did not participate in government investigation, and (2) company would evaluate its obligation to pay legal fees for non-cooperating employees).
- *United States v. Bartlett*, No. 06-CR-273, 2007 WL 1830726, at *1 (E.D. Wis. June 22, 2007) (police department rule requiring officers to "honor all subpoenas for court appearances," combined with rule that failure to follow rules will result in disciplinary action, was not sufficiently specific to constitute involuntary waiver).

The issue of when pressure imposed by the state is so great as to render the claimed waiver of the privilege against self-incrimination involuntary is related to the question, explored in Chapter 2, of when a statement is compelled for purposes of the Fifth Amendment. Just as the test for compulsion is not fixed, so too the test for when a waiver is voluntary is not fixed. Courts must look to the totality of the circumstances to make such determinations.

Waiver Need Not Be Knowing

To waive most constitutional rights, particularly the waiver of "trial rights in a trial type situation," the Supreme Court has required the proponent of waiver to demonstrate that it was the result of an "intentional relinquishment or abandonment of a known right or privilege."

- *Johnson v. Zerbst*, 304 U.S. 458, 464 (1938) (requiring the government to demonstrate the "intentional relinquishment or abandonment of a known right or privilege" in the context of whether the defendant waived his Sixth Amendment right to counsel in a federal criminal trial).
- *Adams v. United States ex rel. McCann*, 317 U.S. 269, 275 (1942) (applying *Johnson* criteria to waiver of right to a jury trial).
- *Brookhart v. Janis*, 384 U.S. 1, 4 (1966) (applying *Johnson* criteria to waiver of right to confrontation of witnesses).
- *Barker v. Wingo*, 407 U.S. 514, 525–26 (1972) (applying *Johnson* criteria to waiver of right to a speedy trial).
- *United States v. Olano*, 507 U.S. 725, 733 (1993) (distinguishing between forfeiture, described as "the failure to make the timely assertion of a right," and waiver, described as "intentional relinquishment or abandonment of a known right").

Indeed, in many other contexts not involving constitutional rights, courts require the government to prove that a defendant's waiver was not only voluntary, but knowing.

- *United States v. Mezzanatto*, 513 U.S. 196, 210 (1995) ("an agreement to waive the exclusionary provisions of the plea-statement rules is valid," absent an indication that the agreement was entered into unknowingly or involuntarily).
- *United States v. Velez*, 354 F.3d 190, 196 (2d Cir. 2004) (government required to demonstrate that waiver provision in a proffer agreement was entered into knowingly and voluntarily; where government can make such demonstration, the waiver provision is constitutional).

In *Minnesota v. Murphy*, 465 U.S. 420, 435–36 (1984), however, the Supreme Court ruled that the state may compel a probationer to answer certain questions posed by his probation officer without demonstrating that the probationer knew he had a right to assert the Fifth Amendment to other questions. The three dissenters in the case, led by Justice Marshall, argued that "the State was obliged to prove that Murphy was aware of his constitutional rights and freely waived them; by showing nothing more than that Murphy failed to assert his privilege before answering, the State failed to carry its burden." *Id.* at 443. As a result of Justice Marshall's dissent, the majority spent a fair amount of energy reviewing its prior cases and stating that the "general rule," subject to an exception for situations governed by *Miranda*, is that "an individual may lose the benefit of the [Fifth Amendment] privilege without making a knowing and intelligent waiver." *Id.* at 427–28 (citations omitted). *See also Garner v. United States*, 424 U.S. 648, 654 n.9 (1976) ("We recently have made clear that an individual may lose the benefit of the privilege without making a knowing and intelligent waiver.") (citing *Schneckloth v. Bustamonte*, 412 U.S. 218, 222–27 (1973)). In the more recent case of *Salinas v. Texas*, 570 U.S. 178 (2013), the Court also remarked that forfeiture of the privilege need not be knowing. *Id.* at 190. The plurality argued that the suspect's failure to assert the privilege as his reason for remaining silent during a non-custodial police interrogation constituted an implied waiver of the right against self-incrimination. *Id.* at 186.

Although none of these cases involved a true waiver—where the court was faced with the issue of whether or not a witness may cease communicating after having made some potentially incriminating remarks—they appear to indicate that the Supreme Court does not consider it necessary for a waiver to be a knowing one in any circumstances other than after a suspect receives *Miranda* warnings.

The absence of a knowledge requirement for waiving the Fifth Amendment privilege does not mean that the privilege is waived for all purposes whenever the witness makes any disclosures. Rather, the consensus is that even a witness who testifies about a subject does not waive the privilege until he makes some self-incriminating admissions and that the waiver is limited to questions about incriminating facts about which the witness has already testified. Because only the witness knows whether the disclosure sought is likely to incriminate, the witness arguably retains a significant degree of control over the waiver determination—even if the witness never actually knew of the privilege against self-incrimination and never consciously or intentionally chose to waive it.

- *McCarthy v. Arndstein*, 262 U.S. 355, 359 (1923) ("[W]here the previous disclosure by an ordinary witness is not an actual admission of guilt or incriminating facts, he is not deprived of the privilege of stopping short in his testimony whenever it may fairly tend to incriminate him.").
- *In re Hitchings*, 850 F.2d 180, 181 (4th Cir. 1988) (overturning contempt citation where witness, having answered some questions without revealing self-incriminating information, refused to answer further questions).
- *United States v. MacCloskey*, 682 F.2d 468, 478 n.18 (4th Cir. 1982) ("[T]he privilege is waived only if the prior testimony revealed incriminating facts.") (citation omitted).
- *United States v. James*, 609 F.2d 36, 45 (2d Cir. 1979) ("[O]ur examination of [witness's] testimony shows that he disclosed nothing that might be characterized as incriminating. Therefore, he did not waive his privilege, which he properly invoked in response to other questions.") (citations omitted).
- *In re Vitamins Antitrust Litig.*, 120 F. Supp. 2d 58, 67 (D.D.C. 2000) ("It is clear that a witness does not lose his Fifth Amendment privilege unless he testifies to an incriminating fact.") (citing *Rogers v. United States*, 340 U.S. 367, 372–73 (1951)).
- *Krasney v. Nam (In re Gi Yeong Nam)*, 245 B.R. 216, 227, 234 (Bankr. E.D. Pa. 2000) (because facts revealed by debtor at hearing were incriminating of his son, but not self-incriminating, prior disclosures did not constitute a waiver of debtor's Fifth Amendment privilege).

A more difficult question is presented when the witness makes some statements that could arguably form a link in the chain of incrimination and then attempts to invoke the privilege to prevent answers that are more directly incriminating. The proponent of waiver will argue that the witness has waived the privilege against self-incrimination by disclosing a "link in the chain," and some cases take the position that "link in the chain" statements may constitute a broad testimonial waiver.

- *In re Oxford Royal Mushroom Prods., Inc.*, 46 B.R. 77, 79–80 (Bankr. E.D. Pa. 1985) (even though debtor's former president's testimony at a hearing revealed essentially non-incriminating information, president had waived the privilege by volunteering the information and would have to provide details to the trustee).
- *Nutramax Labs., Inc. v. Twin Labs., Inc.*, 32 F. Supp. 2d 331, 334 (D. Md. 1999) (by giving self-serving speech at end of deposition and by submitting affidavits, the defendant in a patent infringement case was held to have waived the right against self-incrimination and could not refuse to supply further details related to the same subject matter).
- *Presser v. United States*, 284 F.2d 233, 235 (D.C. Cir. 1960) (by answering that he had complied with a congressional subpoena to the best of his ability and had produced every responsive document available to him, a congressional witness subjected himself to cross-examination with respect to how he had complied with the subpoena and waived his privilege on whether he had destroyed any responsive documents).

However, the better-reasoned decisions place a heavier burden on the proponent of waiver and uphold the witness's right to invoke the privilege even after making some comments that contain "links in the chain" of incriminating admissions. The rationale against inferring waiver from testimony that does not directly incriminate was explained in *Klein v. Harris*, 667 F.2d 274, 287 (2d Cir. 1981). In responding to the defendant's argument that a witness had waived the privilege by testifying earlier in the trial and that his testimony should have been struck when he later asserted the privilege against self-incrimination, the court remarked:

> There is no doubt that a waiver of the fifth amendment's privilege against self-incrimination may, in an appropriate case, be inferred from a witness' [sic] prior statements with respect to the subject matter of the case, without any inquiry into whether the witness, when he made the statements, actually knew of the existence of the privilege and consciously chose to waive it. However, such a "testimonial waiver" is not to be lightly inferred, and the courts accordingly indulge every reasonable presumption against finding a testimonial waiver. Indeed, we read the prior decisions of the Supreme Court and the courts of this Circuit to hold that a court should only infer a waiver of the fifth amendment's privilege against self-incrimination from a witness' prior statements if (1) the witness' prior statements have created a significant likelihood that the finder of fact will be left with and prone to rely on a distorted view of the truth, and (2) the witness had reason to know that his prior statements would be interpreted as a waiver of the fifth amendment's privilege against self-incrimination. . . . The requisite reason to know that a waiver might be inferred should be found only if the witness' prior statements were (a) "testimonial," meaning that they were voluntarily made under oath in the context of the same judicial proceeding, and (b) "incriminating," meaning that they did not merely deal with matters "collateral" to the events surrounding commission of the crime.

Id. at 287–88 (citations omitted).

The *Klein v. Harris* "distortion" test has attracted a large number of adherents.

- *United States v. Davenport*, 929 F.2d 1169, 1174 (7th Cir. 1991) (citing *Klein* in discussing the "distortion of facts" that could arise from allowing a defendant to select any stopping place in his testimony).
- *United States v. Singer*, 785 F.2d 228, 241 (8th Cir. 1986) (stating that the *Klein* two-part test was "useful" and applying it to hold that a government witness in a criminal case did not waive his Fifth Amendment privilege).

- *In re Saunders*, 528 B.R. 860, 868 (Bankr. N.D. Ga. 2015) (applying *Klein* to uphold debtor's right not to answer deposition questions about matters previously testified to in her statement of financial affairs at creditors' meeting).
- *In re Vitamins Antitrust Litig.*, 120 F. Supp. 2d 58, 66 (D.D.C. 2000) (citing *Klein* two-part test for waiver).
- *In re Gi Yeong Nam*, 245 B.R. 216, 228 (Bankr. E.D. Pa. 2000) (indicating that although *Klein* formula had not been expressly adopted by the Third Circuit, it had gained widespread acceptance by other courts).

Under the *Klein* test, the danger of being deemed to have waived the right against self-incrimination by volunteering some potentially incriminating facts is often too great to justify trying to walk the line. There is simply no clear line that can always be determined in advance of which testimony about a potentially criminal subject will be deemed to constitute a waiver and which will not. *Compare Cartier v. Micha, Inc.*, 2008 WL 2061386 (S.D.N.Y. May 12, 2008) (freely testifying about when he obtained Cartier watches in trademark infringement case did not prevent civil defendant from asserting privilege against self-incrimination when asked about adding diamonds to Cartier watches) *with Thorne v. Loews Philadelphia Hotel, Inc.*, No. 15–3837, 2016 WL 4011332 (E.D. Pa. July 27, 2016) (testifying about how he had massaged plaintiff's buttocks waived a civil defendant's right to assert a privilege against self-incrimination in a suit for assault and other torts). Thus, most careful lawyers will advise their clients to assert the self-incrimination privilege to any question that could conceivably be viewed as calling for a link in a chain of evidence that could possibly be incriminating. The client will be required to assert the privilege on a question-by-question basis, rather than make a blanket assertion, as previously discussed.

Many courts appear to follow a "further incrimination" test to determine waiver, focusing on whether the witness might risk further incrimination based on his additional testimony. This test is based on language in the Supreme Court's decision in *Rogers v. United States*, 340 U.S. 367, 374 (1951), in which the Supreme Court remarked that a witness has no Fifth Amendment right where the witness has already so thoroughly incriminated himself that the answer to any additional questions on the same topic cannot further incriminate him. But *Rogers*, as described in the next section, did not announce a test, but simply focused on whether further details appreciably increased the risk of incrimination. The lower courts have nonetheless used the "further incrimination" test to rule both in favor of a party who seeks to stop making further statements as well as to rule that the witness has waived the privilege and must continue to testify.

- *In re Seper*, 705 F.2d 1499, 1501–02 (9th Cir. 1983) (stating that "[t]he issue here is whether Seper was withholding mere 'details' or evidence which would 'further incriminate' him," and holding that although Seper testified that he had received confidential taxpayer information from two IRS agents, he did not waive his privilege with respect to the identity of those agents because disclosure of that information under the circumstances "would further incriminate him by providing links in the essential chain of proof").
- *In re Folding Carton Antitrust Litig.*, 609 F.2d 867, 873 (7th Cir. 1979) ("[A]s to each question to which a claim of privilege is directed, the court must determine whether the answer to that particular question would subject the witness to a 'real danger' of further incrimination.") (quoting *Rogers v. United States*, 340 U.S. 367, 374 (1951)).
- *United States v. LaRiche*, 549 F.2d 1088, 1096 (6th Cir. 1977) ("Although disclosure of an incriminating fact generally waives the privilege as to details, waiver does not occur where further disclosure carries a risk of incrimination beyond that raised by previous testimony. Since disclosure of the details of Flott's participation in unreported criminal activity would present a real and appreciable danger of criminal prosecution not raised by his testimony on direct, the Court was not in error in upholding his right to refuse to respond.") (internal citations omitted).
- *In re Master Key Litig.*, 507 F.2d 292, 294 (9th Cir. 1974) ("[A]n ordinary witness may . . . refuse to answer any questions about

a matter already discussed, even if the facts already revealed are incriminating, as long as the answers sought may tend to *further* incriminate him.") (emphasis added) (citations omitted).

- *Hashagen v. United States*, 283 F.2d 345, 352 (9th Cir. 1960) ("The touchstone in *Rogers*, is the adjective 'further,' and thus an admission of a criminating fact may waive the privilege as to the details of that fact so long as they d[o] not further incriminate, but where those detai[l]s would so incriminate, the privilege is not waived.") (citations omitted).
- *United States v. Wilson*, No. 04-CR-1016 (NGG), 2013 WL 3243630, at *1 (E.D.N.Y. June 26, 2013) ("[A]bsent some indication that his current testimony might subject him to *further* incrimination, a witness may not invoke his Fifth Amendment right after having already testified about the events in question.") (citations omitted).
- *SEC v. Parkersburg Wireless Ltd. Liab. Co.*, 156 F.R.D. 529, 536–37 (D.D.C. 1994) ("As a general rule, where as here [the witness] waived her privilege by raising a subject, she cannot then invoke the privilege with respect to the particulars. This is true unless the related questions further incriminate the witness.") (citations omitted).

Regardless of the test applied, it would seem to be easily established that a person compelled to appear as a witness may proclaim his or her innocence without fear of waiving the privilege against self-incrimination.

The attempt by a former senior IRS official to assert her Fifth Amendment privilege before a congressional committee while also proclaiming her innocence, discussed in Chapter 5, was met by claims that she had thereby waived her privilege and could be compelled to testify. Although the House of Representatives found the IRS official in contempt for refusing to testify after asserting her innocence, the U.S. Attorney for the District of Columbia subsequently notified the House Speaker that his office would not present the contempt citation to a federal grand jury, thereby ending any potential criminal prosecution for contempt. The letter from the U.S. Attorney correctly found that assertion of innocence did not constitute a waiver. *See* Letter from Ron Machen, U.S. Attorney for D.C. to Hon. John

Boehner, House of Representatives (Mar. 31, 2015), available at https://www.npr.org/sections/thetwo-way/2015/04/01/396872364/justice-department-wont-charge-irs-lois-lerner-with-criminal-contempt. In addition to the cases previously cited, the following cases would appear to support that conclusion.

- *Emspak v. United States*, 349 U.S. 190, 193, 195–98 (1955) (a witness appearing before a House committee answered 171 questions about his union and its ties to the Communist Party, but then invoked the Fifth Amendment not to answer 68 questions about his associations and affiliations; the Court held that when the witness answered "No" to whether revealing his knowledge of people associated with the Communist Party "would subject [him] to criminal prosecution," he did not waive his privilege).
- *McCarthy v. Arndstein*, 262 U.S. 355, 359 (1923) (citing with approval the holding of the highest court of New York that "a witness by answering questions exonerating himself in general terms from all connection with a criminal transaction does not thereby waive his right to remain silent").

Waiver in Various Contexts

Just as the right to assert the privilege is best considered in the various contexts in which it may be raised, the issue of waiver should be considered in context as well.

Waiver of *Miranda* Rights

Waivers of a suspect's *Miranda* rights are an exception to the general rule that waiver of Fifth Amendment self-incrimination rights need not be knowing. A defendant's waiver of *Miranda* rights must be both "voluntary in the sense that it was the product of a free and deliberate choice" and "made with a full awareness both of the nature of the right being abandoned and the consequences of the decision to abandon it." *Colorado v. Spring*, 479 U.S. 564, 573 (1987) (quoting *Moran v. Burbine*, 475 U.S. 412, 421 (1986)).

Waiver of a person's *Miranda* rights is a necessary precondition to the admission of a suspect's statement made during a custodial interrogation. As indicated in *Berghius v. Tompkins*, 560 U.S. 370, 382 (2010), "[E]ven absent the accused's invocation of the right to remain silent, the accused's statement during a custodial interrogation is inadmissible at trial unless the prosecution can establish that the accused 'in fact knowingly and voluntarily waived [*Miranda*] rights' when making the statement." Furthermore, a waiver of *Miranda* rights does not act as a true waiver that thereafter forbids the subject from ceasing to make incriminating remarks. Indeed, as mentioned previously in Chapter 3, a suspect can stop talking at any time and invoke his/her *Miranda* rights, once "waived."

The burden of proof is clearly on the government to demonstrate a *Miranda* waiver.

- *Colorado v. Connelly*, 479 U.S. 157, 168–69 (1986) (the government must prove by a preponderance of the evidence that the suspect waived his *Miranda* rights).
- *Tague v. Louisiana*, 444 U.S. 469, 470–71 (1980) (summarily reversing where lower court had indicated burden was on defendant claiming lack of mental capacity necessary to knowingly waive *Miranda* rights).

The Supreme Court has held that determinations regarding a *Miranda* waiver are to be made based on the "totality of the circumstances."

- *Moran v. Burbine*, 475 U.S. 412, 421 (1986) (court must find that waiver of *Miranda* rights was a product of a free and deliberate choice, considering the totality of the circumstances).
- *Fare v. Michael C.*, 442 U.S. 707, 725 (1979) (totality of circumstances approach is adequate even in determinations of whether a juvenile has waived *Miranda* rights).

Thus, the background, experience, and competence of the person waiving his or her *Miranda* rights are critical considerations.

- *J.D.B. v. North Carolina*, 564 U.S. 261, 273–76 (2011) (holding that a child's age may properly be taken into consideration in determining whether a juvenile was in custody for purposes of *Miranda*).
- *Mincey v. Arizona*, 437 U.S. 385, 399–400 (1978) (waiver invalid because hospitalized defendant complained of excruciating pain while hooked to at least six tubes and nodded off during four hours of interrogation).
- *Harris v. Bornharst*, 513 F.3d 503, 512 (6th Cir. 2008) (waiver invalid for a 12-year-old defendant without experience in criminal justice system, when he was separated from his mother and subjected to intense interrogation).
- *United States v. Garibay*, 143 F.3d 534, 537 (9th Cir. 1998) (no effective waiver by defendant who had a low IQ and barely spoke English).
- *Smith v. State*, 918 A.2d 1144, 1147, 1149 (Del. 2007) (no effective waiver by defendant with diminished capacity, IQ of 65, and mental age of 11 to 12).

While the competency of the defendant will be important to the determination of whether the defendant "knowingly and intelligently" waived his or her *Miranda* rights, the government must also demonstrate that the conduct of the police did not interfere with the suspect's voluntary waiver of the privilege.

- *Guidry v. Dretke*, 397 F.3d 306, 328–29 (5th Cir. 2005) (*Miranda* waiver invalid where police falsely told defendant that they had contacted defendant's attorney, who had approved his cooperation).
- *Hart v. Attorney Gen.*, 323 F.3d 884, 894–95 (11th Cir. 2003) (*Miranda* waiver invalid where police told defendant that lawyer would disadvantage him and "honesty wouldn't hurt him.").
- *State v. Stanga*, 617 N.W.2d 486, 490–91 (S.D. 2000) (incriminating statement should have been suppressed when interrogating police officer deceived suspect into believing that any statement he made was solely between the officer and suspect).

There is language in *Miranda* indicating that the Supreme Court requires an express waiver in the context of custodial interrogation: "[W]here in-custody interrogation is involved, there is no room for the contention that the privilege is waived if the individual answers some questions or gives some information on his own prior to invoking his right to remain silent when interrogated." 384 U.S. at 475–76. However, in *North Carolina v. Butler*, 441 U.S. 369 (1979), the Supreme Court retreated from this passage in a case in which the suspect made an incriminating statement after indicating he understood the warnings and would talk but not sign the waiver form. Although the North Carolina Supreme Court had reversed Butler's convictions based on its reading that *Miranda* required a specific "oral waiver," the U.S. Supreme Court rejected this reading and held that "an explicit statement of waiver is not invariably necessary to support a finding that the defendant waived the right to counsel guaranteed by the *Miranda* case." *Id.* at 376. Thereafter, many courts held that when a suspect makes an incriminating statement—after expressing his understanding of the *Miranda* warnings—the incriminating statements are admissible, absent police coercion, because the suspect has implicitly waived his or her *Miranda* rights.

In *Berghuis v. Thompkins*, 560 U.S. 370 (2010), the Court finished overruling the *Miranda* requirement of express waiver. After issuing a *Miranda* warning and obtaining an acknowledgment by Thompkins that he understood his rights, the police began talking to him about the case. Thereafter, Thompkins was silent for two hours and 45 minutes. However, when asked if he prayed to God to forgive him for the shooting, Thompkins responded "Yes." This answer was introduced at his trial as an admission of guilt. Picking up on the implicit waiver language in *Butler*, the five-member majority, over a vigorous dissent, ruled: "In sum, a suspect who has received and understood the *Miranda* warnings, and has not invoked his *Miranda* rights, waives the right to remain silent by making an uncoerced statement. . . ." *Id.* at 388–89. As previously mentioned, this "waiver" authorized the admissibility of *Berghuis*'s admission, nothing more.

Subsequent to *Berghuis*, most courts have found it easy to deny suppression motions made by defendants who made statements to the police after being advised of their *Miranda* rights. *See, e.g.*, *United States v.*

Quiroz, 874 F.3d 562, 567–68 (7th Cir. 2017); *United States v. Peter*, 2018 WL 5282878 at *4 (S.D.N.Y. Oct. 24, 2018).

If officers misrepresent the nature of the *Miranda* rights or the consequences of waiving them, a subsequent *Miranda* waiver may be deemed invalid on the grounds that it was not knowing and intelligent. However, a *Miranda* waiver will generally not be invalidated on grounds that the police lied to the suspect about other matters. *See, e.g., Illinois v. Perkins*, 496 U.S. 292, 297 (1990) ("Ploys to mislead a suspect or lull him into a false sense of security that do not rise to the level of compulsion or coercion to speak are not within *Miranda*'s concerns.").

In addition to being "knowing and intelligent," *Miranda* waivers must be "voluntary." To be voluntary, the waiver must be "a free and deliberate choice rather than [the result of] intimidation, coercion or deception." *Berghuis v. Thompkins*, 560 U.S. 320, 380 (2010). The voluntariness of a *Miranda* waiver is determined by the same factors as the courts use to determine the voluntariness of a confession as a matter of due process.

- *Colorado v. Spring*, 479 U.S. 564, 573–74 (1987) ("There is no doubt that *Spring*'s decision to waive his Fifth Amendment privilege was voluntary. He alleges no coercion of a confession by means of physical violence or other deliberate means calculated to break his will.").
- *Colorado v. Connelly*, 479 U.S. 157, 169–70 (1986) ("There is obviously no reason to require more in the way of a 'voluntariness' inquiry in the *Miranda* waiver content than in the Fourteenth Amendment confession context.").

The one tactic the Supreme Court has invalidated as a means of obtaining a valid waver is the so-called two step, in which officers would interrogate the suspect before giving *Miranda* warnings and then seek a waiver and have the suspect repeat earlier admissions. *See Missouri v. Seibert*, 542 U.S. 600, 616 (2004).

Testimonial Waiver in Grand Jury Proceedings

A witness appearing before a grand jury may relinquish his privilege against self-incrimination without an express acknowledgment that he is waiving a known right, simply by answering a question and providing incriminating information. In *Rogers v. United States*, 340 U.S. 367, 368, 370 (1951), the witness testified before the grand jury that while she had been in possession of the records of the Communist Party of Denver, she had transferred the records to another person. She refused to identify the person, asserting the information would be incriminating. A divided Court affirmed her contempt conviction, holding that having already incriminated herself by admitting Communist Party membership and possession of the records, she could not claim the privilege as to "details." *Id.* at 373. To uphold such a claim would, according to the majority, "open the way to distortion of facts by permitting a witness to select any stopping place in the testimony." *Id.* at 371.

Rogers is described as the leading case on testimonial waiver, and courts often cite it as establishing a "fact-detail" test for determining whether a party has waived his or her Fifth Amendment privilege by making some incriminating revelations. A careful reading of *Rogers*, however, does not support the "fact-detail" distinction as the sole basis for the decision. Rather, *Rogers* also articulated both a "distortion" and a "further incrimination" test for determining waiver, which is more protective of the witness's ability to decide when to answer a question and when to assert his privilege against self-incrimination.

In *Rogers*, the Supreme Court affirmed the district court's contempt sentence not because it thought Rogers had waived her Fifth Amendment right, but because the Court did not believe the revelation of the name of the individual to whom she had transferred the records would further incriminate her. *Id.* at 374–75. After worrying about how the invocation of the privilege might open the way to distortion, the Court articulated the grounds for its ruling by stating:

> Requiring full disclosure of details after a witness freely testifies as to a criminating fact does not rest upon a further "waiver" of the privilege against self-incrimination. Admittedly, petitioner had already "waived" her privilege of silence when she freely answered criminating questions relating to her connection with the Communist Party. But when petitioner was asked to furnish the name of the person to whom she

> turned over Party records, the court was required to determine, as it must whenever the privilege is claimed, whether the question presented a reasonable danger of *further crimination* in light of all the circumstances, including any previous disclosures. As to each question to which a claim of privilege is directed, the court must determine whether the answer to that particular question would subject the witness to a "real danger" of *further crimination*. After petitioner's admission that she held that office of Treasurer of the Communist Party of Denver, disclosure of acquaintance with her successor presents no more than a "mere imaginary possibility" of increasing the danger of prosecution.

Id. at 374–75 (emphasis added).

In the grand jury context, courts generally err on the side of permitting the witness to determine when answering a question will further incriminate.

- *In re Seper*, 705 F.2d 1499, 1502 (9th Cir. 1983) (although witness had "provide[d] a basis" on which to charge him with a crime through his testimony, conviction was far enough from being certain that witness was justified in invoking the privilege when he did).
- *United States v. Chase*, 281 F.2d 225, 230 (7th Cir. 1960) (where defendants had invoked privilege at the beginning of their testimony and later testified only about those items which did not incriminate them, defendants did not waive their Fifth Amendment privilege).
- *In re Grand Jury Subpoena*, No. M11–189 (JSR), 2003 WL 21373497, at *1 (S.D.N.Y. June 10, 2003) (granting access by lawyer to transcript of grand jury witness's prior testimony to demonstrate that prior testimony did not waive privilege against self-incrimination as to government's questions in new grand jury proceeding).
- *Grand Jury Investigation in re Teamsters League of Phila. & Vicinity*, 204 F. Supp. 147, 149–50 (E.D. Pa. 1962) (when the focus of the inquiry shifted from labor law violations to tax law violations, the information the witness was asked for became potentially incriminating, and he had not waived the privilege against self-incrimination by responding to the earlier inquiries).

Particularly in a grand jury proceeding, the decisions just cited appear sound. Nonetheless, careful lawyers will most often advise their clients not to risk waiver by testifying to some facts in the grand jury but refusing to answer other questions, unless the distinctions between the potentially criminal subjects and the non-criminal subjects is extremely clear.

Waiver by Pleading Guilty

In *Mitchell v. United States*, 526 U.S. 314, 327 (1999) the Supreme Court held that a plea of guilty is not a waiver of a defendant's Fifth Amendment privilege at sentencing, resolving a split in the circuits. The Court rejected the government's contention that the guilty plea waived the privilege with respect to all crimes comprehended in the plea and specifically interpreted the words "any criminal case" in the text of the Self-Incrimination Clause to include sentencing proceedings, ensuring that the "core" right against self-incrimination applied until a final judgment is entered (and confirmed on appeal).

The *Mitchell* Court's comments on waiver are useful to consider in a broader context. In its ruling, the Court indicated that its prior Fifth Amendment waiver cases, including *Rogers v. United States*, 340 U.S. 367 (1951) and *Brown v. United States*, 356 U.S. 148 (1958), were primarily concerned with the danger that the grand jury or fact-finder would be misled by selective disclosure, whereby the defendant might testify to some facts but unfairly refuse to testify to other facts within the scope of relevant cross-examination. 526 U.S. at 321–22. The Court indicated that a plea colloquy presented little of these same dangers.

Waiver in Criminal Trials

During a criminal trial, the courts are justifiably concerned about allowing the adversarial process for determining truth to be distorted by allowing testimony as to some facts, but preventing cross-examination about those facts on the basis of the Fifth Amendment privilege against self-incrimination. Thus, the courts are critical of allowing the trial witness to pick the point beyond which he or she will not testify. Justice Frankfurter's decision in *Brown v. United States*, 356 U.S. 148 (1958), though a civil denaturalization proceeding, explains this distortion of the truth approach to waiver in a criminal trial. Justice Frankfurter remarked:

> When a witness voluntarily testifies, the privilege against self-incrimination is amply respected without need of accepting testimony freed from the antiseptic test of the adversary process. The witness himself, certainly if he is a party, determines the area of disclosure and therefore of inquiry. Such a witness has the choice, after weighing the advantage of the privilege against self-incrimination against the advantage of putting forward his version of the facts and his reliability as a witness, not to testify at all. He cannot reasonably claim that the Fifth Amendment gives him not only this choice but, if he elects to testify, an immunity from cross-examination on the matters he has himself put in dispute. It would make of the Fifth Amendment not only a humane safeguard against judicially coerced self-disclosure but a positive invitation to mutilate the truth a party offers to tell.... The interests of the other party and regard for the function of courts of justice to ascertain the truth become relevant, and prevail in the balance of considerations determining the scope and limits of the privilege against self-incrimination.

Id. at 155–56 (citation omitted).

As a result of *Brown*'s distortion of truth approach, once a defendant takes the stand and testifies to the merits, he generally will be held to have "waived" the privilege against self-incrimination as to any question properly within the scope of cross-examination. *See also Caminetti v. United States*, 242 U.S. 470, 493 (1917) ("Where a defendant elects to go upon the witness stand and testify, he then subjects himself to the same rule as that applying to any other witness, and if he has failed to deny or explain acts of an incriminating nature ... such failure may not only be commented upon, but may be considered by the jury with all the other circumstances in reaching their conclusion as to his guilt or innocence. . . .").

The scope of proper cross-examination under Federal Rule of Evidence 611(b) and its state counterparts is broad, and once the defendant testifies, the rules of evidence would appear to apply to him just like any other party.

- *United States v. Musk*, 719 F.3d 962, 965–67 (8th Cir. 2013) (a defendant who testifies at trial waives his privilege against self-incrimination and may be cross-examined about other matters beyond the scope of direct examination related to his credibility, which he placed in issue by taking the stand).
- *United States v. Fernandez*, 559 F.3d 303, 330–31 (5th Cir. 2009) (defendant who testified was subject to cross-examination on all matters relevant to scope of direct examination).
- *United States v. Crockett*, 435 F.3d 1305, 1312–13 (10th Cir. 2006) (accused waives privilege by testifying and is subject to cross-examination on all relevant facts, and district court did not abuse its discretion when it allowed the defendant to be questioned about his failure to file his own tax return to rebut defendant's assertion on direct that he would never help anyone cheat on his taxes).
- *United States v. Ellis*, 951 F.2d 580, 584 (4th Cir. 1991) ("A defendant who testifies waives his Fifth Amendment privilege in all areas subject to proper cross-examination. Proper cross-examination—and therefore waiver—reaches all subject matters relevant to the direct examination.") (citation omitted).
- *United States v. Pilcher*, 672 F.2d 875, 877 (11th Cir. 1982) ("[O]nce [the accused] took the stand voluntarily to testify in his own behalf, he waived the Fifth Amendment privilege to refuse to answer questions properly within the scope of cross-examination under Rule 611(b) of the Federal Rules of Evidence.").
- *United States v. Beechum*, 582 F.2d 898, 907–09 (5th Cir. 1978) (en banc) (waiver of privilege and permissible cross-examination of defendant are determined by whether government's questions are reasonably related to defendant's testimony).
- *United States v. Hearst*, 563 F.2d 1331, 1339–42 (9th Cir. 1977) (because government questions on cross-examination were "reasonably related" to subjects covered by the defendant's testimony, the trial court did not abuse its discretion in allowing the government to

ask questions about a time period that the defendant, Patty Hearst, failed to mention in her direct testimony).

- *But cf.* Fed. R. Evid. 611 advisory committee's notes: "The extent of the waiver of the privilege against self-incrimination ought not to be determined as a by-product of a rule on scope of cross-examination."

In many states, the applicable rules and statutes appear to provide for an even broader waiver. *See, e.g.*, Mass. R. Evid. 511(c)(1): "When a defendant voluntarily testifies in a criminal case, . . . the defendant may be cross-examined on all relevant and material facts regarding that case."

Similarly, when a defendant introduces testimony concerning his or her mental state, he or she may not invoke the Fifth Amendment to keep the prosecution from rebutting that evidence with statements made by the defendant during prior court-ordered mental examinations.

- *Buchanan v. Kentucky*, 483 U.S. 402, 421–24 (1987) (introduction of a psychological report for limited rebuttal purposes did not constitute a violation of the accused's Fifth Amendment rights when the accused asserted a mental status defense).
- *Estelle v. Smith*, 451 U.S. 454, 465, 466 n.10 (1981) (citing, with apparent approval, cases holding that a defendant who asserts the insanity defense and introduces psychiatric testimony in support can be required to submit to a sanity exam by a government-appointed psychiatrist).

However, both the Federal Rules of Criminal Procedure and most state rules that conform to the Federal Rules protect statements made in the context of court-ordered mental examinations from being used against the defendant in criminal proceedings, except to rebut an issue that the defendant puts in issue. Fed. R. Crim. P. 12.2(c)(4):

> No statement made by a defendant in the course of any examination conducted under this rule [authorizing courts to order psychiatric examinations upon notice of an insanity defense and/or notice of expert evidence of a mental condition] . . . , no testimony by the expert based

> on the statement, and no other fruits of the statement may be admitted into evidence against the defendant on any criminal proceeding *except* on an issue regarding mental condition on which the defendant:
>
> (A) has introduced . . . evidence requiring notice under [the rule], or
>
> (B) has introduced expert evidence in a capital sentencing proceeding requiring notice under [the rule].

In 2013, the Supreme Court unanimously decided *Kansas v. Cheever*, overturning a decision that the state had violated the defendant's Fifth Amendment privilege against self-incrimination by introducing evidence obtained from a court-ordered mental health evaluation. The Court decided that there was no violation of the Self-Incrimination Clause when the court-ordered evaluation was used to rebut testimony from a defense expert that the defendant lacked the required mental state to commit murder by virtue of his intoxication. 571 U.S. 87 (2013). The Court relied on its prior decision in *Buchanan v. Kentucky*, 483 U.S. 402 (1987) and remanded the case to determine if the rebuttal testimony exceeded the scope allowed, by the Fifth Amendment or state evidentiary rules, which was the harder issue presented by the case. On remand, the Kansas Supreme Court upheld the conviction and ruled that the prosecution's expert did not exceed the scope allowed as it justifiably addressed matters that Cheever himself had put at issue. *Kansas v. Cheever*, 284 P.3d 1002 (Kan. 2012).

It is worth noting that to safeguard a defendant's privilege against self-incrimination during mental examinations conducted under Federal Rule of Criminal Procedure 12.2, at least two courts have ordered audiotaping of all interviews and testing of the defendant, with the tapes to be provided to defense counsel. *See United States v. Johnson*, 362 F. Supp. 2d 1043, 1082–85 (N.D. Iowa 2005); *United States v. Sampson*, 335 F. Supp. 2d 166, 247–48 (D. Mass. 2004). Other courts have required the appointment of a taint team to prevent the trial prosecutors from obtaining advance knowledge of information pertinent only to penalty-related issues. *See United States v. Williams*, 731 F. Supp. 2d 1012, 1020 (D. Haw. 2010).

A defendant who takes the stand and testifies has not, however, necessarily waived his right to object on the basis of the Fifth Amendment privilege against self-incrimination to questions about his past criminal conduct to which liability could still attach.

- Fed. R. Evid. 608(b): "By testifying on another matter, a witness does not waive any privilege against self-incrimination for testimony that relates only to the witness's character for truthfulness."
- *United States v. McClurge*, 311 F.3d 866, 874 (7th Cir. 2002) (citing to commentary to Rule 608(b), which states that the rule "constitutes a rejection of the doctrine . . . that any past criminal act relevant to credibility may be inquired into on cross-examination, in apparent disregard of the privilege against self-incrimination").

Defendants may also take the stand at trial to demonstrate their physical characteristics without waiving their Fifth Amendment rights or subjecting themselves to cross-examination, since the physical demonstration does not constitute testimony.

- *United States v. Williams*, 461 F.3d 441, 448 (4th Cir. 2006) (Fifth Amendment rights violated when court required defendant to be cross-examined as a condition of admitting his demonstration that the fanny pack did not fit him).
- *United States v. Bay*, 762 F.2d 1314, 1315 (9th Cir. 1984) (where an accused bank robber displayed his tattoos to show that he was not the person identified by eyewitnesses, defendant was entitled to refuse to be cross-examined by the prosecutor).
- *Commonwealth v. Poggi*, 761 N.E.2d 983, 985–86 (Mass. App. Ct. 2002) (defendant's proposed display of tattoos on his forearm was non-testimonial and did not entitle prosecutor to cross-examine him); *State v. Martin*, 519 So. 2d 87 (La. 1988) (same).
- *Taylor v. United States*, 601 A.2d 1060, 1065–66 (D.C. 1991) (defendant who wanted to recite words said by purported criminal on tape should have been allowed to do so in court, without being required to expose himself to cross-examination).

An ordinary witness, not a defendant, is generally held to a standard of waiver more accommodating to the witness's right not to answer questions properly within the scope of cross-examination. Thus, a witness may generally refuse to answer questions about an incriminating matter already disclosed, as long as the answers sought may tend to further incriminate the witness.

- *United States v. Seifert*, 648 F.2d 557, 561 (9th Cir. 1980) ("Our rule is that, whatever the standard of waiver for defendants who voluntarily testify, an ordinary witness may pick the point beyond which he will not go, and refuse to answer any questions about a matter already discussed, even if the facts already revealed are incriminating, as long as the answers sought may tend to further incriminate him.") (citations and internal quotation marks omitted).
- *United States v. LaRiche*, 549 F.2d 1088, 1096 (6th Cir. 1977) ("Although disclosure of an incriminating fact generally waives the privilege as to details, waiver does not occur where further disclosure carries a risk of incrimination beyond that raised by previous testimony. Since disclosure of the details of [the witness's] participation in unreported criminal activity would present a real and appreciable danger of criminal prosecution not raised by his testimony on direct, the Court was not in error in upholding his right to refuse to respond.") (citations omitted).

However, the defendant has a Sixth Amendment right to confront witnesses against him. Thus, when a prosecution witness testifies on direct and invokes the privilege against self-incrimination on cross-examination, the appropriate relief is ordinarily to strike the direct testimony of the witness.

- *United States v. Baskin*, 424 F.3d 1, 3 (1st Cir. 2005) (court properly struck witness's direct testimony because witness invoked Fifth Amendment privilege during cross-examination related to details of direct testimony).
- *United States v. Wilmore*, 381 F.3d 868, 872–73 (9th Cir. 2004) (court should have struck witness's testimony when witness invoked

Fifth Amendment privilege on cross-examination and refused to answer questions on matters in dispute).

- *Carlos v. Wyrick*, 753 F.2d 691, 693–94 (8th Cir. 1985) (in prosecution for murder, trial court should have struck direct testimony of prosecution witness when the witness refused to answer questions directly related to the circumstances surrounding the murder).
- *United States v. Lyons*, 703 F.2d 815, 819 (5th Cir. 1983) (district court properly concluded that the defendant's Sixth Amendment right to confrontation were violated by witness's refusal to testify based on her Fifth Amendment privilege against self-incrimination on cross-examination, and district court adequately protected defendant's right by striking witness's direct testimony).
- *United States v. Seifert*, 648 F.2d 557, 561 (9th Cir. 1980) ("Where a witness asserts a valid privilege against self-incrimination on cross-examination, all or part of that witness's testimony must be stricken if invocation of the privilege blocks inquiry into matters which are direct and not merely collateral.") (citation and internal quotation marks omitted).
- *Funches v. Commonwealth*, 397 N.E.2d 1097, 1102–03 (Mass. 1979) (holding it was prejudicial error for the trial judge to deny striking the testimony of the prosecution's chief witness after his proper invocation of his privilege against self-incrimination on cross-examination, where the cross-examination related to the crucial sequence of events in the case).
- *But cf. Douglas v. Alabama*, 380 U.S. 415, 416–18 (1965) (court reversed a conviction on the basis that the defendant's right to confront witnesses was violated where witness invoked his privilege against self-incrimination and refused to answer 21 questions on cross-examination).

Courts often distinguish between "direct testimony" and "collateral matters" and refuse to strike testimony when the witness has asserted his Fifth Amendment privilege only about collateral matters.

- *United States v. Rivera Rangel*, 466 F.3d 158, 160–62 (1st Cir. 2006) (not error for court to have allowed prosecution witness to assert

Fifth Amendment on cross-examination about payments he had received when he was a government official, years before the conduct charged in the indictment).

- *United States v. Duverge Perez*, 295 F.3d 249, 255 (2d Cir. 2002) (trial court properly refused to strike testimony of witness who asserted Fifth Amendment privilege only on collateral matters and was otherwise subject to full and fair cross-examination).
- *United States v. Kaufmann*, 985 F.2d 884, 898 (7th Cir. 1993) ("However, where the witness' [sic] refusal to answer relates only to collateral matters, such as credibility, there is little danger to the defendant.") (citation omitted).
- *Bagby v. Kuhlman*, 932 F.2d 131, 135 (2d Cir. 1991) ("If the court determines that the [Fifth Amendment] privilege has been invoked with respect to a collateral matter . . . no corrective action is necessary.").
- *United States v. Zapata*, 871 F.2d 616, 623–25 (7th Cir. 1989) (because witness refused to answer questions that were collateral and not directly related to direct testimony, lower court did not err in refusing to strike witness's testimony).

Similar questions arise when the defense calls a witness to testify and the witness invokes his Fifth Amendment right against self-incrimination, thereby preventing the prosecution from exercising its non-constitutional rights to cross-examine the witness. In these cases, the defendant's Sixth Amendment right "to have compulsory process for obtaining witnesses in his favor," conflicts with the prosecution's right, as a matter of the Federal Rules of Evidence, to cross-examine the witness. Although this subject is beyond the scope of this book, readers may find the case *United States v. Gary*, 74 F.3d 304 (1st Cir. 1996), a useful starting point.

Testimonial Waivers in Legislative Proceedings

As with a grand jury proceeding, a witness testifying in a legislative proceeding ordinarily is compelled by subpoena to appear, and there is no judge immediately available to determine if the witness has waived his or her Fifth Amendment privilege by giving some testimony. When

Congress has challenged a witness as having waived the privilege, most of the reported decisions have ruled for the witness.

- *United States v. Hoag*, 142 F. Supp. 667, 669–71 (D.D.C. 1956) (a witness appearing before a Senate committee who testified that she had "never engaged in espionage nor sabotage" did not waive her Fifth Amendment privilege because she "did not testify as to any criminating fact . . .").
- *Jackins v. United States*, 231 F.2d 405, 408–09 (9th Cir. 1956) (a congressional witness who testified at length about his work did not waive his Fifth Amendment privilege with respect to follow-up questions about his work's ties to the Communist Party, because his testimony "was in no sense or manner incriminating").
- *United States v. Costello*, 198 F.2d 200, 202–03 (2d Cir. 1952) (a congressional witness who testified that he had "always upheld the Constitution and the laws" and answered questions about his assets did not waive his constitutional privilege, because his testimony did not "constitute[] an admission or proof of any crime. . .").

See also

- *Emspak v. United States*, 349 U.S. 190, 193, 197–98 (1955) (A witness appearing before a House committee answered 171 questions about his union and its ties to the Communist Party but then invoked the Fifth Amendment not to answer 68 questions about his associations and affiliations that "were of an incriminatory character." The Court held that the witness did not waive his privilege when he answered "No" to whether revealing his knowledge of people associated with the Communist Party would subject him to criminal prosecution.).

As previously addressed in Chapter 5, a congressional witness should be allowed to state his innocence in general terms and refuse to answer any congressional inquiries on matters that could result in potential incrimination, without risk of waiving his Fifth Amendment rights.

Waiver in Other Non-Criminal Proceedings

In general, the waiver principles discussed previously apply in non-criminal proceedings just as they do in criminal proceedings. For example, in non-criminal proceedings, the Supreme Court has made the distinction between a witness who testifies on his own behalf and a witness who is compelled to testify. In *Arndstein v. McCarthy*, 254 U.S. 71 (1923), Arndstein was adjudicated an involuntary bankrupt and compelled to appear before a special bankruptcy examiner, where he invoked his Fifth Amendment privilege not to answer any questions. *Id.* at 72. After filing sworn schedules of his assets and liabilities, Arndstein was recalled for further examination, where he again refused to answer any questions on Fifth Amendment grounds. *Id.* Holding that Arndstein did not waive his privilege, the Supreme Court explained that "[t]he schedules . . . did not amount to an admission of guilt or furnish clear proof of crime, and the mere filing of them did not constitute a waiver of the right to stop short whenever the bankrupt could fairly claim that to answer might tend to incriminate." *Id.* (citations omitted). On remand, Arndstein testified as to some of the matters in question, including denying that he had certain assets in his possession, before invoking his Fifth Amendment privilege. *McCarthy v. Arndstein*, 262 U.S. 355, 357 (1923). Holding again that Arndstein did not waive his privilege, the Supreme Court held that "where the previous disclosure by an ordinary witness is not an actual admission of guilt or incriminating facts, he is not deprived of the privilege of stopping short in his testimony whenever it may fairly tend to incriminate him." *Id.* at 359.

In *Brown v. United States*, 356 U.S. 148 (1958), Brown took the stand in a denaturalization proceeding initiated against her and testified that she had resigned from the Young Communist League many years earlier, had not engaged in any Communist activities since then, and had never taught or advocated for the overthrow of the government. *Id.* at 150. On cross-examination, Brown refused to answer questions relating to her Communist activities on Fifth Amendment grounds. *Id.* at 152. Distinguishing between a "witness who is compelled to testify" and one who "voluntarily testifies," the Supreme Court held that Brown had waived her Fifth Amendment privilege by taking the stand in her own defense: "Petitioner, as a party to the suit, was a voluntary witness. She could not take the stand to testify in her own behalf and also claim the right to be free from cross-examination on matters raised by her own testimony on direct examination." *Id.* at 155–56.

It is worth noting that in non-criminal proceedings where the defendant does not have a constitutional right to confront the witnesses against him, a judge has substantial discretion in determining when the witness has waived the Fifth Amendment privilege against self-incrimination by testifying to certain matters. Given the discretion, it is very difficult for lawyers to advise a witness whether a disclosure—such as answering a complaint, answering questions during a deposition, or responding to interrogatories—will be deemed to constitute a waiver and thereby require the party or witness to make further incriminating revelations. Justice Black's dissent in *Rogers v. United States*, 340 U.S. 367 (1951), described the problem correctly as follows:

> Apparently, the Court's holding is that at some uncertain point in petitioner's testimony, regardless of her intention, admission of associations with the Communist Party automatically effected a "waiver" of her constitutional protection as to all related questions. To adopt such a rule for the privilege against self-incrimination, when other constitutional safeguards must be knowingly waived, relegates the Fifth Amendment's privilege to a second-rate position. Moreover, today's holding creates this dilemma for witnesses: On the one hand, they risk imprisonment for contempt by asserting the privilege prematurely; on the other, they might lose the privilege if they answer a single question. The Court's view makes the protection depend on timing so refined that lawyers, let alone laymen, will have difficulty in knowing when to claim it.

Id. at 377–78.

Lawyers must exercise great care in advising clients in civil cases where the potential for criminal prosecution is real. Erring on the side of caution and invoking the privilege in civil cases is usually the best way to proceed unless and until the risk of criminal prosecution has passed. Chapter 3 addressed the consequences for asserting the privilege against self-incrimination in non-criminal proceedings.

Waiver in Connection with Production of Documents

Waiver in the context of the production of documents is particularly problematic. When a witness fails to invoke the attorney-client privilege upon delivery of documents to the opposing party, it is generally the rule that he has waived the attorney-client privilege as to other documents concerning the same subject matter, for all purposes, including in separate proceedings.

- *In re Pac. Pictures Corp.*, 679 F.3d 1121, 1127–28 (9th Cir. 2012) (citing decisions from other circuits in agreement, the court rejected the selective waiver doctrine and required production of attorney-client privileged documents in civil litigation that were previously voluntarily disclosed in a government investigation).
- *Fort James Corp. v. Solo Cup Co.*, 412 F.3d 1340, 1349 (Fed. Cir. 2005) (citing circuit court cases holding that the "standard for determining the scope of a waiver of attorney-client privilege is that the waiver applies to all other communications relating to the same subject matter") (citations omitted).
- *See also* Fed. R. Evid. 502(a): "When the disclosure is made in a federal proceeding . . . the waiver extends to an undisclosed communication or information . . . if (1) the waiver is intentional; (2) the disclosed and undisclosed communications or information concern the same subject matter; and (3) they ought in fairness to be considered together."

Because the Fifth Amendment right against compulsory self-incrimination protects only the act of producing documents, and not their contents, a matter covered in Chapter 8, the "subject matter" test applicable to the attorney-client privilege should not apply to the waiver of the Fifth Amendment act of production privilege. Instead, the waiver of the Fifth Amendment's act of production privilege should be considered on a document-by-document basis, as discussed in Chapter

4. If the document has previously been voluntarily produced, it would stand to reason that it cannot be withheld on the grounds of the Fifth Amendment, because the existence, possession, and authentication of the compelled production of the same document is a foregone conclusion. See discussion in Chapter 8. If the document has not been previously produced, however, its production may still be self-incriminating—that is, reveal its existence or the producing party's possession—even if other documents regarding the same subject matter have been produced.

CHAPTER 8

Documents and the Fifth Amendment: The Act of Production Privilege

The language of the Self-Incrimination Clause prohibits compelling a person to be "a witness against himself." In one of the first cases interpreting the clause, *Boyd v. United States*, 116 U.S. 616, 634–35 (1886), the Supreme Court unanimously held that the Fifth Amendment protected against compelled production of books and papers, linking its interpretation to the understanding that being a witness against oneself included furnishing incriminating evidence as well as giving testimony. As Justice Thomas remarked in his concurring opinion in *United States v. Hubbell*, 530 U.S. 27, 50–51 (2000), the Founders may have used the word "witness" to be synonymous with the phrase "to give evidence" or "to furnish evidence."

Although the Supreme Court has never expressly overruled *Boyd* and squarely held that the contents of all voluntarily created documents are unprotected by the Fifth Amendment, the Supreme Court has now effectively dismantled the Fifth Amendment's application to the incriminating contents of voluntarily created documents that it set forth in *Boyd*. The modern Supreme Court has limited the application of the Fifth Amendment to the act of producing documents in response to compulsion. Only where the act of production is incriminating—by implicitly admitting the existence or possession of the documents sought, or the documents are authentic—does the Fifth Amendment provide protection.

In the *Boyd* case, the government sought to obtain documents from a partnership in the course of forfeiture proceedings. The Supreme Court agreed with Boyd that the incriminating contents of the requested documents were protected from compelled production by the Self-Incrimination Clause, observing that there is no difference between compelling a person to produce his incriminating private books and papers and compelling the person to incriminate himself through oral testimony. *Id.* at 633–35.

In *Fisher v. United States*, 425 U.S. 391 (1976), the Supreme Court significantly restricted *Boyd*'s application of the Fifth Amendment to the contents of voluntarily created documents. The *Fisher* opinion reasoned that unless the government requires an individual to prepare the papers subject to production, or to affirm the truth of their incriminating contents, no self-incriminating information contained within them is covered by the privilege. Instead, *Fisher* limited the definition of "compelled testimony" to the act of producing documents demanded by a subpoena or other legal process, reasoning that the act of production "tacitly concedes the existence of the papers demanded and their possession or control by the [producing party]," as well as indicating the person's belief that the documents produced are those requested by the subpoena. *Id.* at 409–10.

The Supreme Court's application of the Fifth Amendment since *Fisher* confirms that the only privilege applicable to demands for documents is an "act of production" privilege. In *United States v. Doe*, 465 U.S. 605 (1984) (*Doe I*), the Court considered a grand jury subpoena for the business records of a sole proprietorship. The lower court had quashed the subpoena, holding that the papers were protected under *Boyd* because their contents were potentially self-incriminating and because the act of producing them to the grand jury would admit their existence and authenticity. *Id.* at 607–08. The Supreme Court squarely rejected the first ground of decision, holding that because the documents were created voluntarily and because the subpoena did not require the witness to restate, repeat, or affirm the truth of their contents, no Fifth Amendment privilege existed on that basis. *Id.* at 611–12. Justice O'Connor, concurring, wrote separately "just to make explicit what is implicit in [the Court's] opinion: that the Fifth Amendment provides absolutely no protection for the contents of private papers of any kind." *Id.* at 618. However, the Court accepted the findings of the lower court that, in the particular circumstances of the case, the witness's act of producing the documents would involve testimonial self-incrimination—by admitting their existence and his possession of them, as well as by authenticating them through his production. *Id.* at 613–14 and nn.11–13.

In *Boyd*, the Court explicitly articulated a privacy rationale for the protection of voluntarily created documents, which rationale was repeated in subsequent decisions. *See Murphy v. Waterfront Comm'n of N.Y. Harbor*, 378 U.S. 52, 55 (1964); *Bellis v. United States*, 417 U.S. 85, 91 (1974). The privacy rationale led many commentators to hypothesize that even after *Fisher* and *Doe I*, there was a distinction between the protection afforded the contents of private documents, such as diaries, and the contents of business records. However, since *Fisher* and *Doe I*, the vast majority of courts have concluded that as long as the government has not compelled the creation of the document, even distinctly private or personal documents may be compelled to be produced—despite their incriminating contents.

- *Packwood v. Senate Select Comm. on Ethics*, 510 U.S. 1319, 1321–22 (1994) (Rehnquist, Circuit J.) (denying Senator Packwood's application for a stay pending appeal of a decision enforcing a subpoena duces tecum for his diaries and stating that certiorari was not likely to be granted on Senator Packwood's claim that the Fifth Amendment privilege prevented their compelled production).
- *In re Grand Jury Subpoena Duces Tecum*, 1 F.3d 87, 90 (2d Cir. 1993) (Fifth Amendment does not protect defendant's personal calendar).
- *United States v. Wujkowski*, 929 F.2d 981, 983 (4th Cir. 1991) (contents of desk calendars, pocket calendars, appointment books, and planners are not privileged).
- *In re Grand Jury Proceedings on Feb. 4, 1982*, 759 F.2d 1418, 1420–21 (9th Cir. 1985) (contents of personal journal not protected by Fifth Amendment).

- *In re Steinberg*, 837 F.2d 527, 529–30 nn.3–4 (1st Cir. 1988) (reviewing cases on issue of whether Fifth Amendment protected voluntarily created personal documents).
- *Moyer v. Commonwealth*, 531 S.E.2d 580, 583–89 (Va. Ct. App. 2000) (denying motion to suppress diaries that appellant argued were seized in violation of his Fourth and Fifth Amendment rights).

Of course, the act of production doctrine may nonetheless provide a valid objection to the production of voluntarily created personal papers or other tangible items.

- *In re Grand Jury Proceedings, Subpoenas for Documents*, 41 F.3d 377, 382–84 (8th Cir. 1994) (reversing district court refusal to quash wide-ranging IRS subpoena for taxpayer business records on basis that act of production would testify as to possession and existence of the documents as well as authenticate these voluntarily created records).
- *People v. Havrish*, 866 N.E.2d 1009, 1015 (N.Y. 2007) (suppressing an unregistered handgun turned over to the police pursuant to a protective order directing the defendant to surrender any firearms, on the basis that the act of producing the gun "involved the commission of a crime in the presence of the police").
- *Skakel v. State*, No. FSTCV 054006524S, 2006 WL 2773470, at *3 (Conn. Super. Ct. Sept. 12, 2006) (denying motion to compel production of personal telephone records, e-mail correspondence, diaries, and other personal documents, based on act of production privilege).
- *Commonwealth v. Hughes*, 404 N.E.2d 1239, 1245–46 (Mass. 1980) (order requiring defendant to produce a certain firearm was vacated, where the act of production would make an implicit statement about the existence, location, possession, and authenticity of the weapon, thereby incriminating the defendant).

The "Foregone Conclusion" Exception to the Act of Production Privilege

The Supreme Court's focus on the extent to which the act of production involves a testimonial communication has generated a number of difficult issues for the lower courts. In *Fisher v. United States*, the Supreme Court based its determination that the act of production would not incriminate the taxpayer on the ground, at least in part, that the existence and possession of the records called for by the subpoena (tax returns, accountant work papers, correspondence between the taxpayer and his accountant) were already known by the government, or as described by the Court, were a "foregone conclusion." 425 U.S. at 411 (concluding it was "doubtful that implicitly admitting the existence and possession of the papers rises to the level of testimony within the protection of the Fifth Amendment" because "[t]he existence and location of the papers are a foregone conclusion and the taxpayer adds little or nothing to the sum total of the Government's information by conceding that he in fact has the papers"). Thus, where the government already knows that the documents exist and that defendant possessed the documents sought by the subpoena, the act of production was not deemed "testimonial."

By contrast, in *United States v. Hubbell*, 530 U.S. 27, 45–46 (2000), the Supreme Court affirmed the dismissal of an indictment on the grounds that the government (an independent counsel) was precluded by an order of immunity from making direct use or derivative use of the immunized witness's act of production. The Court emphasized that Hubbell's assembling of 13,000 documents responsive to a wide-ranging subpoena duces tecum was a testimonial act for which Hubbell enjoyed Fifth Amendment protection. The Court cited the necessity of Hubbell "to make extensive use of 'the contents of his own mind' in identifying the hundreds of documents responsive to the requests in the subpoena," *id.* at 43 (citations omitted), describing the assembly of the documents as "tantamount to answering a series of interrogations asking a witness to disclose the existence and location of particular documents fitting certain broad descriptions." *Id.* at 41.

Thus, lower courts must define when a subpoena or other demand for production of documents simply seeks the surrender of documents, the existence and possession of which are a foregone conclusion, on the one hand, and when a compelled production of documents would instead require a party to use the contents of his own mind in identifying and producing responsive documents, thereby constituting Fifth Amendment–protected "testimony," on the other hand. The lines drawn are very fact-specific, but the following cases provide substantial guidance.

- *United States v. Greenfield*, 831 F.3d 106, 110, 128 (2d Cir. 2016) (following the "reasonable particularity standard" adopted by other circuits, the court held that the government failed to demonstrate that taxpayers' possession and control of the documents covered by the summons was a foregone conclusion).
- *United States v. Sideman & Bancroft, LLP*, 704 F.3d 1197, 1202–03 (9th Cir. 2013) (determining that the "'quantum of information' possessed by the [IRS] prior to its issuance of the summons as to the existence and possession of the summonsed document[s]" was sufficient to establish that the "foregone conclusion" exception to the act of production privilege applied).
- *In re Grand Jury Subpoena Duces Tecum Dated Mar. 25, 2011*, 670 F.3d 1335, 1344 n.20 (11th Cir. 2012) (adopting the "reasonable particularity" standard to describe the quantum of knowledge that the government must possess to satisfy the foregone conclusion rationale and finding government failed to satisfy the standard).
- *United States v. Bright*, 596 F.3d 683, 693–94 (9th Cir. 2010) (court concludes that "foregone conclusion" exception applies to some but not all credit card records, and that government failed to show that it was aware of certain records and the defendant's possession of them prior to issuance of an IRS summons).
- *United States v. Ponds*, 454 F.3d 313, 324, 329 (D.C. Cir. 2006) (applying the lessons of *Fisher* and *Hubbell* to determine whether defendant's act of production in response to a subpoena duces tecum was a foregone conclusion or was testimonial, the court reversed the district judge's determination and held that the government had failed to show with reasonable particularity that it had prior knowledge of the existence and location of the documents produced by defendant to the grand jury).
- *In re Grand Jury Subpoena Dated Apr. 18, 2003*, 383 F.3d 905, 911 (9th Cir. 2004) (concluding that the subpoena "far exceeded government's knowledge about the actual documents that [grand jury witness] created or possessed during his former employment and that he retained after he terminated his employment," and thereby granting witness's motion to quash the grand jury subpoena).

- *In re Subpoena Duces Tecum Dated Oct. 29, 1992*, 1 F.3d 87, 93 (2d Cir. 1993) (existence of pocket calendar was a "foregone conclusion" where owner previously produced a copy to the SEC).
- *United States v. Stone*, 976 F.2d 909, 911 (4th Cir. 1992) ("We agree with the district court's conclusion that although the documents are personal, they are unprotected by the privilege against self-incrimination because their existence, possession, and authentication are a foregone conclusion; their production adds little or nothing to the sum total of the Government's information.") (citations and internal quotation marks omitted).
- *Freedom Med. Inc. v. Gillespie*, Civil Action No. 06–3195, 2006 WL 3791339, at *2–3 (E.D. Pa. Dec. 21, 2006) (granting a protective order in favor of the defendant from having to respond to plaintiff's document requests, where requests were not sufficiently targeted at documents whose existence and possession were a foregone conclusion).

Similarly, even if the existence and possession of the documents is a foregone conclusion, the courts have struggled over whether the witness can still claim that the act of production has some testimonial value in authenticating the records. Many courts have taken the position that if the subpoenaed witness prepared the documents in question, the production of the documents would always constitute an "implicit authentication" sufficient to trigger Fifth Amendment protection.

- *In re Grand Jury Proceedings*, 41 F.3d 377, 381 (8th Cir. 1994) (because the breadth of the subpoena necessarily required taxpayer to discriminate among documents, "thereby providing identifying information that is relevant to the authenticity of the documents," the act of production was deemed protected by the Fifth Amendment privilege).
- *United States v. Fox*, 721 F.2d 32, 36 (2d Cir. 1983) (recognizing that even when the existence and location of documents are known to the government, a person may still refuse to produce documents, if by doing so, he will be providing the government with evidence it

can later use to authenticate the records as having been the records requested).

- *In re Sambrano Corp.*, 441 B.R. 562, 566 (Bankr. W.D. Tex. 2010) (after granting trustee's motion to compel production of certain records on the basis of the foregone conclusion doctrine and required records exception, the court ruled that implicit authentication of certain financial records from their compelled production was protected by the Fifth Amendment).

However, other courts have reasoned that "implicit authentication" is insufficient to constitute protected testimony, at least when the government can demonstrate its ability to authenticate the documents produced through other witnesses or other means.

- *United States v. Bright*, 596 F.3d 683, 693 (9th Cir. 2010) (expressing satisfaction that government could authenticate some of the credit cards the court ordered to be produced through the card servicing company, and did not need to rely on the act of production for authentication).
- *United States v. Fishman*, 726 F.2d 125, 127 (4th Cir. 1983) (upholding district court's order holding doctor in contempt for refusing to produce records when government could use other witnesses who worked in doctor's office to authenticate the records subject to the grand jury subpoena).
- *United States v. Pearson*, No. 1:04-CR-340, 2006 U.S. Dist. LEXIS 32982, at *62–63 (N.D.N.Y. May 24, 2006) (reserving decision on whether government could authenticate encrypted password from source other than through witness's compliance with grand jury subpoena, therefore rendering act of production a foregone conclusion).
- *United States v. Walker*, 982 F. Supp. 288, 292 (S.D.N.Y. 1997) (while agreeing that government could call former employees to authenticate the documents as business records and that defendant thereby had no Fifth Amendment privilege in their production, the court conditioned its ruling on the government granting the defendant act of production immunity).

- *In re Application to Quash a Grand Jury Subpoena Duces Tecum*, 597 N.Y.S.2d 557–58, 563, 157 Misc. 2d 432, 441–42 (N.Y. Crim. Ct. 1993) (imposing burden of proof on the government to demonstrate that tape recordings could be authenticated by persons other than the person who taped the calls and deciding that, if government complied, the Fifth Amendment claim by the person producing the tape recordings would be eliminated).

The courts have struggled to apply the foregone conclusion exception to orders and subpoenas seeking to compel suspects to either provide passcodes to their computers or smartphones to law enforcement or to decrypt the documents on these devices. As previously mentioned, the vast majority of courts have accepted that either the act of entering a memorized passcode in order to open encrypted files or giving the passcode to law enforcement is a Fifth Amendment–protected testimonial act. The courts have therefore been required to define when such "testimony" is a "foregone conclusion."

- *United States v. Apple MacPro Computer*, 851 F.3d 238, 247–48 (3d Cir. 2017) (appearing to agree with Eleventh Circuit that the suspects' compelled decryption and production of the contents of the computer drives would be testimonial, despite upholding district court's finding, on plain error review, that the government had demonstrated that the existence and production of the documents was a foregone conclusion).
- *In re Grand Jury Subpoena Duces Tecum Dated Mar. 25, 2011*, 670 F.3d 1335, 1337 (11th Cir. 2012) (court found that the suspect's compelled decryption and production of documents on his computer would be testimonial and that factual communications associated with the decryption were not a foregone conclusion).
- *United States v. Kirshner*, 823 F. Supp. 665, 669 (E.D. Mich. 2010) (quashing a subpoena requiring the defendant to give up his password to encrypted computer files on the basis that such revelation would be constitutionally protected testimony).
- *Commonwealth v. Gelfgatt*, 11 N.E.3d 605, 613 (Mass. 2014) (allowing compelled decryption when accused admitted all his

documents were on his computer, that all documents were encrypted, and that he knew the passcode).

- *But cf. State v. Stahl*, 206 So. 3d 124, 134 (Fla. 2d DCA 2016) (deciding that the suspect's passcode was not testimonial and that, in any event, the state had established that the existence, possession, and authenticity of the documents on the computer was a foregone conclusion).

The courts have struggled to define which facts the government must prove in order to demonstrate that the compelled decryption rendered the "testimony" a foregone conclusion. Although many courts focus on whether the government can demonstrate with reasonable particularity the existence and possession of the actual files or evidence on the locked device, others have focused on whether the government can simply show that the suspect has the passcode and can access the files. Until the question is addressed by the Supreme Court, the following decisions can be used for guidance:

- *United States v. Apple MacPro Computer*, 851 F.3d 283, 247–48 & n.7 (3d Cir. 2017) (not deciding whether it was the government's knowledge of the contents of the devices or merely the government's knowledge of whether the subject knew the password that should be the focus of the foregone conclusion analysis, and instead deciding under the plain error standard of review that the district court had not made an obvious error).
- *In re Grand Jury Subpoena Duces Tecum Dated Mar. 25, 2011*, 670 F.3d 1335, 1337 (11th Cir. 2012) (finding that the government had failed to show with reasonable particularity whether any files existed on the hard drives or that the suspect could access the encrypted portion of the drives and thereby finding the foregone conclusion exception inapplicable).
- *SEC v. Huang*, 2015 U.S. Dist. LEXIS 127853 at 3–7 (E.D. Pa. 2015) (denying request to compel corporate employees to give government their personal passcodes to their smartphones because government

could not demonstrate the existence of the specific documents they were seeking were located on the smartphones).

- *United States v. Gavegnano*, 305 F. App'x 954, 956 (4th Cir. 2009) (deciding that "[a]ny self-incriminating testimony that [the defendant] may have provided by revealing the password was already a 'foregone conclusion' because the Government independently proved that [the defendant] was the sole user and possessor of the computer").
- *Commonwealth v. Jones*, 117 N.E.3d 702, 710–11 (Mass. 2019) (holding that the only fact conveyed by compelling a defendant to enter the password to an encrypted electronic device is that the defendant knows the password and that the government had demonstrated such beyond a reasonable doubt, by virtue of various prior admissions of the defendant and the statements of witnesses).
- *G.A.Q.L. v. Florida*, 257 So. 3d 1058 (Fla. Dist. Ct. App. 2018) (denying request to compel minor to provide passcode on the basis that the government could not demonstrate with reasonable particularity the contents of the documents sought that were behind the passcode wall).
- *Commonwealth v. Baust*, 89 Va. Cir. 267 (2014) (foregone conclusion not proven by government because lack of evidence that documents sought existed on the specific device).

Interestingly, at least two courts have required the government to prove the foregone conclusion beyond a reasonable doubt. *See, e.g.*, *United States v. Spencer*, 2018 WL 1964588, at *2 (N.D. Cal. 2018); *Commonwealth v. Jones*, 117 N.E.3d 702, 714 (Mass. 2019).

A subsidiary question raised by the foregone conclusion exception is whether the government can introduce at trial the fact that the defendant produced the documents because the government satisfied the foregone conclusion exception. The better-reasoned decisions appear to say no. *See, e.g.*, *United States v. Spencer*, 2018 WL 1964588, at *3 (N.D. Cal. 2018); *United States v. Friscou*, 841 F. Supp. 2d 1232, 1237–38 (D. Colo. 2012).

Application of the Act of Production Privilege to Demands for Documents Made to Third Parties

Fact-intensive issues arise where a party intervenes to quash a demand for production of documents directed to a third party who is arguably holding documents on behalf of the intervenor. Since the Fifth Amendment right is one concerning compelled self-incrimination, it generally follows that material owned by one person may, in certain circumstances, be subpoenaed from a third party in possession of the owner's documents, without impinging on the Fifth Amendment rights of the owner. *See, e.g., Fisher v. United States*, 425 U.S. at 397 (enforcement of subpoena to obtain taxpayer's accountant's work papers from taxpayer's attorney "would not compel the taxpayer to do anything" and does not offend the Fifth Amendment); *Couch v. United States*, 409 U.S. 322, 329 (1973) (taxpayer's accountant and not the taxpayer was the subject of the IRS demand for production, and therefore the enforcement of the subpoena did not offend the Fifth Amendment because "the ingredient of personal compulsion against an accused is lacking"). But where the owner/intervenor claims that the records demanded from the third party are in his "constructive possession," the court must determine if compelling the third party to produce the documents actually results in incriminating the owner/intervenor, which could protect the documents from production.

- *Couch v. United States*, 409 U.S. at 329 (recognizing that "situations may well arise where constructive possession is so clear or the relinquishment of possession is so temporary and insignificant as to leave the personal compulsions upon the accused substantially intact") (citation omitted).
- *In re Grand Jury Subpoena John Doe*, 584 F.3d 175, 187–88 (4th Cir. 2007) (upholding government subpoena to a congressman's staff member on the basis that the congressman had shared the documents with other staff, and moreover that the staff member subject to the demand for production had actual possession and was directly responsible for preparing and maintaining the requested records).
- *In re Grand Jury Subpoena Duces Tecum Dated May 29, 1987*, 834 F.2d 1128, 1133 (2d Cir. 1987) (because corporate president

allowed his administrative assistant to possess and maintain his personal checking account records, the president had no Fifth Amendment claim to object to a subpoena for such records directed to his administrative assistant).

- *United States v. Kent (In re Grand Jury Subpoena)*, 646 F.2d 963, 970 (5th Cir. 1981) (holding that a sole proprietor could invoke his Fifth Amendment privilege to preclude his employee from producing documents that the employee had neither prepared, filed, nor maintained, but to which the employee merely had access).
- *In re Grand Jury Subpoena (ABC, Inc.)*, 668 F. Supp. 2d 307, 312–13 (D. Mass. 2009) (a tally sheet sought by a grand jury subpoena directed to the target's former administrative assistant was enforced where the owner of the business had asked the administrative assistant to create and maintain the document in her private, password-protected folder on the company server; court decided that owner had failed to demonstrate the necessary constructive possession to be able to demonstrate that the subpoena compelled him to incriminate himself by the document's production).
- *See also Waymo, LLC v. Uber Techs., Inc.* 870 F.3d 1350, 1364–65 (Fed. Cir. 2017) (agreeing with district court that intervenor did not have constructive possession of a report entitling him to object on Fifth Amendment grounds to its production from his corporate employer in civil litigation between his former and current employer).

The "Required Records" Exception to the Act of Production Privilege

Another issue raised by the act of production doctrine is the extent to which it is compatible with the Supreme Court's prior decisions eliminating all Fifth Amendment protection for so-called required records. In *Shapiro v. United States*, 335 U.S. 1, 32–35 (1948), the Supreme Court held, in a closely divided case, that Shapiro could not rely on the Fifth Amendment privilege to resist production of business records he was required to maintain by law—subject to criminal sanction—relating to the federal regulation of prices during wartime, analogizing the records to "public records." The Supreme Court reasoned that the government may compel persons to prepare and maintain certain records so that they can be examined at any time, where the purpose of the requirement is essentially regulatory. As the majority explained, if Congress has the power to prohibit an activity altogether, then Congress may legitimately impose record-keeping, registration, and inspection requirements as a condition of engaging in that regulated (and not purely private) activity.

Shapiro, however, does not mean that the government may require citizens to keep a diary of their crimes, and the Supreme Court thereafter limited the required records exception to self-reporting schemes that do not purport to regulate inherently criminal activity. *See Marchetti v. United States*, 390 U.S. 39, 55–57 (1968) (limiting *Shapiro*'s "required records" exception to requests not directed to persons suspected of criminal activity); *Grosso v. United States*, 390 U.S. 62, 67–69 (1968) (same); *Haynes v. United States*, 390 U.S. 85, 96–97 (1968) (holding that the required records doctrine did not extend to a statute requiring registration of illegal firearms). For the required records exception to apply, three requirements must be satisfied: (1) the purpose of the record-keeping requirement is "essentially regulatory," rather than criminal; (2) the records contain the type of information that the regulated party customarily would keep; and (3) the records have "public aspects" that render them "analogous to public documents." *Grosso*, 390 U.S. at 67–68; *In re Grand Jury Subpoena*, 21 F.3d 226, 228 (8th Cir. 1994); *In re Grand Jury Subpoena Duces Tecum Served (Underhill)*, 781 F.2d 64, 67 (6th Cir. 1986).

In contrast, if a self-reporting statute is (1) directed at a highly selected group inherently suspect of criminal activities, (2) asserted in an essential non-criminal and regulatory area of inquiry, and (3) would create a substantial likelihood of prosecution, the Fifth Amendment is presumed to apply. *Alberton v. Subversive Activities Control Bd.*, 382 U.S. 70, 79 (1965); *Marchetti*, 390 U.S. at 57. *See also Leary v. United States*, 395 U.S. 6, 16 (1969) (reversing conviction under Marijuana Tax Act, which required marijuana dealers to register and pay and transfer tax on grounds that statute "compelled petitioner to expose himself to real and appreciable risk of self-incrimination . . ."). Chapter 3 discusses the Fifth Amendment in response to government reporting demands.

The required records exception developed when the content of voluntarily created documents was protected by the Fifth Amendment. However, the Supreme Court has since limited the Fifth Amendment protection for documents to the act of producing them. Thus, it has been argued that a required records exception to the act of production privilege is unnecessary. In fact, a compelling argument can be made that the required records exception is inconsistent with the concept that the testimonial aspects of production, rather than the nature of the regulatory scheme requiring the creation of the records, is determinative of the Fifth Amendment right against compelled self-incrimination.

Despite these arguments, courts have found nothing in the act of production doctrine to be incompatible with the required records doctrine.

- *In re Grand Jury Subpoena*, 21 F.3d 226, 229 (8th Cir. 1994) (reversing district court order quashing a grand jury subpoena, and holding that required records exception applied to a sole proprietor's production of records maintained under federal and state law despite the self-incriminating and testimonial aspects of the act of production).
- *In re Grand Jury Subpoena, Underhill*, 781 F.2d 64, 70 (6th Cir. 1986) (compelling production of odometer statements from sole proprietorships under the required records exception, even though the act of production was incriminating).
- *United States v. Lehman*, 887 F.2d 1328, 1332–34 (7th Cir. 1989) (affirming district court's order enforcing a subpoena for records related to livestock transactions, holding that required records exception remained viable and defendant could not invoke act of production privilege).
- *In re Two Grand Jury Subpoenae Duces Tecum*, 793 F.2d 69, 73 (2d Cir. 1986) ("*Doe* did not involve required records . . . and we find nothing in its 'act of production' analysis that can be construed as weakening the required records exception.").

- *In re Two Subpoenas to Testify Before a Grand Jury*, 252 F. Supp. 3d 170, 179–82 (E.D.N.Y. 2017) (finding record-keeping requirements for retail liquor stores were directed at implementing a valid taxation scheme and had a necessary public aspect qualifying them as required records).
- *United States v. Bell*, 217 F.R.D. 335, 340–41 (M.D. Pa. 2003) (required records exception applies to documents that income tax preparer is required to keep).
- *Thomas v. Tyler*, 841 F. Supp. 1119, 1127 (D. Kan. 1993) (drivers' logs and vehicle condition reports are required records, so civil defendant could not exercise his Fifth Amendment privilege).

Indeed, in 1990, the Supreme Court actually expanded the application of the required records doctrine. In *Baltimore City Department of Social Services v. Bouknight*, 493 U.S. 549 (1990), the Court applied the required records exception to a juvenile court order demanding that a mother, Bouknight, produce her child to the Department of Social Services. In the case, the Court assumed that Bouknight's compliance with the production order would compel the incriminating communication that she exercised control over the child—evidence that the state could later use in a prosecution for child abuse. *Id.* at 555. Nonetheless, the Court ruled that "[Bouknight] may not invoke the privilege to resist the production order because she has assumed custodial duties related to production and because production is required as part of a noncriminal regulatory scheme." *Id.* at 555–56. According to the Court, because the child was the legitimate object of the government's non-criminal regulatory interests, the child was subject to inspection, just like the required records at issue in *Shapiro*. *Id.* at 555–59.

In recent years, the required records doctrine has been tested in connection with subpoenas demanding the production of records that a person who holds a foreign bank account is required to keep and maintain for inspection under the Bank Secrecy Act. Because failing to report the existence of a foreign bank account to the federal government is a criminal offense, compelling a foreign account holder who has failed to report his or her account to produce the account records essentially proves the government's case through the act of production. Nevertheless, the federal appellate courts that have considered this issue have unanimously rejected Fifth Amendment objections to the production of the required foreign bank account records. The most common rationale of the appellate courts is that by voluntarily choosing to engage in an activity that imposes record-keeping requirements under a valid civil regulatory scheme, the foreign account holder "waives" any act of production privilege under the Fifth Amendment.

- *United States v. Chabot*, 793 F.3d 338 (3d Cir. 2015) (agreeing with other circuits that required records doctrine mandated taxpayer to produce foreign bank account records in response to IRS summons).
- *In re Grand Jury Subpoena Dated Feb. 2, 2012*, 741 F.3d 339, 345–49 (2d Cir. 2013) (affirming a district court holding that the required records exception applied to a grand jury subpoena demanding that Doe produce records of his foreign bank accounts).
- *United States v. Under Seal*, 737 F.3d 330 (4th Cir. 2013) (upholding a district court ruling that the required records exception applied to a grand jury subpoena seeking records of the Does' Swiss bank account).
- *In re Grand Jury Proceedings No. 4–10*, 707 F.3d 1262, 1270–75 (11th Cir. 2013) (affirming a district court ruling that the required records doctrine applied to a subpoena duces tecum issued to target and his wife requiring them to produce records concerning their foreign bank accounts).
- *In re Grand Jury Subpoena*, 696 F.3d 428, 433–36 (5th Cir. 2012) (reversing a district court decision that the required records doctrine did not apply to a grand jury subpoena issued to target requiring him to produce records relating to his foreign bank account).
- *In re Special Feb. 2011–1 Grand Jury Subpoena Dated Sept. 12, 2011*, 691 F.3d 903, 905–09 (7th Cir. 2012) (overturning a district court ruling that the required records doctrine did not apply to records relating to a foreign bank account).
- *In re M.H.*, 648 F.3d 1067, 1071–79 (9th Cir. 2011) (denying Fifth Amendment challenge to a Bank Secrecy Act subpoena and holding that the required records doctrine applied).

In each of these cases, the appellate courts found that the Bank Secrecy Act subpoena satisfied the three requirements for the required records exception. In holding that the record-keeping requirements are essentially regulatory and not directed at activity that is inherently criminal, the courts agreed that the record-keeping requirements in the Bank Secrecy Act "target[] those engaged in the lawful activity of owning a foreign bank account," *In re Grand Jury Subpoena Dated Feb. 2, 2012*, 741 F.3d 339, 348 (2d Cir. 2013) and that "there is nothing inherently illegal about having or being [a] beneficiary of an offshore foreign bank account." *In re Grand Jury Subpoena*, 696 F.3d at 435 (quoting *In re M.H.*, 648 F.3d at 1074). *Cf. Grosso*, 390 U.S. at 68 (holding that the required records doctrine did not apply to the requirement that the petitioner file returns with the IRS reporting his wagering income, in part because the requirement was "directed almost exclusively to individuals inherently suspect of criminal activities"); *Marchetti*, 390 U.S. at 57 (same). Although the legislative history of the Bank Secrecy Act indicates that it also has some criminal purposes, the courts agreed that this was not enough to strip the statute of its essentially regulatory character. *In re Grand Jury Subpoena Dated Feb. 2, 2012*, 741 F.3d at 348; *In re Grand Jury Proceedings No. 4–10*, 707 F.3d at 1270. With respect to the third requirement, the courts also agreed that where personal information is required to be maintained in furtherance of a regulatory scheme, "that information assumes a public aspect." *United States v. Under Seal*, 737 F.3d 330, 336–37 (4th Cir. 2013); *In re Grand Jury Proceedings No. 4–10*, 707 F.3d at 1275 (quoting *In re M.H.*, 648 F.3d at 1077). This suggests that when the first requirement of the required records doctrine is satisfied, the third requirement is automatically satisfied. Three of the courts also addressed the relationship between the act of production privilege and the required records doctrine, finding that the required records doctrine applies even where the act of producing the records in question would be compelled, testimonial, and self-incriminating. *In re Grand Jury Subpoena Dated Feb. 2, 2012*, 741 F.3d at 345–46; *In re Special February 2011–1 Grand Jury Subpoena*, 691 F.3d at 906–09; *In re Grand Jury Proceedings No. 4–10*, 707 F.3d at 1274–75.

These decisions, which concern the private activity of owning a foreign bank account, appear to be a substantial erosion of the Fifth Amendment. In his dissent in *Shapiro*, Justice Felix Frankfurter pointed out the concern that these decisions demonstrate. He wrote: "[I]f Congress by the easy device of requiring a man to keep the private papers that he has customarily kept can render such papers 'public' and non-privileged, there is little left to either the right of privacy or the constitutional privilege." *Shapiro v. United States*, 335 U.S. at 70 (Frankfurter, J. dissenting).

Not all court decisions applying the required records exception favor the government, however. For instance, in 2018, the Idaho Supreme Court held that the state-imposed duty to promptly notify law enforcement authorities of the discovery or custody of a dead body violated the Fifth Amendment rights of a defendant criminally charged for failing to report. *See State v. Akins*, 423 P.3d 1026 (Idaho 2018). The court correctly reasoned that the reporting requirement was not simply a reasonable regulatory measure but was intentionally directed to detect criminal activity, thereby removing it from the required records exception.

CHAPTER 9

Immunity

Use and Derivative Use Immunity Is Constitutional

Both the federal and state governments may extinguish a person's valid Fifth Amendment privilege against self-incrimination by granting the witness immunity from having his testimony (or any information directly or indirectly derived from such testimony) used against him in a criminal prosecution. *Kastigar v. United States*, 406 U.S. 441 (1972) (upholding a federal immunity statute prohibiting use of any testimony or information compelled under an immunity order, or any information directly or indirectly derived therefrom, in any criminal case); *Zicarelli v. New Jersey*, 406 U.S. 472 (1972) (upholding a state immunity statute providing for use and derivative use immunity). "[W]hen granted immunity, a witness once again owes the obligation imposed upon all citizens the duty to give testimony since immunity substitutes for the privilege." *United States v. Mandujano*, 425 U.S. 564, 576 (1976).

Until 1970, the federal immunity statutes guaranteed that witnesses compelled to testify under their terms could not be prosecuted for any transaction about which the witness testified. This type of immunity, known as transactional immunity, is still required by several states as the only form of immunity sufficient to overcome a witness's assertion of the privilege against self-incrimination in state criminal cases.

- *State v. Thrift*, 440 S.E.2d 341, 351 (S.C. 1994) (South Carolina's use immunity statute held unconstitutional, because state constitutional article prohibiting compelled self-incrimination requires transactional immunity).

- *State v. Gonzalez*, 853 P.2d 526, 533 (Alaska 1993) (Alaska's use immunity statute held unconstitutional under self-incrimination clause of Alaska constitution).
- *Wright v. McAdory*, 536 So. 2d 897, 903–04 (Miss. 1988) (Mississippi constitutional provision that the accused shall not be compelled to give evidence against himself required a grant of transactional immunity to compel self-incriminating testimony).
- *State v. Soriano*, 693 P.2d 26, 26 (Or. 1984) (under Oregon constitution, only transactional immunity is permissible).
- *Attorney Gen. v. Colleton*, 444 N.E.2d 915, 921 (Mass. 1982) (refusing to compel a witness to testify under a grant of use and derivative use immunity, finding that such immunity was inadequate to displace the defendant's right against self-incrimination under Article 12 of the Massachusetts Declaration of Rights).
- *State v. Miyasaki*, 614 P.2d 915, 924 (Haw. 1980) (reversing an order denying the motion to dismiss the indictment, and ruling that Hawaii's use immunity statute was inadequate to terminate the defendant's right against self-incrimination under the Hawaii constitution).

Many states provide for transactional immunity through legislation, as well.

- *People v. Schmidt*, 455 N.W.2d 430, 434 (Mich. Ct. App. 1990) (interpreting Mich. Comp. Laws Ann. § 780.701).
- *State v. McCullough*, 744 P.2d 641, 642 (Wash. Ct. App. 1987) (interpreting Superior Ct. Crim. R. 6.14).
- *People v. Campbell*, 187 Cal. Rptr. 340, 346–47, 137 Cal. App. 3d 867, 877–78 (1982) (interpreting Cal. Penal Code § 1324).
- *State ex rel. Brown v. MacQueen*, 285 S.E.2d 486, 490 (W. Va. 1981) (interpreting W. Va. Code § 57–5-2).
- *People ex rel. Cruz v. Fitzgerald*, 363 N.E.2d 835, 837 (Ill. 1977) (interpreting 725 ILCS 5/106–2, codified at the time of the case as Ill. Rev. Stat. 1975, ch. 38, ¶ 106–2).

- *State v. Paquette*, 369 A.2d 1096, 1099 (R.I. 1977) (interpreting R.I. Gen. Laws 1956 § 12–17–15).
- *State v. Hanson*, 342 A.2d 300, 304 (Me. 1975) (interpreting 15 Me. Rev. Stat. Ann. § 1314-A).
- *Dutton v. Dist. Court*, 518 P.2d 1182, 1184–86 (Idaho 1974) (referring to Idaho Code § 19–1115).

Although *Murphy v. Waterfront Commission of New York*, 378 U.S. 52, 79 (1964) guarantees that whenever one state grants immunity to a witness and compels the person to give self-incriminating testimony all other state and federal jurisdictions are forbidden from using the witness's testimony (and the fruits derived therefrom) in a subsequent prosecution, the grant of transactional immunity by a state does not entitle the witness to transactional immunity in every other jurisdiction. Rather, the grant of transactional immunity by a state is limited to that state, and the transactionally immunized witness is entitled only to use and derivative use immunity for the testimony compelled by the transactional immunity in a prosecution by other states and the federal government. *See, e.g.*, *State v. Finley*, 337 P.3d 527 (Alaska Ct. App. 2014); *In re Vaccari*, 955 N.E.2d 266, 269–70 (Mass. 2011); *Batlioni v. Chief of Police of Salem*, 656 N.E.2d 1223, 1226 (Mass. 1995).

In 1970, Congress enacted the statute whose constitutionality was upheld in *Kastigar*. This statute, 18 U.S.C. § 6002, provides in pertinent part as follows:

> Whenever a witness refuses, on the basis of his privilege against self-incrimination, to testify or provide other information in a proceeding before or ancillary to—
>
> (1) a court or grand jury of the United States,
>
> (2) an agency of the United States, or
>
> (3) either House of Congress, a joint committee of the two Houses, or a committee or a subcommittee of either House,
>
> and the person presiding over the proceeding communicates to the witness an order issued under this title, the witness may not refuse

> to comply with the order on the basis of his privilege against self-incrimination; but no testimony or other information compelled under the order (or any information directly or indirectly derived from such testimony or other information) may be used against the witness in any criminal case, except a prosecution for perjury, giving a false statement, or otherwise failing to comply with the order.

Despite having previously held in *Counselman v. Hitchcock*, 142 U.S. 547, 586 (1892), that a statutory grant of immunity in conformance with the Fifth Amendment "must afford absolute immunity against future prosecution for the offense to which the question relates," the *Kastigar* Court determined that transactional immunity offers greater protection than is constitutionally necessary and that use and derivative use immunity provided by 18 U.S.C. § 6002 was co-extensive with the privilege against self-incrimination. The five member majority reasoned:

> We hold that such immunity from use and derivative use is coextensive with the scope of the privilege against self-incrimination, and therefore is sufficient to compel testimony over a claim of the privilege. While a grant of immunity must afford protection commensurate with that afforded by the privilege, it need not be broader. Transactional immunity, which accords full immunity from prosecution for the offense to which the compelled testimony relates, affords the witness considerably broader protection than does the Fifth Amendment privilege. The privilege has never been construed to mean that one who invokes it cannot subsequently be prosecuted. Its sole concern is to afford protection against being "forced to give testimony leading to the infliction of 'penalties affixed to . . . criminal acts.'" Immunity from the use of compelled testimony, as well as evidence derived directly and indirectly therefrom, affords this protection. It prohibits the prosecutorial authorities from using the compelled testimony in any respect, and it therefore insures that the testimony cannot lead to the infliction of criminal penalties on the witness.

Kastigar, 406 U.S. at 453 (citations omitted).

The federal use and derivative use immunity statute contains several important limitations. First, 18 U.S.C. § 6002 protects the witness only from use or derivative use of his testimony in a future criminal case and does not protect the witness from numerous other collateral consequences resulting from compelled testimony. Because the Fifth Amendment also does not protect a witness from fear of consequences other than domestic criminal prosecution, neither the Supreme Court nor other courts have been troubled by this limitation.

- *Piemonte v. United States*, 367 U.S. 556, 559 n.2 (1961) (immunity is constitutionally adequate even if it does not protect against violent reprisal against the witness or his family by the persons against whom the testimony is offered).
- *Ullman v. United States*, 350 U.S. 422, 430–31 (1956) (discharge from employment, expulsion from a labor union, and loss of passport eligibility are non-criminal sanctions and therefore did not render the grant here of transactional immunity inadequate under the Fifth Amendment).
- *Senate Impeachment Trial Comm. on the Articles of Impeachment Against Judge G. Thomas Porteous, Jr. of the E. Dist. of La.*, 111th Cong. 1970–71 (Aug. 25, 2010) (Disposition of Pre-Trial Motions) (deciding that judge's prior immunized testimony may be used against him in Senate impeachment proceeding, which is not a criminal case).
- *United States v. Mahler*, 567 F. Supp. 82, 87 (M.D. Pa. 1983) (affirming order of immunity requiring witness to answer civil discovery, and ruling that such immunized testimony could be used to import civil liability on party for violations of Clean Water Act).
- *Childs v. McCord*, 420 F. Supp. 428, 435–36 (D. Md. 1976) (use of immunized testimony in attorney disbarment proceedings does not violate either immunity order or the Fifth Amendment privilege against self-incrimination).
- *In re Pressman*, 658 N.E.2d 156, 159 (Mass. 1995) (an attorney may be disciplined by the Board of Bar Overseers based solely on testimony that the attorney gave pursuant to a federal immunity order).

Second, 18 U.S.C. § 6002 does not protect against a prosecution for perjury committed or the making of false statements during the testimony, just as the Fifth Amendment provides no right to lie. In *United States v. Apfelbaum*, 445 U.S. 115, 126–27 (1980), the Supreme Court held that perjury prosecutions are permissible when a witness gives false answers under oath following a grant of immunity. There, the witness made statements before the grand jury that formed the basis for a perjury indictment. When the government sought at trial to use other immunized statements made before the same grand jury to prove that the witness had made the allegedly perjured statements knowingly, the defendant objected on the ground that the immunity pursuant to 18 U.S.C. § 6002 prevented the government from using at trial the immunized statements not alleged to have been false. Resolving a conflict between the circuits, the Court reversed, holding that it was constitutionally permissible to use all of a witness's immunized grand jury testimony at a subsequent prosecution for false swearing during the immunized testimony.

On the other hand, immunized testimony cannot be used in prosecutions for false statements made before the immunity order.

- *United States v. DeSalvo*, 26 F.3d 1216, 1221 (2d Cir. 1994) (immunized testimony in second grand jury appearance cannot be used to prove witness committed perjury in first grand jury appearance).
- *In re Grand Jury Proceedings (Kopkowski)*, 819 F.2d 981, 983 (11th Cir. 1987) (grand jury testimony given under immunity could not subject witness to prosecution for false statements made during previous interview with prosecutor).
- *United States v. Doe*, 819 F.2d 11, 11 (1st Cir. 1987) (affirming district court's contempt order on basis that "immunized testimony in a future appearance before the grand jury cannot be used as evidence to prove a charge of perjury in giving false testimony in his prior appearance") (citations omitted).
- *United States v. Cintolo*, 818 F.2d 980, 988 n.5 (1st Cir. 1987) ("The law is settled that a grant of immunity precludes the use of immunized testimony in a prosecution for *past* perjury (though affording no protection against *future* perjury).") (citation omitted).

- *United States v. Alter*, 482 F.2d 1016, 1028 (9th Cir. 1973) (immunized trial testimony cannot be used in prosecution for perjury based on prior false statement).

Because an immunized witness cannot be prosecuted for perjury based on the inconsistency between prior testimony and subsequent immunized testimony, the immunized witness may not assert the Fifth Amendment privilege against self-incrimination solely on the basis that the immunized testimony will reveal his false prior testimony on the same subject.

- *United States v. McDougal (In re Grand Jury Subpoena)*, 97 F.3d 1090, 1093–94 (8th Cir. 1996) (affirming district court's contempt order for an immunized witness's refusal to testify before a grand jury, when refusal was based on her claim that the prosecutor would not believe her testimony).
- *In re Grand Jury Proceedings (Kopkowski)*, 819 F.2d 981, 983 (11th Cir. 1987) (rejecting argument that immunized witness could avoid testifying based on fear that prosecutor would disbelieve testimony, claiming that the argument "would provide practically all potential grand jury witnesses with a fool-proof escape from testifying simply by claiming that the grand jury or a prosecutor might disagree with their version of the truth") (citation omitted).

Of course, providing a person with use immunity, without derivative use, or issuing a protective order preventing sharing of his testimony with prosecutors are both insufficient to supplant the witness's Fifth Amendment privilege.

- *State v. Delacruz*, 411 P.3d 1207, 1209 (Kan. 2018) (per curiam) (reversing contempt order for witness who refused to testify after being granted only use, without derivative use, immunity).
- *State ex rel. Nothum v. Walsh*, 380 S.W.3d 557, 565 (Mo. 2012) (en banc) (statute that granted only use immunity was insufficient to justify compelling a judgment debtor's testimony).

- *Andover Data Servs. v. Statistical Tabulating Corp.*, 876 F.2d 1080, 1084 (2d Cir. 1989) (holding that a Rule 26(c) protective order is inadequate to overcome a witness's right against compulsory self-incrimination).

The Use of Evidence Obtained Through Immunity Granted Pursuant to 18 U.S.C. § 6002

While 18 U.S.C. § 6002 does not prohibit the prosecution of a witness who provides immunized testimony, the statute makes post-immunity prosecution difficult by prohibiting the use in any criminal case of "any information directly or indirectly derived from such testimony." In *Kastigar v. United States*, 406 U.S. 441, 460 (1972), the Court placed the burden on the prosecutor "to prove that the evidence it proposes to use is derived from a legitimate source wholly independent of the compelled testimony." This burden will often effectively preclude any prosecution from seeking the testimony of a previously immunized witness.

Perhaps the most renowned instance of a grant of immunity precluding a future prosecution was the case of Oliver North. North testified before Congress pursuant to a grant of immunity pursuant to 18 U.S.C. § 6005. The independent counsel scrupulously sealed all of its previously obtained evidence and demonstrated to the satisfaction of the district court that all of its evidence had been obtained before North's congressional testimony. Nonetheless, because the prosecution called witnesses at trial whose testimony was influenced by having heard North's immunized testimony, the District of Columbia Circuit reversed the conviction. *See United States v. North*, 920 F.2d 940, 942 (D.C. Cir. 1990), amending *United States v. North*, 910 F.2d 843 (D.C. Cir. 1990) (holding that Fifth Amendment is violated "whenever the prosecution puts on a witness whose testimony is shaped, directly or indirectly, by compelled testimony, regardless of how or by whom he was exposed to that compelled testimony"). *See also United States v. Poindexter*, 951 F.2d 369, 373 (D.C. Cir. 1991) ("[A] prohibited 'use' occurs if a witness's recollection is refreshed by exposure to the defendant's immunized testimony, or if his testimony is in any way 'shaped, altered, or affected,' by such exposure.") (citation omitted).

Although *Kastigar* places a difficult burden on the prosecution, there are cases affirming convictions on the basis that the government's trial evidence was sufficiently independent of the defendant's prior immunized testimony.

- *United States v. Romano*, 583 F.2d 1, 6 (1st Cir. 1978) (defendant's conviction upheld when government's trial evidence had been derived from defendant's proffer to congressional investigators, which preceded his immunized testimony before Congress).

See also

- *United States v. Pham*, 463 F.3d 1239, 1244 (11th Cir. 2006) (no Fifth Amendment violation during sentencing because government proved that evidence it used was derived from sources independent of immunized testimony).

Following *Kastigar* (and before *United States v. Hubbell*, 530 U.S. 27 (2000)), most federal circuits had ruled that non-evidentiary or tactical uses of immunized disclosures were not invariably prohibited.

- *United States v. Nanni*, 59 F.3d 1425, 1443 (2d Cir. 1995) (holding harmless the use of immunized testimony to obtain a search warrant and precluding suppression of evidence gathered in the search).
- *United States v. Montoya*, 45 F.3d 1286, 1296–97 (9th Cir. 1995) (use of immunized testimony to obtain Department of Justice approval to prosecute the witness is not prohibited, and subsequent indictment is not tainted by the testimony's use).
- *United States v. Velasco*, 953 F.2d 1467, 1474 (7th Cir. 1992) (assuming that prosecution used defendant's proffer of testimony "to shape [its] trial strategy," the court ruled that *Kastigar* did not prohibit such use, reasoning that "mere tangential influence that privileged information may have on the prosecutor's thought process in preparing for trial is not an impermissible 'use' of that information") (citations omitted).

- *United States v. Serrano*, 870 F.2d 1, 17–18 (1st Cir. 1989) (rejecting the view that Fifth Amendment is violated "merely because the immunized testimony might have tangentially influenced the prosecutor's thought processes in preparing the indictment and preparing for trial") (citation and internal quotation marks omitted).
- *United States v. Mariani*, 851 F.2d 595, 601 (2d Cir. 1988) ("In view of the government's convincing proof that the evidence upon which it based its prosecution of Mariani came from legitimate independent sources, we cannot see how the government prosecutor's knowledge of Mariani's immunized testimony could be considered an impermissible use of that testimony.").
- *United States v. Crowson*, 828 F.2d 1427, 1431–32 (9th Cir. 1987) (declining to decide whether non-evidentiary use comes within the prohibition of section 6002, but suggesting that, so long as government proves a prior, independent source for its evidence, any non-evidentiary use will be harmless).
- *United States v. Byrd*, 765 F.2d 1524, 1532 (11th Cir. 1985) (examining whether "[exposure] to the immunized testimony during the course of the governmental investigation" would be improper use under *Kastigar*; concluding that "a violation of the privilege against self-incrimination would not occur in any event unless such 'use' of the immunized testimony resulted in the introduction of evidence not obtained wholly from independent sources").
- *United States v. Sasson*, 334 F. Supp. 2d 347, 357 (E.D.N.Y. 2004) (immunized testimony used in part to obtain court authorization for a wiretap did not warrant suppression of evidence secured from wiretaps).

The Eighth and Third Circuits had prohibited the government from using immunized testimony for any purpose in connection with a criminal prosecution, a result that appears supported by *United States v. Hubbell*, discussed in the next section of this chapter.

- *United States v. Abanatha*, 999 F.2d 1246, 1249 (8th Cir. 1993) (although defendant was not prejudiced by the error and his sentence was affirmed on appeal, court ruled it was error to include

information provided under immunity about the defendant's prior involvement in drug dealing in his pre-sentence investigation report).
- *United States v. Semkiw*, 712 F.2d 891, 894–95 (3d Cir. 1983) (requiring government to show no non-evidentiary use of immunized testimony).
- *United States v. McDaniel*, 482 F.2d 305, 311 (8th Cir. 1973) (reasoning that prosecutor's exposure to immunized testimony could assist the prosecutor in "focusing the investigation, deciding to initiate prosecution, refusing to plea-bargain, interpreting evidence, planning cross-examination, and otherwise generally planning trial strategy" and finding such uses impermissible).
- *See also State v. Gault*, 551 N.W.2d 719, 725 (Minn. Ct. App. 1996) (prohibiting use of immunized testimony in choosing to prosecute).

Despite the Supreme Court's decision in *Hubbell*, reversing a conviction for non-evidentiary uses of the immunized production of documents, some courts have continued to rule that certain non-evidentiary uses of immunized testimony are permissible.

- *United States v. Slough*, 641 F.3d 544, 553–54 (D.C. Cir. 2011) (deciding the issue left open by *North I* by finding error in lower court's ruling that prosecutors had improperly used immunized testimony to make the decision to prosecute).
- *United States v. Cozzi*, 613 F.3d 725, 728–29 (7th Cir. 2010) (holding that *Kastigar* is not concerned with the exercise of prosecutorial discretion).

Courts have also disagreed on the government's burden of proof to demonstrate that its evidence or its witness's testimony was not tainted by immunized testimony and was derived from a wholly independent, legitimate source. While most federal courts have required the government to prove the absence of taint by a preponderance of the evidence, several state courts have required "clear and convincing" proof, and others have upheld state statutes that require that the state's proof meet an elevated standard of "beyond a reasonable doubt."

- *United States v. North*, 910 F.2d 843, 872–73, *opinion withdrawn and superseded in part on reh'g by* 920 F.2d 940 (D.C. Cir. 1990) (prosecution must show by a preponderance of the evidence that no immunized testimony was used).
- *United States v. Zielezinski*, 740 F.2d 727, 733–34 (9th Cir. 1984) (a defendant indicted by the same grand jury that heard his immunized testimony is entitled to a hearing at which the prosecutor would have to demonstrate by a preponderance of the evidence that grand jury indictment rested only on independent sources).
- *Kansas v. Carapezza*, 272 P.3d 10, 15 (Kan. 2012) (upholding lower court decision that state had failed to meet its burden of proof in *Kastigar* hearing, regardless of whether statutory standard of clear and convincing evidence or preponderance standard was applicable).
- *State v. Ely*, 708 A.2d 1332, 1334 (Vt. 1997) (upholding, under Vermont Constitution, a statute requiring proof beyond a reasonable doubt that all evidence used in criminal prosecution was derived independently of immunized testimony).
- *Commonwealth v. Swinehart*, 664 A.2d 957, 957, 969 (Pa. 1995) (state must prove "by the heightened standard of clear and convincing evidence, that the evidence upon which a subsequent prosecution is brought arose *wholly* from independent sources").
- *State v. Strong*, 542 A.2d 866, 872 (N.J. 1988) (to ensure that use and derivative use immunity provides equivalent protection to a self-incrimination privilege, court requires clear and convincing proof that evidence used by prosecutors was derived from wholly independent sources from immunized testimony).

When the government uses immunized testimony or evidence derived therefrom in a criminal prosecution, most courts have held the violation may constitute harmless error under *Chapman v. California*.

- *United States v. Allen*, 864 F.3d 63, 97 (2d Cir. 2018) ("When tainted evidence is presented at trial, we will deem the error harmless if we are 'persuaded beyond a reasonable doubt that the jury would have reached the same verdict even without consideration of the tainted evidence.'").

- *United States v. Ponds*, 454 F.3d 313, 316 (D.C. Cir. 2006) (reversing judgment of conviction based upon violation of act of production immunity order, but remanding case to the district court to determine if the government's impermissible use of the documents was harmless beyond a reasonable doubt).
- *United States v. Schmidgall*, 25 F.3d 1523, 1529, 1531 n.10 (11th Cir. 1994) (remanding for further hearings to determine if the government can make the showing required by *Kastigar* and for determining whether any use of evidence tainted by the defendant's immunized testimony was harmless beyond a reasonable doubt).
- *United States v. Serrano*, 870 F.2d 1, 16 (1st Cir. 1989) ("While the reference to Serrano's immunized testimony was clearly improper, we do not think the district court's finding of harmless error was clearly erroneous given the substantial untainted evidence presented to the grand jury and the tangential nature of the reference in relation to the indictment returned in this case.").
- *United States v. Gallo*, 859 F.2d 1078, 1083 (2d Cir. 1988) (Van Graafeiland, J., concurring) ("I conclude that the use of immunized testimony in this case constituted harmless error beyond a reasonable doubt. Here the record plainly indicates that, except for the single paragraph in question, the government's information came from reliable FBI informants other than appellant, and from direct surveillance, and that the paragraph in question was of negligible significance.") (citations omitted).
- *United States v. Beery*, 678 F.2d 856, 859–60 (10th Cir. 1982) (recognizing that a bankrupt's testimony given during certain hearings, and evidence derived from it, cannot be used against the individual in a grand jury proceeding or in a criminal trial pursuant to 11 U.S.C. § 25(a)(10), but remanding for a determination if error was harmless beyond a reasonable doubt).
- *Aiken v. United States*, 30 A.3d 127, 133 (D.C. 2011) (noting that "even if immunized testimony was impermissibly used, vacation of

the conviction is not necessary where the use is found to be harmless beyond a reasonable doubt") (citations omitted).

When the government uses immunized testimony or evidence derived from it to obtain an indictment, some courts have required the indictment to be dismissed.

- *United States v. Hubbell*, 530 U.S. 27, 42–45 (2000) (Court required the dismissal of the indictment that had been obtained using the immunized person's act of producing subpoenaed documents).
- *United States v. Allen*, 864 F.3d 63, 74–75 (2d Cir. 2018) (citing to prior Second Circuit opinions and distinguishing others, court dismisses indictment procured on the basis of testimony tainted by prior immunized testimony).
- *State v. Jackson*, 927 N.E.2d 574, 581 (Ohio 2010) (remanding the case for dismissal of the indictment because "whenever compelled testimony is used against the witness who provided it, any error cannot be held harmless") (citation omitted).
- *State v. Conrad*, 552 N.E.2d 214, 217 (Ohio 1990) (rejecting the state's harmless error argument because the state's use of the defendant's immunized testimony at the grand jury hearing "alone ends the inquiry of whether use of the defendant's immunized testimony constituted error").

To determine whether the prosecutor's evidence is tainted by testimony obtained under a grant of immunity and that the government has satisfactorily demonstrated that "the evidence it proposes to use is derived from a legitimate source wholly independent of the compelled testimony," *Kastigar*, 406 U.S. at 460, a trial court must generally hold a "Kastigar" hearing at which the defendant is entitled to examine witnesses. Because such hearings can concern not only the direct uses of immunized testimony but also derivative evidentiary or non-evidentiary uses—such as exposure of witnesses to immunized testimony or use of immunized testimony to obtain investigatory leads—these hearings require detailed fact-finding. For instance, in *United States v. Slough*,

677 F. Supp. 2d 112 (D.D.C. 2009), the district judge held hearings for three weeks to determine whether the defendants' statements constituted compelled statements under *Garrity v. New Jersey*, 385 U.S. 493 (1967), and whether the government made impermissible use of such immunized statements. Despite the district court's careful fact-finding, the D.C. Circuit reversed and remanded, ruling that the trial court had made certain errors in determining whether evidence presented to the grand jury was tainted by the defendants' *Garrity* immunized statements and had failed to separately assess for each defendant the presence, extent, and possible harmfulness of the taint. *United States v. Slough*, 641 F.3d 544, 551–55 (D.C. Cir. 2011). The detailed instructions provided by the D.C. Circuit on how to conduct a proper *Kastigar* hearing illustrate the intensive fact-finding involved in this exercise.

The Use of Documents Obtained Through Immunity Granted Pursuant to 18 U.S.C. § 6002

In *United States v. Hubbell*, 530 U.S. 27 (2000), the Supreme Court considered the interplay between the act of production doctrine and the protections afforded to the use of immunized testimony under *Kastigar*. In the case, the independent counsel granted Hubbell immunity pursuant to 18 U.S.C. § 6002–03, in connection with his production of various records in response to a grand jury subpoena. Upon inspection of the documents, the independent counsel discovered various tax offenses for which it later indicted Hubbell. Hubbell argued that the independent counsel, by reviewing the contents of the documents, had used the documents in deciding to prosecute him, in violation of *Kastigar*. The independent counsel argued that because it did not intend either to use Hubbell's testimonial act of production to prove its criminal case or to admit the documents produced to the grand jury into evidence, it had not violated the terms of the immunity order.

The Supreme Court agreed with the lower court and upheld the dismissal of the indictment on the basis that the government had improperly made derivative use of the immunized act of production. According to the Court, "[i]t is abundantly clear that the testimonial aspect of respondent's act of producing subpoenaed documents was the first step in a chain of evidence that led to this prosecution." *Hubbell*, 530 U.S. at 42. The Court ruled that even if the independent counsel did not intend to make "direct use" of the documents in its prosecution, in procuring Hubbell's indictment the independent counsel had made "derivative use" of Hubbell's act of producing the documents compelled by the order of immunity. *Id.* at 42–43. Because the independent counsel could not demonstrate that the evidence it used in obtaining the indictment was derived from legitimate sources "wholly independent" of the testimonial aspects of Hubbell's immunized act of production, *Kastigar* prohibited his prosecution. *Id.* at 45–46.

Although *Hubbell* suggested that the government's use of the contents of documents also would have violated *Kastigar*, it did not directly address whether *Kastigar* prohibited the derivative use of the contents of documents produced through act of production immunity. However, subsequent decisions have ruled that whenever the government grants immunity to a witness in connection with the production of documents, it may not use the contents of the documents in connection with any future prosecution, directly or indirectly.

- *In re Grand Jury Subpoena Dueces Tecum Dated March 25, 2011*, 670 F.3d 1335, 1351–52 (11th Cir. 2012) (defendant who received act of production immunity to decrypt his computer may not thereafter have the contents used against him, as the decrypted files represent the indirect use of his immunized act of production).
- *United States v. Ponds*, 454 F.3d 313, 328–29 (D.C. Cir. 2006) (reversing conviction and remanding for determination whether use was harmless beyond a reasonable doubt, where government used contents of the documents obtained under court-ordered immunity to prosecute defendant).

In other words, although the contents of voluntarily created documents are not protected by the Fifth Amendment privilege, the contents of documents produced pursuant to an order of immunity may not be used—directly or derivatively—against the producer. In such circumstances, the government will be reluctant to confer act of production immunity on any witness it may later want to prosecute.

18 U.S.C. § 6002 and "Ancillary Proceedings"

Immunity pursuant to 18 U.S.C. § 6002 applies to testimony given in congressional proceedings (18 U.S.C. § 6005), certain administrative proceedings (18 U.S.C. § 6004), and court and grand jury proceedings (18 U.S.C. § 6003), as well as to that given in a proceeding "ancillary to" such proceedings. However, the statute does not define "ancillary" proceedings. While the legislative history of section 6002 cites pretrial depositions as the sole example of what could constitute an ancillary proceeding, there are no reported decisions deciding what constitutes an ancillary proceeding for the purpose of the federal immunity statute.

The absence of a clear definition is of more than academic interest. Prosecutors will often want to interview, outside of the grand jury, a witness who has been granted statutory immunity to testify before the grand jury. Is such a debriefing an ancillary proceeding covered by the order of immunity? Similarly, investigators for congressional committees often want to prepare an immunized witness before the witness gives testimony before a committee. Is such a preparation session an ancillary proceeding? There is no clear answer, leaving immunized witnesses arguably able to resist such debriefings on the basis of their Fifth Amendment right against self-incrimination. Many attorneys seek separate "letter" immunity for such debriefings.

"Garrity" Immunity

In *Garrity v. New Jersey*, 385 U.S. 493, 495–98 (1967), the Supreme Court considered a case in which a police department compelled officers to answer self-incriminating questions by threatening to fire them for any refusal to answer. When the officers answered the questions, their responses were used in subsequent prosecutions against them. The Supreme Court decided that the option of losing one's job was coercive, and that unless the government was prohibited from using the statements obtained in subsequent criminal proceedings, the process violated the Fifth Amendment. The Court reasoned: "The option to lose their means of livelihood or pay the penalty of self-incrimination is the antithesis of free choice to speak out or to remain silent." *Id.* at 497.

As described the same day by Justice Fortas's concurring opinion in *Spevack v. Klein*, 385 U.S. 511, 519–20 (1967), *Garrity* did not necessarily prohibit public employees from being discharged for refusing to testify to conduct relating to their employment. Rather, it decided that if public employees were forced to answer under threat of being fired for refusing to answer, such statements cannot be used against them in subsequent criminal proceedings. *See also Lefkowitz v. Cunningham*, 431 U.S. 801, 805–06 (1977) (unless public employees are immunized from subsequent use of their statements in a criminal prosecution, any statements procured through threats of discipline, sanction, or loss of employment for failure to waive the privilege against self-incrimination are coerced and violate the Fifth Amendment). Thus, *Garrity* established that public employees receive the equivalent of use and derivative use immunity before being compelled to answer questions under threat of termination or other similarly direct adverse employment action. The Supreme Court crafted such use and derivative use immunity despite holding in other contexts that immunity is an executive function and that courts are normally without authority to grant immunity. Nonetheless, statements compelled under threat of employment termination are entitled to the full panoply of protections that *Kastigar* applies to statements immunized under 18 U.S.C. § 6002–05.

- *United States v. Moten*, 551 F.3d 763, 766 (8th Cir. 2008) (holding that if the employee demonstrates that she was compelled by her government employer to testify under threat of termination, "the government must show [under *Kastigar*] that any evidence used or derived has a legitimate source wholly independent of the compelled testimony") (citations and internal quotation marks omitted).
- *Sher v. U.S. Dep't of Veterans Affairs*, 488 F.3d 489, 501 (1st Cir. 2007) ("*Garrity* and *Gardner* stand for the proposition that a government employee who has been threatened with an adverse employment action . . . for failure to answer questions put to her by her employer receives immunity from the use of her statements or their fruits in subsequent criminal proceedings. . . .").

- *Kinamon v. United States (In re Grand Jury Proceedings)*, 45 F.3d 343, 348 (9th Cir. 1995) (holding that statements obtained from an employee who was required to answer questions under a threat of dismissal were subject to use and derivative use immunity).
- *In re Grand Jury Subpoenas (Stover)*, 40 F.3d 1096, 1103 (10th Cir. 1994) (holding that "[i]f an officer, whose compelled statement [under *Garrity*] has been considered by the grand jury, ultimately is indicted, . . . the government will be required to prove that its evidence derives entirely from legitimate sources or that the grand jury's exposure to the officer's statement was harmless") (citations omitted).
- *State v. Jackson*, 927 N.E.2d 574, 579–81 (Ohio 2010) (when agent testified before grand jury after reviewing defendant's *Garrity* statement, state was required to satisfy *Kastigar* in order to prosecute the agent).

See also

- *Carney v. Springfield*, 532 N.E.2d 631, 635–36 (Mass. 1988) (deciding that, under Article 12 of the Massachusetts Declaration of Rights, a public employee compelled to speak under threat of discipline is entitled to transactional immunity). *But cf. State v. Burris*, 187 A.3d 830 (N.H. 2018) (disagreeing with *Carney* under identical language under New Hampshire Constitution).

Several courts have required that government agencies conducting investigations of employees first give warnings about the consequences for remaining silent before questioning the employee, at least if the employee is unrepresented by counsel.

- *Atwell v. Lisle Park Dist.*, 286 F.3d 987, 990 (7th Cir. 2002) (while recognizing that its rule requiring prior notice has been rejected by other circuits and is contrary to the prevailing law, court says its rule is justified because "uncounselled persons . . . may instinctively 'take the Fifth' and by doing so unknowingly set themselves up to be fired without recourse").

- *Modrowski v. Dep't of Veterans Affairs*, 252 F.3d 1344, 1350–53 (Fed. Cir. 2001) (finding that agency's refusal to delay interview to allow targeted employee to meet with his lawyer was arbitrary and capricious and reversing portion of Merit Systems Protection Board's decision adverse to the federal employee).
- *Kalkines v. United States*, 473 F.2d 1391, 1393 (Cl. Ct. 1973) (employer must, at time of interrogation, specify to the employee the precise repercussions that will result if the employee refuses or fails to respond).

See also

- *Lybarger v. City of L.A.*, 710 P.2d 829, 40 Cal. 3d 822 (1985) (construing the Public Safety Officers Procedural Bill of Rights to require that before the employee could be disciplined for failing to cooperate with the investigation, he must be advised that his statements could not be used against him in a subsequent criminal proceeding).

Courts agree that statements made by a public employee under threat of automatic job termination or other discipline may not be used—directly or indirectly—in a subsequent criminal prosecution against the employee, and that the employee cannot be fired for refusing to waive such immunity. *See Uniformed Sanitation Men Ass'n v. Commissioner*, 392 U.S. 280 (1968) (holding that the termination of public employees for refusing to waive their Fifth Amendment privilege against self-incrimination in advance of answering questions was unlawful). Nevertheless, courts have struggled to determine when the employee may be lawfully fired for refusing to answer incriminating questions about his job performance.

Compare

- *Gardner v. Broderick*, 392 U.S. 273, 278 (1968) (stating in dictum that if the public employee in question "had refused to answer questions specifically, directly, and narrowly relating to the performance of his official duties, without being required to waive his immunity with respect to the use of his answers or the fruits thereof in a criminal prosecution of himself," then "the privilege against self-incrimination would not have been a bar to his dismissal") (citation omitted).

- *Nelson v. County of Los Angeles*, 362 U.S. 1, 6–7 (1960) (upholding the termination of state employees who refused on Fifth Amendment grounds to answer questions posed to them by the House Committee on Un-American Activities because the state statute under which they were terminated was not based on their assertion of the Fifth Amendment but rather on their refusal to answer "on any ground whatsoever" questions relating to subversion, and because the statute did not result in an adverse inference being made against them).
- *Aguilera v. Baca*, 510 F.3d 1161, 1171 (9th Cir. 2007) (holding that the state may fire public employees for refusing on Fifth Amendment grounds to answer specific job-related questions even though the state did not advise the employees of their *Garrity* immunity, provided the state does not explicitly demand that they waive immunity regarding their answers).
- *Sher v. U.S. Dep't of Veteran Affairs*, 488 F.3d 489, 504–05 (1st Cir. 2007) (the government may lawfully fire a public employee represented by counsel without informing the employee of his *Garrity* immunity because while "the circuits have reached different conclusions about the notice, if any, that the government employer must give to an unrepresented employee about his *Garrity* immunity[,] . . . no court has held that the government employer must give notice of *Garrity* immunity to an employee represented by counsel").
- *Harrison v. Wille*, 132 F.3d 679, 683 (11th Cir. 1998) (the termination of a public employee who refused to answer questions on Fifth Amendment grounds was not unlawful even though the employee was not informed that he had *Garrity* immunity).
- *Hill v. Johnson*, 160 F.3d 469, 472 (5th Cir. 1998) (the firing of a public employee for refusing to answer questions was not unlawful, because the "mere failure" to advise him of his *Garrity* immunity was "not an impermissible attempt to compel a waiver of immunity").

- *Gulden v. McCorkle*, 680 F.2d 1070, 1075 (5th Cir. 1982) (failure to inform public employee of his *Garrity* immunity did not make his termination for refusing to answer questions unlawful).

With

- *Franklin v. City of Evanston*, 384 F.3d 838, 844–45 (7th Cir. 2004) (city violated an employee's procedural due process rights by not advising him that he had immunity for any statements made during a disciplinary hearing and effectively forcing him to choose between his job and his Fifth Amendment rights).
- *Weston v. U.S. Dep't of Hous. & Urban Dev.*, 724 F.2d 943, 948 (Fed. Cir. 1983) ("Invocation of the *Garrity* rule for compelling answers to pertinent questions about the performance of an employee's duties is adequately accomplished when that employee is duly advised of his options to answer under the immunity granted or remain silent and face dismissal.") (citation omitted).
- *Kalkines v. United States*, 473 F.2d 1391, 1393–94 (Ct. Cl. 1973) (invalidating the firing of a federal government employee for refusal to answer questions when investigator failed to advise employee that answers and their fruits could not be used against him in a criminal prosecution).
- *Spielbauer v. County of Santa Clara*, 199 P.3d 1125, 1130, 45 Cal. 4th 704, 713 (2009) (state may fire its employee for exercising his Fifth Amendment rights so long as the employee is not required, as a condition of retaining his job, to surrender his right against criminal use of the statements obtained—at least where the employee is specifically advised that he retains that right).

A *Garrity* violation does not automatically entitle a defendant protection from being prosecuted; it merely entitles the defendant protection from having the unconstitutionally compelled statements from being used directly or indirectly against him. In the recent case of *United States v. Connolly,* Chief Judge McMahon denied defendant Black's request for relief, despite finding he had been forced, in violation of *Garrity*, to make self-incriminating statements during his employer's internal investigation.

Judge McMahon determined that because the prosecutors had made no use of his statements, directly or indirectly, at trial or before the grand jury, there was not even a need to hold a *Kastigar* hearing. Mem. Decision and Order Den. Def. Gavin Black's Mot. for *Kastigar* Relief, *United States v. Connolly*, No. CR 0370(CM) slip op. at 40–45 (S.D.N.Y. May 2, 2019).

It is useful to note that *Garrity* is not the only case in which a court has imposed the equivalent of use and derivative use immunity in exchange for compelling a witness to make self-incriminating statements. Various state supreme courts, either explicitly or implicitly noting the U.S. Supreme Court's creation of immunity for public employees threatened with losing their jobs, have created similar forms of immunity in other circumstances. *See, e.g.*, *People v. Garcia*, 2 Cal. 5th 292, 216 Cal. Rptr. 3d 76, 86, 391 P.3d 1153, 1162 (2017) (construing the requirement of California law that convicted sex offenders answer all questions posed by the supervising officer as meaning that compelled responses cannot be used against the probationer in any subsequent criminal proceedings and that the burden will be on the state "to demonstrate that its evidence was untainted by the defendant's prior statements," citing *Kastigar*).

It is also worth noting that *Garrity* does not extend to job applicants who are compelled as a condition of obtaining employment to make potentially incriminating statements. *Vogt v. City of Hays*, 844 F.3d 1235, 1248–49 (10th Cir. 2017).

Informal Use and Derivative Use or "Letter" Immunity

It is common practice for an attorney for the United States to informally agree to provide protection to a witness consistent with that provided by 18 U.S.C. § 6002, instead of obtaining an order of immunity from the court, as required by the statute. Such agreements may take the form of a letter and most often contain a statement acknowledging that the immunity accorded under the agreement will be identical to what is available under 18 U.S.C. § 6002.

- *United States v. Palumbo*, 897 F.2d 245, 247 (7th Cir. 1990) (prosecutor offered witness "informal use and derivative use immunity for his proffer, tantamount to the protections provided by 18 U.S.C. 6002").

The courts have treated such informal agreements as binding contracts that "must be scrupulously performed and kept." *United States v. Cahill*, 920 F.2d 421, 425 (7th Cir. 1990) (citation and internal quotation marks omitted). *See generally Santobello v. New York*, 404 U.S. 257 (1971) (requiring sentence to be vacated where prosecutor breached the terms of a plea agreement, reasoning that a prosecutor must scrupulously honor promises made in plea agreements).

- *United States v. Farmer*, 543 F.3d 363, 374 (7th Cir. 2008) (proffer agreements are binding contracts and bargaining process must not be unfair to the defendant).
- *United States v. Aleman*, 286 F.3d 86, 90 (2d Cir. 2002) ("Due Process not only requires that the government adhere to the terms of any . . . immunity agreement it makes, but also requires us to construe the agreements strictly against the government in recognition of its superior bargaining power. . . .") (citation and internal quotation marks omitted).
- *United States v. Fitch*, 964 F.2d 571, 574 (6th Cir. 1992) ("An agreement not to prosecute is contractual in nature, and subject to contract law standards.") (citation omitted).
- *State v. Bryant*, 42 P.3d 1278, 1285–86 (Wash. 2002) (en banc) (requiring dismissal of indictment issued by county prosecutor using statements obtained from contract of immunity entered into by another county prosecutor, on grounds of fundamental fairness).

Informal letter immunity necessarily provides the witness with less protection, however, than immunity issued by a court pursuant to 18 U.S.C. § 6002. Whereas court-ordered immunity binds all federal and state prosecutors, an informal immunity agreement binds only the authority that enters into the agreement.

Compare

- *Murphy v. Waterfront Comm'n of N.Y. Harbor*, 378 U.S. 52, 77–79 (1964) (A state witness could not be compelled to give testimony that might be incriminating under federal law unless the compelled testimony and its fruits could not be used in any way by federal officials in a criminal prosecution against the state witness. Court declared that "there is no continuing legal vitality to, or historical justification for, the rule that one jurisdiction . . . may compel a witness to give testimony which could be used to convict him of a crime in another jurisdiction.").

- *Tracy v. Superior Court*, 810 P.2d 1030, 1049–50 (Ariz. 1991) (concluding that the *Murphy* doctrine applies in a federal court proceeding to bar the use of immunized testimony given in a tribal court).

With

- *United States v. Brown*, 400 F.3d 1242, 1255–56 (10th Cir. 2005) (immunity agreement that, by its terms, applied only to state prosecution did not bar federal prosecution even though state officials shared information obtained pursuant to immunity with federal officials).
- *Taylor v. Singletary*, 148 F.3d 1276, 1284–85 (11th Cir. 1998) (informal immunity agreement was specifically limited to U.S. Attorney's Office for the Southern District of Florida and did not prohibit state of Florida from using statements made pursuant to the agreement against defendant).
- *United States v. Gregory*, No. 96–1186, 1997 WL 561422, at *6–7 (6th Cir. Sept. 9, 1997) (federal prosecutors who were not parties to defendant's informal immunity agreement with state prosecutors did not have to abide by the agreement).
- *United States v. Bryant*, 905 F. Supp. 2d 877, 891 (C.D. Ill. 2012) (defendant could be prosecuted in federal court with statements given pursuant to state immunity agreement, even if federal prosecutors had recommended state criminal investigation).

But cf.

- *State v. Bryant*, 42 P.3d 1278, 1283, 1285–86 (Wash. 2002) (informal agreement providing use and derivative use immunity for statements made to one state prosecutor did not apply to sister county prosecutor, but fundamental fairness nonetheless prohibited immunized statements from being used by sister county prosecutor).

Informal grants of use immunity often do not bar the prosecution's use of the immunized testimony at sentencing, whereas 18 U.S.C. § 6002 provides that immunized testimony may not be used in any "criminal case," which includes sentencing.

Compare

- *United States v. Oyegoke-Eniola*, 734 F.3d 1262, 1268 (10th Cir. 2013) (where letter immunity agreement barred use of defendant's statements in government case-in-chief only, the defendant's statements to federal agents could be used against him at sentencing).

With

- *United States v. Abanatha*, 999 F.2d 1246, 1249 (8th Cir. 1993) (statutory immunized testimony "may not be used to affect a subsequent sentence of the testifier (or allowed to affect conditions and terms of confinement)") (citations omitted).

See also

- U.S. Dep't of Justice, Justice Manual Title 9, Criminal Resource Manual at 725 ("[I]f the witness for whom [statutory] immunity has been authorized is awaiting sentencing, the prosecutor should ensure that the substance of the witness's compelled testimony is not disclosed to the sentencing judge unless the witness indicates that he or she does not object.").

Furthermore, informal immunity agreements may contain provisions that impose obligations beyond those imposed by a formal order of immunity pursuant to 18 U.S.C. § 6002. For instance, prosecutors often include language in informal immunity agreements about "full and truthful cooperation," thereby retaining an ability to prosecute the witness for the underlying conduct if they are dissatisfied with the witness's cooperation.

- *United States v. Santiago*, 566 F.3d 65, 69–70 (1st Cir. 2009) (explaining that a grant of immunity to a government informant for "specifically authorized" acts "gave no protection to [the informant] as to related criminal conduct not authorized by the [government] agents").
- *United States v. Fitch*, 964 F.2d 571, 574 (6th Cir. 1992) (government required to demonstrate that defendant's lack of candor was material and substantial under terms of informal immunity agreement before being allowed to prosecute the defendant for violating an informal immunity letter).
- *United States v. Skalsky*, 857 F.2d 172, 176 (3d Cir. 1988) (where government and defendant entered into informal agreement that required defendant to provide "complete, truthful and accurate information and testimony" in order to avoid prosecution, defendant's breach of agreement by lying allowed government to prosecute the defendant for underlying offenses as well as perjury).
- *United States v. Irvine*, 756 F.2d 708, 711–12 (9th Cir. 1985) (defendant could be prosecuted where immunity agreement allowed for it if he provided untruthful information).
- *In re Grand Jury Subpoena to John Doe*, 41 F. Supp. 2d 616, 624 (W.D. Va. 1999) (Doe, who wore body wire and made two cocaine purchases as part of cooperation deal with government, had no fear of prosecution regarding the cooperative conduct justifying assertion of Fifth Amendment).

Most importantly, an informal grant of immunity is a negotiated agreement and does not involve compulsion, as would be the case for testimony compelled pursuant to 18 U.S.C. § 6002. Thus, a prosecutor seeking to prosecute a person who provides testimony or documents under an informal immunity letter should not, at least as a constitutional matter, be required to show that a subsequent prosecution was based on evidence wholly independent from the immunized testimony.

- *United States v. Gregory*, No. 96–1186, 1997 WL 561442, at *6 (6th Cir. Sept. 9, 1997) (court did not abuse discretion by refusing to hold *Kastigar* hearing in case of alleged breach of informal immunity agreement, because such testimony was not compelled).

Rather, in a case involving an informal grant of immunity, the burden should arguably be on the defendant to demonstrate breach of the contract. However, a number of circuits have applied *Kastigar*'s protections to prosecutions resulting from breaches of informal immunity agreements, despite the absence of compulsion.

- *United States v. Hill*, 643 F.3d 807, 877–78 (11th Cir. 2011) (requiring district court to hold *Kastigar* hearing for allegedly violating terms of its proffer agreement with the defendant).
- *United States v. Mendoza*, 78 F.3d 460, 464 (9th Cir. 1996) (deciding that when government informally promises that statements will not be used against the defendant, *Kastigar* governs despite absence of compulsion).
- *United States v. Kilroy*, 27 F.3d 679, 684–87 (D.C. Cir. 1994) (while the court stated that the defendant bears the burden of proving a breach of an informal immunity agreement made as part of a plea bargain, it nonetheless examines the evidence "as if the government ha[s] the burden [under *Kastigar*]" to demonstrate that it did not use any evidence against the defendant obtained directly or indirectly from his self-incriminating statements).
- *United States v. Quintanilla*, 2 F.3d 1469, 1483 (7th Cir. 1993) ("[I]nformal grants of use and derivative use immunity are fully enforceable and implicate the provisions of *Kastigar*.") (citation omitted).
- *United States v. Harvey*, 869 F.2d 1439, 1443–44 (11th Cir. 1989) (en banc) (applying same rules and methods of analysis to an informal oral grant of immunity as to a formal grant "because due process requires us to enforce the government's agreement with [the witness]. . . .").

Prosecutors and defendants often enter into cooperation agreements in which the defendant cooperates with the government's continuing investigation hoping to obtain a reduction of his sentence. In federal cases, those agreements often cite to and are governed by section 1B1.8 of the U.S. Sentencing Guidelines. These agreements are binding, even after *United States v. Booker*, 543 U.S. 220 (2005), which made the federal sentencing guidelines advisory. *See United States v. Milan*, 398 F.3d 445, 455–56 (6th Cir. 2005). This section provides that the court cannot use self-incriminating information obtained under such agreements "in determining the applicable guidelines range," but can consider self-incriminating statements "in determining whether, or to what extent, a downward departure from the guidelines is warranted. . . ." *Id.* at 455 n.8 (citing U.S. Sentencing Commission, *Guidelines Manual* § 1B1.8). Courts have turned away arguments from cooperating witnesses pursuant to such agreements that the court violated their Fifth Amendment rights when determining whether or to what extent to depart downward from the otherwise applicable sentencing guidelines range by considering the cooperator's self-incriminating statements.

- *United States v. McFarlane*, 309 F.3d 510, 515–16 (8th Cir. 2002) (holding that an agreement pursuant to section 1B1.8 does not violate the Fifth Amendment by allowing the sentencing court to consider the self-incriminating information provided by a cooperating defendant to determine whether a downward departure was warranted).

However, where plea agreements promise that a defendant's further cooperation will not be used against him, the courts specifically enforce such prohibitions and construe the cooperation agreements against the government by prohibiting such cooperative statements from being used to sentence more harshly.

- *United States v. Chavful*, 781 F.3d 758 (5th Cir. 2015) (government breached plea agreement cooperation provision and USSG Section 1B1.8 by introducing information about an intervening drug sale at sentencing).
- *United States v. Harper*, 643 F.3d 135, 143 (5th Cir. 2011) (where prosecution used immunized statements to advocate for higher

guideline level and sentence, the court concluded that the government had breached the plea agreement and that defendant was entitled to be resentenced before a different judge).

- *United States v. Farmer*, 543 F.3d 363, 375 (7th Cir. 2008) (defendant was entitled to be resentenced when government submitted statements protected under a proffer agreement to the probation officer who prepared the Presentence Investigation Report).
- *United States v. Milan*, 398 F.3d 445, 456 (6th Cir. 2005) (concluding that the district court could not consider the defendant's proffer statements for the purposes of departing upward from the applicable guideline range).

The targets of criminal investigations often make statements to prosecutors under so-called proffer agreements that provide only for use immunity, without derivative use protection. As is the case with other forms of informal immunity, courts typically construe these agreements against the government and prevent use of the statements made at the proffer session whenever the agreement can be construed to protect against the use.

- *United States v. Jiménez-Bencevi*, 788 F.3d 7, 16–17 (1st Cir. 2015) (where proffer agreement prohibited trial court's use of any statements, it was reversible error for trial judge to allow government to use the proffer to cross-examine or impugn the defense expert).
- *United States v. Melvin*, 730 F.3d 29, 37 (1st Cir. 2013) (when proffer agreement granted use immunity, it was error for trial court to allow testimony from an agent that he was able to identify the defendant's voice on recorded wiretaps as a result of having heard the same voice during the proffer session).
- *United States v. Hill*, 643 F.3d 807, 879 (11th Cir. 2011) (where proffer agreement contained contradictory language regarding derivative use, the court interpreted the agreement to require the government to make a *Kastigar* showing before being allowed to use the proffered statements or their fruits at trial).

Court Authority to Grant or Deny Immunity

Criminal defendants have a Sixth Amendment right to compulsory process to obtain witnesses in their favor. When those witnesses indicate an intention to invoke their Fifth Amendment right against self-incrimination, defendants often request the court to grant such witnesses immunity and compel their (presumably) favorable testimony. As discussed in preceding chapters, the United States Supreme Court has created various forms of immunity for witnesses, and defendants have argued that courts have the inherent authority to protect their rights to a fair trial by granting favorable witnesses immunity from prosecution.

However, the federal courts have universally held that a federal district court judge does not, absent exceptional circumstances, have the authority to grant immunity from prosecution to a defense witness.

- *United States v. Quinn*, 728 F.3d 243, 251–53 (3d Cir. 2013) (en banc) (ruling that the courts lack inherent authority to grant use immunity to a defense witness and disapproving of its prior decisions recognizing that the court could grant immunity to assure an effective defense).
- *United States v. Serrano*, 406 F.3d 1208, 1217 (10th Cir. 2005) (noting that every circuit (except the Third at that time) has held that a federal district court lacks authority to compel a prosecutor to grant statutory immunity, absent exceptional circumstances).
- *United States v. Bowling*, 239 F.3d 973, 976 (8th Cir. 2001) (restating the settled rule that "[t]he district court did not have the authority to grant [the witness] immunity . . .") (citation omitted).
- *United States v. Perkins*, 138 F.3d 421, 424 (D.C. Cir. 1998) (supporting judge's inaction and finding that "[u]nder circuit precedent, therefore, the district judge lacked authority to grant [the witness] use immunity").
- *United States v. Mackey*, 117 F.3d 24, 27 (1st Cir. 1997) (remarking that the concern with interfering with future prosecutions of culpable parties is "a major reason why judges have not shared the enthusiasm of student law review editors for creating a 'right' of defendants to insist on immunity for defense witnesses").

- *United States v. Abbas*, 74 F.3d 506, 511–12 (4th Cir. 1996) (finding no merit in defendant's assertion that refusal to grant co-defendant immunity was a deliberate attempt to distort the fact-finding process).
- *United States v. Bahadar*, 954 F.2d 821, 825–26 (2d Cir. 1992) (while indicating that judges may be able to use their coercive powers to force government to grant immunity in rare circumstances, "as we have repeatedly held, the fifth amendment does not require that defense witness immunity must be ordered whenever it seems fair to grant it") (citation and internal quotation marks omitted).
- *United States v. Mohney*, 949 F.2d 1397, 1401 (6th Cir. 1991) ("We [have] rejected [the effective defense] theory because it would violate separation of powers to recognize an inherent judicial right to grant immunity when immunity is a legislative creation explicitly entrusted to the executive branch.") (citation omitted).
- *United States v. Hooks*, 848 F.2d 785, 798–99 (7th Cir. 1988) (holding that court lacks both authority to grant immunity or to compel government to seek immunity for a defense witness who exercises his Fifth Amendment right).
- *United States v. Sawyer*, 799 F.2d 1494, 1506–07 (11th Cir. 1986) (upholding conclusion of prior Fifth Circuit precedent that district courts have no authority to grant immunity to a defense witness).
- *United States v. Mendia*, 731 F.2d 1412, 1414 (9th Cir. 1984) (court has neither power to grant immunity nor power to compel government to grant it).
- *United States v. Thevis*, 665 F.2d 616, 638–41 (5th Cir. 1982) (rejecting various policy arguments for allowing judges to grant immunity to defense witness with exculpatory testimony who plans to assert privilege against self-incrimination).
- *United States v. Turkish*, 623 F.2d 769, 778 (2d Cir. 1980) (recognizing that in cases where defendant seeks to have court require the government to grant immunity to witness, prosecutor need only "present to the court *in camera* an *ex parte* affidavit setting forth the circumstances that support the prosecutor's suspicion of the witness's criminal activity" to justify its refusal).

On the other hand, most of the federal circuits and some state courts have indicated that, in narrow circumstances, a district court can force the government to choose between providing immunity for defense witnesses or proceeding with the prosecution, as a matter of due process. Although the courts differ somewhat in the language they use to describe this authority, they all agree that a court can act if the government has abused its authority to grant immunity by "intentionally" attempting to distort the fact-finding process.

- *United States v. Quinn*, 728 F.3d 243, 247–48, 251 (3d Cir. 2013) (en banc) (describing a five-part test for deciding if the prosecution is violating a defendant's due process rights by deliberately intending to distort the fact-finding process by denying defense witness immunity).
- *United States v. Straub*, 538 F.3d 1147, 1156–57 (9th Cir. 2008) (prosecutor's refusal to grant immunity to the one defense witness who could have discredited the testimony of an immunized prosecution witness had effect of distorting fact-finding process, denying the defendant due process).
- *United States v. Stapleton*, 297 F. App'x 413, 432 (6th Cir. 2008) (recognizing a prosecutorial misconduct exception to the bar against judicial grants of defense witness immunity, but finding it inapplicable in the case).
- *United States v. LaHue*, 261 F.3d 993, 1014 (10th Cir. 2001) (court could force government to choose between conferring immunity and acquittal if prosecutor's denial of immunity was attempt to distort fact-finding process).
- *United States v. Dolah*, 245 F.3d 98, 106 (2d Cir. 2001) ("[W]e have consistently assumed that, in some limited circumstances, using the immunity device in a one-sided manner can result in a basic unfairness that rises to the level of a violation of procedural due process.").
- *United States v. Angiulo*, 897 F.2d 1169, 1190–92 (1st Cir. 1990) (recognizing that in extreme cases of prosecutorial misconduct, the government's refusal to grant immunity could justify a court's refusal to allow the prosecution to proceed).

- *United States v. Capozzi*, 883 F.2d 608, 613–14 (8th Cir. 1989) (while recognizing that a showing of prosecutorial misconduct in making its immunity decisions could support a due process violation, court found such suggestion without merit in the case).
- *United States v. Frans*, 697 F.2d 188, 191 (7th Cir. 1983) (requiring a defendant to show "that the government intended to distort the judicial fact-finding process" by refusing to immunize a defense witness after immunizing a prosecution witness).
- *Commonwealth v. Brewer*, 34 N.E.3d 314, 318 (Mass. 2015) (noting that unique circumstances may arise where the government's "deliberate intent to distort the fact-finding process" warrants immunizing a defense witness).
- *State v. Belanger*, 210 P.3d 783, 789–90 (N.M. 2009) (granting courts the unilateral power to grant defense witness immunity in limited circumstances, particularly where prosecutor's actions deliberately disrupt the fact-finding process).
- *United States v. Carter*, 684 A.2d 331, 341–44 (D.C. 1996) (the court may fashion a remedy, including dismissing the case, where a defense witness possesses material, exculpatory, and non-cumulative evidence unobtainable from any other source and government can provide no justifiable reason for not granting use immunity).

Two circumstances may substantiate the necessary governmental abuse: (1) when the government has intimidated or harassed a potential defense witness and thereby encouraged the witness to invoke his Fifth Amendment privilege; and (2) when the government has deliberately withheld immunity from a prospective witness for the sole purpose of keeping relevant exculpatory evidence from the jury.

- *United States v. Westerdahl*, 945 F.2d 1083, 1086–87 (9th Cir. 1991) (ruling that "an evidentiary hearing should have been held to determine whether the government intentionally distorted the fact-finding process," where it granted immunity to one witness but refused to grant immunity to second witness whose testimony contradicted that of the immunized witness).

- *United States v. Angiulo*, 897 F.2d 1169, 1192–93 (1st Cir. 1990) (describing the two circumstances and citing illustrative cases from various circuits, but holding that the defendants failed to make an adequate showing of either type of prosecutorial misconduct).
- *United States v. Burns*, 684 F.2d 1066, 1077 (2d Cir. 1982) (requiring that government had "engaged in discriminatory use of immunity to gain a tactical advantage or, through its own overreaching, has forced the witness to invoke the Fifth Amendment . . .") (citations omitted).
- *People v. Shapiro*, 409 N.E.2d 897, 904 (N.Y. 1980) ("[I]n cases in which witnesses favorable to the prosecution are accorded immunity while those whose testimony would be exculpatory of the defendant are not . . . due process may be violated.").

The number of times a federal judge has granted a defense witness immunity is extraordinarily small. In a high-profile prosecution in the case against Broadcom, however, the district judge granted immunity to a defense witness because prosecutorial misconduct distorted the fact-finding process and compromised the integrity of the trial. *See, e.g.*, Tr. 5195–97, *United States v. Ruehle*, No. SACR 08–001390-CJC (C.D. Cal. Dec. 15, 2009), available at http://www.google.com/url?sa=t&rct=j&q=&esrc=s&frm=1&source=web&cd=1&cad=rja&ved=0CCQQFjAA&url=http%3A%2F%2Fjenner.com%2Fsystem%2Fassets%2Fassets%2F3768%2Foriginal%2FUnited_States_v._Ruehle.pdf%3F1319647752&ei=r0b-UsPUCaXx0gH7-oGIBQ&usg=AFQjCNFCD8mzxF4CMLAAe4iWHgLWHA61bw.

The vast majority of federal and state courts have also ruled that judges lack the discretion to deny a properly pled motion or application by a prosecutor to grant immunity to a witness, reasoning that the decision is solely an executive function. *See In re Sealed Case*, 791 F.2d 179, 181 (D.C. Cir. 1986); *In re Grand Jury Investigation*, 657 F.2d 88, 90–91 (6th Cir. 1981); *United States v. Hollinger*, 553 F.2d 535, 548 (7th Cir. 1977); *State v. Rice*, 136 A.3d 720 (Md. 2015); *In re Tuso*, 376 A.2d 895, 896 (N.J. 1977).

CHAPTER 10

The Future of the Fifth Amendment

Future advances in cognitive neuroscience will likely test the Fifth Amendment's core values. Current neurotechnologies are already able to peer inside our brains and produce significant evidence about our memories and our thoughts—even if the reliability of the evidence has not yet reached levels making it admissible in courtrooms in the United States.

For instance, commercial enterprises are currently experimenting with so-called brain fingerprinting, which, by measuring certain electrical oscillations emitted by the brain when subjects are presented with certain stimuli, purport to be able to provide an objective scientific way to connect established features of a crime scene with the record of the crime stored in the brain of the perpetrator. This is accomplished by measuring a subject's brain response to stimuli in the form of words or pictures presented on a computer screen. During a brain fingerprinting test, electroencephalography (EEG) signals are recorded from electrodes placed on the scalp. When the subject recognizes a significant stimuli, the brain, it is believed, fires neurons in a specific, identifiable pattern known as a P300-MERMER that can be detected by computer analysis of the EEG signals. If the subject does not possess any knowledge relevant to the stimuli displayed, the P300-MERMER response is absent. In other words, the specific measurable brain response known as P300-MERMER is emitted by the brain of a subject who has the crime scene or its details stored in his brain, but the subject lacking the information will not emit the P300-MERMER response.

Additionally, scientists are using blood-oxygen-level-dependent functional magnetic resonance imaging (BOLD-fMRI), which measures the concentrations of oxygenated blood (oxyhemoglobin) within the brain to detect which regions of the brain are activated by various thought processes. The underlying theory of BOLD-fMRI detection is similar to conventional polygraph testing. However, instead of measuring stress reactions such as heart rate, blood pressure, and respiration thought to be associated with lying, the BOLD-fMRI measures blood-oxygen-level-dependent (BOLD) activity within the regions of the brain. BOLD-fMRI does not depict absolute regional brain activity; rather it indicates relative changes in regional activity over time. By observing the blood-flow responses to known lies and known truth, the BOLD-fMRI scans are, as reported in various studies, able to detect lying more reliably than polygraph tests.

While each of these and other experimental neurotechnologies focus on measuring the brain's reactions to some outside input, it is not science fiction to imagine a future technology able to make reliable observations of the metabolic manifestations of a person's thought patterns or memory simply by placing a human head inside a special device or scanner. In other words, we can expect a future in which we will be able to extract self-incriminating patterns of brain function from a person without requiring the person to speak or even make a responsive gesture.

Obtaining incriminating evidence from an accused's neurological activities raises profound questions about the protections afforded by the Fifth Amendment. As previously observed, the Self-Incrimination Clause protects only "testimonial" or "communicative" disclosures. In other words, if a court-ordered neurological examination could produce reliable evidence of a person's memory of being present at the time and place of a murder, or reliable evidence about whether a person is lying or telling the truth about participating in the murder, the resulting evidence would be banned pursuant to the Fifth Amendment only if it were deemed to constitute testimony.

Current Fifth Amendment jurisprudence provides contradictory insights into whether brain fingerprinting or BOLD-fMRI test results would be constitutionally admissible. On the one hand, the Supreme

Court has ruled that compelled disclosure of purely physical evidence from which science can discern reliable self-incriminating information does not constitute testimony. In *Schmerber v. California*, 384 U.S. 757, 763–65 (1966), the Court announced a distinction between "testimony" and "real or physical evidence." In upholding the use at trial of an alcohol content analysis performed on blood extracted from a suspect without his consent, the Court determined that neither the withdrawal of blood (admittedly by compulsion) nor its use in the analysis of its alcohol content (admittedly producing self-incriminating information) involved protected testimony. As the majority opinion written by Justice Brennan explained:

> Not even a shadow of testimonial compulsion upon or enforced communication by the accused was involved either in the extraction or in the chemical analysis. Petitioner's testimonial capacities were in no way implicated; indeed, his participation, except as a donor, was irrelevant to the results of the test, which depend on chemical analysis and on that alone.

Id. at 765.

On the basis of this rationale, forcing a suspect to submit to a futuristic device that merely measures electrical, chemical, or biological activities of the brain to derive incriminating evidence would seem, at first blush, not to implicate a person's "testimonial capacities." The suspect would—as in *Schmerber*—be no more than a donor of the measurable events emitted by the physical operation of the brain.

On the other hand, the Supreme Court has repeatedly defined testimony in a manner that strongly suggests that evidence derived from brain function is different from evidence derived from other bodily functions. As previously explained, the majorities in both *Doe v. United States*, 487 U.S. 201, 210 n.9 (1988), and *United States v. Hubbell*, 530 U.S. 27, 43 (2000), agreed that testimony results from evidence generated by a witness's use of the "contents of his own mind." Even Justice Brennan's opinion for the then-five-justice majority in *Schmerber* observed in dicta that physical evidence derived from the brain's functioning may be different from evidence derived from other physical bodily functions. In commenting that there will be many cases in which the distinction between real or physical evidence and testimony are not readily drawn, he offered the following example to illustrate this point:

> Some tests seemingly directed to obtain "physical evidence," for example, lie detector tests measuring changes in body function during interrogation, may actually be directed to eliciting responses which are essentially testimonial. To compel a person to submit to testing in which an effort will be made to determine his guilt or innocence on the basis of physiological responses, whether willed or not, is to evoke the spirit and history of the Fifth Amendment. Such situations call to mind the principle that the protection of the privilege "is as broad as the mischief against which it seeks to guard," quoting *Counselman v. Hitchcock*.

Schmerber, 384 U.S. at 764.

These statements suggest that the majority in *Schmerber*, Justice Brennan and the four dissenting justices, actually considered the Fifth Amendment to provide protection against the compelled extraction of information about brain function, even if it does not protect from the compelled extraction of other physical evidence.

While it is impossible to predict a future court's ruling on evidence derived from a brain fingerprint or BOLD-fMRI assessment of a lie, there can be little doubt that more sophisticated noninvasive neurological technologies to access and measure brain activities will soon be deemed sufficiently reliable to be admissible. A number of defendants have already tried to introduce such test results and expert testimony interpreting the tests in sentencing or the penalty phase of death penalty cases. As these technologies improve, they can be expected to produce admissible evidence about a person's subjective state of mind. When that occurs, the government may well seek to compel persons it suspects of criminal behavior to undergo such procedures. The Fifth Amendment Self-Incrimination Clause will be tested as it has never been before.

Epilogue: A Brief Rejoinder to Justice Thomas

Justice Clarence Thomas's opinions exhibit an interest in narrowing the Supreme Court's current interpretation of the Self-Incrimination Clause in two primary respects. First, Justice Thomas reads the Self-Incrimination Clause as merely "a prohibition on compelling a criminal defendant to testify against himself at trial." *United States v. Patane*, 542 U.S. 630, 630 (2004), citing his plurality opinion for four Justices in *Chavez v. Martinez*, 538 U.S. at 764–68 (2003). According to Justice Thomas, except for prohibiting the use of coercion that produces involuntary statements, the text of the Self-Incrimination Clause says nothing about whether the government may compel a person to make statements against himself outside his criminal trial. *See Chavez v. Martinez*, 538 U.S. at 769 (claiming that "our cases provide that those subjected to coercive police interrogation have an automatic protection from the use of their involuntary statements (or evidence derived from their statements) in any subsequent criminal trial"). According to Justice Thomas, the numerous Supreme Court decisions that have upheld a person's right not to be compelled to give incriminating testimony outside of a criminal trial, or not to have that testimony used against him in a criminal prosecution, are merely court-made "prophylactic rules designed to protect the core privilege against self-incrimination," and to avoid "mak[ing] its invocation useless at a later stage." *United States v. Patane*, 542 U.S. at 638.

Along with this reinterpretation of the Self-Incrimination Clause, Justice Thomas would eliminate altogether one of the so-called prophylactic rules: that the Self-Incrimination Clause prohibits the prosecutor and the judge from commenting about a defendant's decision not to testify at his criminal trial. In *Griffin v. California*, 380 U.S. 609 (1965), the Supreme Court decided that comments allowing a jury to draw an adverse inference from the defendant's decision not to testify in accordance with the Fifth Amendment are a "penalty imposed by courts for exercising a constitutional privilege." Such a penalty "cuts down on the privilege by making its assertion costly." 380 U.S. at 614. Justice Thomas dissented in *Mitchell v. United States*, 526 U.S. 314 (1999), where the Supreme Court extended the *Griffin* "no comment" rule from the trial to the sentencing phase of criminal cases. He argued that *Griffin* "lacks foundation in the Constitution's text, history, or logic" and should be overruled. 526 U.S. at 341. Relying on his view of the text and history of the clause, Justice Thomas further expounded on his reasons for overruling *Griffin* in a separate concurrence in *Salinas v. Texas*, 570 U.S. at 191.

A close examination of Justice Thomas's arguments leads to skepticism regarding his conclusions. First, his interpretation of the clause's text, found in his writings in *Chavez* and *Patane*, is much too narrow. The text reads "[n]o person . . . shall be compelled in any criminal case to be a witness against himself." The clause speaks of any "person," not merely persons charged with crimes. Although Justice Thomas might prefer that the words "in any criminal case to be a witness against himself" be taken to mean only persons who have been charged with a crime, that is, a criminal defendant, the text itself says otherwise. A true literal reading of the text also applies to anyone who is subpoenaed as a witness to appear and give testimony in a criminal case. Indeed, the text speaks about witnessing against oneself in "any" criminal case, not merely one's own criminal case. If the clause meant to apply only to criminal defendants at trial, it would have prohibited compelling a person from "being a witness against himself in *his* criminal case." But the Framers composed the Self-Incrimination Clause differently.

Furthermore, the text is about what is prohibited in "criminal cases," not merely criminal trials. Although the Supreme Court may not ever have decided when a criminal case begins or ends, a "criminal case" consists of more than a trial today, just as it consisted of more than a trial in 1789. Even if the text "witness against himself" were to be interpreted to mean only a criminal defendant, a person charged with a crime is capable of being compelled to be a witness against himself in his "case" long before and long after his trial. Indeed, the Sixth Amendment applies only in "criminal prosecutions." If the Framers and Ratifiers of the Constitution had intended to limit the Self-Incrimination Clause to something less than a "criminal case," they could have used the same words as does the Sixth Amendment. They did not.

When read as a whole, the text of the Fifth Amendment Self-Incrimination Clause is much more than "a prohibition on compelling a criminal defendant to testify against himself at trial." Instead, the text of the clause literally says that no person can be compelled to testify against himself in any criminal case, extending its prohibition to persons other than criminal defendants and to proceedings that occur prior to or after a criminal trial.

Justice Thomas's textual interpretation is often informed by his commitment to interpreting the Constitution in a manner that reflects the intent of those who framed and ratified it, a mode of constitutional interpretation often described as "originalism." For instance, as he explained in his concurrence in *United States v. Hubbell*, 530 U.S. 27, 49–56 (2000), Justice Thomas would be willing to reconsider how the Supreme Court interprets the Self-Incrimination Clause concerning the production of documents, because the act of production doctrine that currently represents the Court's interpretation "may be inconsistent with the original meaning of [the Clause]." 530 U.S. at 49. Justice Thomas is famous for his commitment to originalism as the only legitimate method of constitutional interpretation and has embraced this view in a number of cases involving many different constitutional provisions. But Justice Thomas relies inconsistently on history and the Framers' apparent intent to support his conclusions in the context of the Self-Incrimination Clause.

First, Justice Thomas cites no history to support his construction of the clause in *Chavez* and *Patane*. And no support exists for his interpretation limiting the Fifth Amendment right merely to the prohibition of compelling a defendant to testify against himself in his own criminal trial. As the Supreme Court has explained in *Ferguson v. Georgia*, 365

U.S. 570 (1961), at the time the Constitution was drafted and ratified the criminal defendant was disqualified from testifying under oath at his own trial because of his perceived self-interest. Indeed, the right of a criminal defendant to testify on his own behalf at trial only began to take hold in the United States in 1859, when Maine became the first state to pass a statute overruling the common law prohibition. *See Ferguson*, 365 U.S. at 577. If the Self-Incrimination Clause meant in 1789 only what Justice Thomas claims it means today, there would have been no need for its inclusion in the Bill of Rights.

Further, the Framers were deeply concerned about the use of torture to extract a confession when they included the Self-Incrimination Clause in the Constitution. The history of such concern was spelled out by the Supreme Court in one of its earliest self-incrimination cases, *Bram v. United States*, 168 U.S. 532, 544–545 (1897). Justice Thomas's construction in *Chavez* and *Patane* would eliminate the Fifth Amendment's Self-Incrimination Clause altogether as a source of law prohibiting the use of torture to extract a confession not otherwise used as evidence in a trial. His position would rest the sole limitation on torture to the more ambiguous Due Process Clauses of the Fifth and Fourteenth Amendments. No historical record supports a construction of the Self-Incrimination Clause that eliminates its application to torture used to extract a confession.

Justice Thomas's selective use of history appears again in his argument against *Griffin* and its rule prohibiting juries from making adverse inferences at trial against a non-testifying defendant. In his concurring opinion in *Salinas*, Justice Thomas claims that at the time of the country's founding, "English and American courts strongly encouraged defendants to give unsworn statements and drew adverse inferences when they failed to do so." *Salinas*, 570 U.S. at 192–93. In support of this statement, he cites Justice Scalia's dissent in *Mitchell* and an article by Albert Alschuler. But neither source bears out Justice Thomas's claim. Indeed, Justice Scalia's dissent in *Mitchell* admits that he could find no reported decision during the relevant period referring to the use of an adverse inference at trial against a defendant based on his silence. In fact, Justice Scalia inferred that because criminal defendants throughout the 18th century rarely had the assistance of counsel at trial, they invariably spoke (unsworn) in their own defense, making the adverse inference irrelevant. *Mitchell*, 526 U.S. at 332–36. And Albert Alschuler says nothing supportive of Justice Thomas's claim. Rather, on the Alschuler article's page cited by Justice Thomas, Professor Alschuler merely noted his view that a jury or a judge "*should* be permitted to draw appropriate inference" from a defendant's silence at either his trial or in response to questioning in a pretrial examination; he makes no mention whatsoever of the practice at the time the Constitution was formed. Instead, in a longer published article, Professor Alschuler noted that at the time the Constitution was drafted, suspects were subjected to forceful interrogation outside of court during which the suspects remained unsworn. Albert W. Alschuler, *A Peculiar Privilege in Historical Perspective: The Right to Remain Silent*, 94 Mich. L. Rev. 2625 (1996). In commenting on the possibility that suspects who refused to respond might have suffered "no more severe sanction than the drawing of an adverse inference," he admits that "[o]ne cannot know much, however, about what common law judges would have done if unsworn defendants had refused to answer, for during the centuries prior to the Bill of Rights, *almost none did*." *See A Peculiar Privilege*, n. 98, at 2653 (emphasis added). The history lesson provided by Justice Scalia and Professor Alschuler refutes, rather than supports, Justice Thomas's conclusion.

Further, Justice Thomas's position fails to consider the Supreme Court's recitation in *Ferguson v. Georgia* of the pre- and post-ratification history allowing a defendant to make an unsworn statement in his own defense at trial, as a means of mitigating the harshness of the common-law rule deeming the defendant incompetent as a sworn witness. The history lesson in *Ferguson* makes it reasonably clear that, at the founding and thereafter, there was no common law about the adverse inference to be drawn from a defendant's silence, because neither the defendant's unsworn statement nor his silence was considered to constitute evidence. Instead, only in the late 1800s, when states enacted statutes that granted defendants the right to testify in their defense, did the law begin to recognize the adverse inference, with the majority of states "forbid[ding] comment by the prosecution on the failure of the accused to testify." *Ferguson*, 365 U.S. at 580.

In sum, neither Justice Thomas's reading of the Self-Incrimination Clause, nor his reliance on the history that led the Framers to include the Self-Incrimination Clause in the Constitution, supports his efforts at remaking this area of constitutional law.

Table of Cases

B

C

E

F

L

N

O

Q

R

S

T

V

W

Index